THE CASE FOR THE
Real Jesus

Resources by Lee Strobel

The Case for Christ
The Case for Christ audio
The Case for Christ – Student Edition (with Jane Vogel)
The Case for Christ curriculum (with Garry Poole)
The Case for Christmas
The Case for Christmas audio
The Case for a Creator
The Case for a Creator audio
The Case for a Creator – Student Edition (with Jane Vogel)
The Case for a Creator curriculum (with Garry Poole)
The Case for Easter
The Case for Faith
The Case for Faith audio
The Case for Faith – Student Edition (with Jane Vogel)
The Case for Faith curriculum (with Garry Poole)
The Case for the Real Jesus
The Case for the Real Jesus audio
Discussing the Da Vinci Code curriculum (with Garry Poole)
Discussing the Da Vinci Code discussion guide (with Garry Poole)
Exploring the Da Vinci Code (with Garry Poole)
Experiencing the Passion of Jesus (with Garry Poole)
Faith Under Fire curriculum series
God's Outrageous Claims
Inside the Mind of Unchurched Harry and Mary
Off My Case for Kids
Surviving a Spiritual Mismatch in Marriage (with Leslie Strobel)
Surviving a Spiritual Mismatch in Marriage audio
What Jesus Would Say

Other Resources by Garry Poole

The Complete Book of Questions
Seeker Small Groups
The Three Habits of Highly Contagious Christians
In the Tough Questions Series:
Don't All Religions Lead to God?
How Could God Allow Suffering and Evil?
How Does Anyone Know God Exists?
Why Become a Christian?
Tough Questions Leader's Guide (with Judson Poling)

THE CASE FOR THE
Real Jesus
—

*A Journalist Investigates Current Attacks
on the Identity of Christ*

LEE
STROBEL

ZONDERVAN

The Case for the Real Jesus
Copyright © 2007 by Lee Strobel

This title is also available as a Zondervan ebook.
Visit www.zondervan.com/ebooks.

Requests for information should be addressed to:
Zondervan, *Grand Rapids, Michigan 49530*

This edition: ISBN 978-0-310-33926-7 (softcover)

Library of Congress Cataloging-in-Publication Data

Strobel, Lee, 1952–
        The case for the real Jesus : a journalist investigates current attacks on the
identity of Christ / Lee Strobel.
            p.   cm.
        Includes bibliographical references and index.
        ISBN 978-0-310-24210-9 (hardcover)
            1. Jesus Christ–Historicity. 2. Jesus Christ–Biography–History and criticism.
    I. Title.
    BT303.2.S77   2007
    232.9'08–dc22   2007013737

Cover design: Curt Diepenhorst
Cover photography: Domino / GettyImages®
Interior design: Beth Shagene

Printed in the United States of America

15 16 17 18 19 20 /DCI/ 22 21 20 19 18 17 16 15 14 13 12 11 10 9 8 7 6 5 4 3

For Frank Cate,
who's at Home with the real Jesus

Contents

Searching for the Real Jesus

Much of the history of Christianity has been devoted to domesticating Jesus, to reducing that elusive, enigmatic, paradoxical person to dimensions we can comprehend, understand, and convert to our own purposes. So far it hasn't worked.

Catholic priest Andrew Greeley[1]

Can anybody show me the real *Jesus?*

from a song by Canadian rock band downhere[2]

At first glance, there was nothing unusual about Evergreen Cemetery in Oakland, California. There were the expected rows upon rows of grave markers, some festooned with flowers, others with small American flags hanging limp in the still winter air. I meandered through the property and soon came upon a gently sloping hillside — and there, standing sentry over a wide expanse of grass, was a solitary three-foot headstone. Its stunning inscription: "In Memory of the Victims of the Jonestown Tragedy."

Beneath the ground were the remains of more than four hundred Californians who had followed the siren call of self-proclaimed messiah Jim Jones down to the jungles of South America to build a paradise of racial equality and harmony. Believing his creed of love and equal opportunity, beguiled by his charisma and eloquence, they put their complete faith in this magnetic visionary.

His most audacious boast: he was the reincarnation of Christ — the *real* Jesus.[3]

The pilgrims, intent on living out Jones's doctrine of peace and tolerance, arrived in a remote rainforest of Guyana, only to realize over time that he was building a hellish enclave of repression and violence. When a visiting U.S. congressman and a contingent of journalists threatened him with exposure, Jones ordered them ambushed and killed before they could leave on a private plane.

Then Jones issued his now-infamous command: all of his followers must drink cyanide-laced punch. Syringes were used to squirt the poison into the mouths of infants. Those who refused were shot. Soon more than nine hundred men, women, and children were in the contorted throes of death under the scorching sun, and Jones ended his own life with a bullet to the head.

The bodies of 409 victims, more than half of them babies and children, were shipped back to California in unadorned wooden caskets and buried at Evergreen Cemetery. In the nearly thirty years since the Jonestown tragedy, few have come to visit.

On this day, I stood in silence and reverence. As I shook my head at this senseless loss, one thought coursed through my mind: *Beliefs have very real consequences.*

These victims believed in Jones. They subscribed to his utopian vision. His dogma became their own. But ultimately the truth is this: Faith is only as good as the one in whom it's invested.

Who Is Jesus?

Search for *Jesus* at Amazon.com and you'll find 175,986 books—and, yes, now one more. Google his name and in a blink of the eye you'll get 165 *million* references. Invite people to tell you who they think the *real* Jesus is—as Jon Meacham and Sally Quinn did at *Newsweek*'s website "On Faith" just before Christmas in 2006—and you'll soon be buried in an avalanche of wildly disparate opinions, as these eye-opening excerpts demonstrate:

- "We don't know many historical facts concerning Jesus, but apparently he was a rabbi who was an example of compassion. Since then he has been exploited by Christians, particularly Americans."
- "Jesus is real, in the sense that he exists for those who want him to exist."

- "By today's standards, Jesus was a liberal."

- "Jesus was one of a thousand Jews murdered by the Romans for threatening Roman rule."

- "Jesus is my personal Higher Power. He helps me stay sober one day at a time."

- "Jesus was Everyman. His name could have as well been Morris. Too bad he was in male form this time around. Better luck next time."

- "I believe Jesus is the Son of God. I believe I am a Son of God."

- "Even strict Christians consider Jesus the Son of God only in a symbolic way."

- "Jesus was an enlightened being."

- "Jesus is the Son of God who was born, died, and rose from the dead to save us from our sins. He lives today, and he will come to earth again."

- "It's not even obvious that Jesus was a historical figure. If he was, the legends around him—a Son of God who was born of a virgin, worked miracles, and rose from the dead—were common stories in the ancient Near East. The myths about Jesus are not even original."

- "Jesus is about as 'real' as Santa Claus, the Tooth Fairy, or King Arthur."

- "Jesus was a man who was nailed to a tree for saying how great it would be to be nice to people for a change."

- "So who was Jesus? A highly moral person, much like Teresa of Calcutta. No less, but no more."

- "Jesus was an apocalyptic preacher who thought God would intervene to save Israel from Roman rule and himself from death. God didn't do either. Jesus died disappointed, and that's that. Anything more is fantasy."

- "Honestly—I don't care about Jesus. Who or what he was, is, or isn't doesn't affect me."

- "There is no separation or distinction between where God leaves off and where we begin. We are all One, all Divine, just like Jesus."

- "Jesus was a man we should pity more than revile or worship. He suffered from what contemporary psychologists now know to be delusions of grandeur, bipolar disorder, and probably acute schizophrenia."

- "Jesus is a fairy tale for grown-ups. Unfortunately, he's a fairy tale that leads people to bomb clinics, despise women, denigrate reason, and embrace greed. Any behavior can be justified when you have Jesus as your eternal 'Get out of Jail' card."

- "Who was Jesus? An apocalyptic prophet who bet wrong and died as a result. He should be ignored, not celebrated."[4]

As you can see, after two thousand years there's not exactly a consensus about the founder of Christianity.

"Everyone claims their Jesus is the 'real one,' the only authentic Christ unperverted by secular society or religious institutions," said Chris Suellentrop, who writes for *Slate* and the *New York Times*. "The emergence of Jesus as a computer programmer in *The Matrix* shows how he can be reinvented for any age, even the future."[5]

Jesus has been called an intellectual who spouted pithy aphorisms; a Mediterranean cynic leading a wandering band of proto-hippies; an androgynous feminist and ambassador of Sophia, the female embodiment of divine wisdom; a clever messianic pretender; a gay magician; a peasant revolutionary; and a Jewish Zen master. Asked one philosopher:

> So who was Jesus? Was he a wandering *hasid*, or holy man, as Géza Vermès and A. N. Wilson propose? Was he a "peasant Jewish cynic," as John Dominic Crossan alleges? Was he a magician who sought to lead Israel astray, as the Talmud holds? Was he a self-proclaimed prophet who died in disillusionment, as Albert Schweitzer maintained? Was he some first-century personage whose purported miracles and divinity were mere myths or fabrications by the early church—as David F. Strauss, Rudolf Bultmann, and John Hick suggest? Or was he, as the Gospels assert, "The Christ, the Son of the living God"?[6]

People who have searched for Jesus through history have often discovered exactly who they wanted to find in the first place. "In other words," said Charlotte Allen in *The Human Christ*, "the liberal searchers found a liberal Jesus ... the deists found a deist, the Romantics a Romantic, the existentialists an existentialist, and the liberationists a Jesus of class struggle."[7]

Is it possible to find the *real* Jesus? That depends on how you answer a more foundational question: Are you willing to set aside your preconceptions and let the evidence take you wherever it will? And what about me — am *I* willing to do the same?

I had to honestly ask myself that question when I was an atheist and decided to investigate the identity of Jesus. And more recently, this time as a Christian, I had to face that issue squarely once again when I was confronted by six potent challenges that could undermine everything I had come to believe about him.

Not So Fast ...

If you had asked my opinion about Jesus when I was the legal editor of the *Chicago Tribune*, I would have given you an adamant answer: if he lived, he was undoubtedly a rabble-rousing prophet who found himself on the wrong side of the religious and political leaders of his day. Claims about his divinity clearly were manufactured by his followers long after his unfortunate demise. As an atheist, I ruled out any possibility of the virgin birth, miracles, the resurrection, or anything else supernatural.

It was my agnostic wife's conversion to Christianity and the ensuing positive changes in her character that prompted me to use my legal training and journalism experience to systematically search for the real Jesus. After nearly two years of studying ancient history and archaeology, I found the evidence leading me to the unexpected verdict that Jesus is the unique Son of God who authenticated his divinity by returning from the dead. It wasn't the outcome I was necessarily seeking, but it was the conclusion that I believe the evidence persuasively warranted.

For my book *The Case for Christ*, in which I retraced and expanded upon my original journey, I sat down with respected scholars with doctorates from Brandeis, Cambridge, Princeton, the University of Chicago, and elsewhere, peppering them with the tough questions that had vexed me as a skeptic. I walked away all the more persuaded that the cumulative evidence established the deity of Jesus in a clear and convincing way.[8]

But not so fast ...

That book was published in 1998. Since then the Jesus of historic Christianity has come under increasingly fierce attack. From college classrooms to bestselling books to the Internet, scholars and popular writers are seeking to debunk the traditional Christ. They're capturing the public's imagination with radical new portraits of Jesus that bear scant resemblance to the time-honored picture embraced by the church.

In 2003, Dan Brown's wildly successful novel *The Da Vinci Code* provided a flashpoint for the controversy, bringing jaw-dropping allegations about church history and Jesus' identity into the public's consciousness through an intoxicating brew of fact and fiction. But the issues go much deeper.

For many people, their first exposure to a different Jesus came with extensive news coverage of the Jesus Seminar, a group of highly skeptical professors who captivated the media's attention in the 1990s by using colored beads to vote on what Jesus really said. The group's conclusion: fewer than one in five sayings attributed to Jesus in the Gospels actually came from him. In the Lord's Prayer, the Seminar was confident only of the words "Our Father." There were similar results when the participants considered which deeds of Jesus were authentic.

What made the Jesus Seminar unique was that it bypassed the usual academic channels and instead enthusiastically took its findings directly to the public. "These scholars have suddenly become concerned—to the point of being almost evangelistic—with shaping public opinion about Jesus with their research," said one New Testament expert.[9]

They found a ready audience in many Americans who were receptive to a new Jesus. With the public's appetite whetted, publishers began pumping out scores of popular books touting various revisionist theories about the "real" Christ. At the same time, the Internet spawned a proliferation of websites and blogs that offer out-of-the-box speculation about the Nazarene. An equal-opportunity phenomenon, the World Wide Web doesn't discriminate between sober-minded scholars and delusional crackpots, leaving visitors without a reliable filter to determine what's trustworthy and what's not.

Meanwhile, college classrooms, increasingly dominated by liberal faculty members who grew up in the religiously suspicious 1960s, provided a fertile field for avant-garde beliefs about Jesus and Christianity. According to a landmark 2006 study by professors from Harvard and George Mason universities, the percentage of atheists and agnostics teaching at U.S. colleges is three times greater than in the population as a whole. More than half of college professors believe the Bible is "an ancient book of fables, legends, history, and moral precepts," compared to less than one-fifth of the general population.[10]

In recent years, six major challenges to the traditional view of Jesus have emerged out of this milieu. They are among the most powerful and prevalent objections to creedal Christianity that are currently circulating in popular culture. These issues have left many Christians scratching their heads, unsure how to respond, and have confused countless spiritual seekers about who Jesus is — or whether they can come to any solid conclusions about him at all.

As someone whose road to faith was paved with painstakingly researched facts and logic, I simply could not gloss over these allegations after repeatedly encountering them the last several years. They are too central to the identity of Jesus. I had no choice but to grant them their full weight and open myself to the possibility that they could legitimately undermine the traditional understanding of Christ. For the sake of my own intellectual integrity, I needed answers.

CHALLENGE #1: "Scholars Are Uncovering a Radically Different Jesus in Ancient Documents Just as Credible as the Four Gospels"

Several gospels unearthed in the twentieth century, which some experts date back to the dawning of Christianity, portray Jesus far differently than Matthew, Mark, Luke, and John. The Gospel of Thomas, discovered sixty years ago but only now becoming widely popular, and the Gospel of Judas, whose discovery was announced with much fanfare in 2006, are among the ancient manuscripts fueling a widespread interest in Gnosticism, a movement that its proponents claim is just as valid as mainstream Christianity.

Although Gnosticism is diverse, New Testament scholar N. T. Wright says Gnostics historically have held four basic ideas in common: the world is evil, it was the product of an evil creator, salvation consists of being rescued from it, and the rescue comes through secret knowledge, or *gnosis* in Greek.[11] Said Wright:

> This special *gnosis* is arrived at through attaining knowledge about the true god, about the true origin of the wicked world, and not least about one's own true identity.... What is needed, in other words, is a "revealer" who will come from the realms beyond, from the pure upper spiritual world, to reveal to the chosen few that they have within themselves the spark of light, the divine identity hidden deep within.[12]

For many Gnostics, that revealer is Jesus of Nazareth, who in their view isn't the savior who died for the sins of the world but, rather, was the imparter of secret wisdom who divulged the truth about the divine nature within each of us. Thus, Gnostics aren't as interested in historical claims about Jesus as they are in the private teachings that he supposedly passed along to his most trustworthy followers.

"Gnostic writers tend to view the virgin birth, the resurrection, and other elements of the Jesus story not as literal, historical events but as symbolic keys to a 'higher' understanding," said journalist Jay Tolson in his *U.S. News and World Report* cover story, "In Search of the Real Jesus."[13]

Tolson says that in Princeton religion professor Elaine Pagels' portrayal of them,

> the Gnostics come across as forerunners of modern spiritual seekers wary of institutional religion, literalism, and hidebound traditions. Free of sexism and paternalism and unburdened by an emphasis on guilt and sin, the Gnostics' highly esoteric and intellectual approach to the sacred was one that even enlightened skeptics could embrace.[14]

Canada has already seen the birth of its first Gnostic church.[15] In the United States, "there is a growing, if disconnected and unorganized, Gnostic movement," said Richard Cimino and Don Lattin in their survey of American spirituality.[16] Even if people don't identify themselves as Gnostic, many are freely grafting certain aspects of Gnosticism into their own spirituality. The reason is these elements fit well with the American values of independence and individuality. Said Cimino and Lattin:

> Today's experiential spirituality shares with Gnosticism a need to know God personally without the intermediaries of church, congregation, priests, and scripture. The Gnostic factor can be found in the growth of occult and esoteric teachings and movements, where access to supernatural secrets are available through individual initiation and experience rather than through publicly revealed texts or doctrine.[17]

So which picture of Jesus is true: Is he the one-and-only Son of God who won salvation for humankind through his atoning death on the cross, or is he "an avatar or voice of the oversoul sent to teach humans to find the sacred spark within"?[18] This isn't a matter of merely adding some new brushstrokes or shading to the traditional portrait of Jesus; instead, it's an entirely different canvas and a whole new likeness.

At the heart of this controversy is the reliability of the Gnostic gospels that have been uncovered over the past six decades, many of which were republished in 2007 as a new collection called *The Nag Hammadi Scriptures*.[19] Do they tell a more accurate story about Jesus than the church's official collection of documents that make up the New Testament? Do they support the claims that Gnosticism flourished in the first century when Christianity was being formed? More insidiously, has the church tried to suppress the inconvenient truths contained in the Gnostic texts? If I wanted to discover the "real" Jesus, I simply couldn't avoid this potentially explosive minefield of interrelated issues.

CHALLENGE #2: "The Bible's Portrait of Jesus Can't Be Trusted Because the Church Tampered with the Text"

While popular books point to the Gnostic gospels as revealing the "real" Jesus who has been suppressed by the church, the New Testament's portrayal of him has come under a withering assault by an evangelical-turned-agnostic who is recognized as one of the world's leading authorities on the transmission of the New Testament.

Bart D. Ehrman's surprise bestseller, the provocatively titled *Misquoting Jesus*, has shaken the faith of many Christians and planted seeds of skepticism in spiritual seekers by charging that the scribes who copied the New Testament through the centuries accidentally—and many times, *intentionally*—altered the manuscripts. "In some cases," Ehrman says, "the very meaning of the text is at stake."[20]

How can the New Testament's accounts about Jesus be trusted if the manuscripts are pocked with 200,000 to perhaps 400,000 variants? Are essential teachings about Jesus in jeopardy—for instance, the Trinity and the resurrection? If the Bible contains even a single error, can any of it be trusted at all? What about the inauthentic passages that Ehrman says should never have been included in the Bible in the first place?

I knew that if I were to maintain confidence in the Jesus of the New Testament, these weren't matters that could be blithely swept aside. I would have to face Ehrman's masterfully written critique head-on.

CHALLENGE #3: "New Explanations Have Refuted Jesus' Resurrection"

Two recent *New York Times* bestselling books are only the latest in an escalating battle over the historicity of the resurrection—the pivotal event that, according to Christians, authenticated the divinity of Jesus.

A new generation of aggressive atheists has fashioned fresh and potent objections to the claim that Jesus rose from the dead. At the same time, Muslim apologists, who know that undermining the resurrection casts doubt on all of Christianity, have been more and more outspoken about their belief that Jesus never died on the cross and therefore could not have conquered the grave as the New Testament claims.

In 2007, questions concerning the resurrection received widespread attention when an astounding 57 percent of Americans either saw or heard about a Discovery Channel documentary in which *Titanic* movie director James Cameron and film documentarian Simcha Jacobovici said archaeologists had discovered the tomb of Jesus and his family just south of the old city of Jerusalem.[21] If they really had unearthed his "bone box," or ossuary, then Jesus could not have returned bodily from the dead.

Nothing cuts to the core of Jesus' identity like critiques of his resurrection. If the belief that he rose from the dead is a legend, a misunderstanding, or a deliberate falsehood perpetrated by his followers, then Jesus is quickly demoted from the Son of God to a failed prophet — or worse.

I could not claim to love truth and at the same time turn a blind eye toward the most serious charges against the resurrection. How strong — *really* — is the affirmative case that Jesus returned from the dead? Can the resurrection be established by using historical evidence that the vast majority of scholars in the field — including fair-minded skeptics — would accept as being true? And do any of the most current alternative theories finally succeed in putting Jesus back in his grave?

CHALLENGE #4: "Christianity's Beliefs about Jesus Were Copied from Pagan Religions"

The argument is simple but powerful: a whole bevy of mythological characters were born of virgins, died violently, and were resurrected from the dead in antiquity, but nobody takes them seriously. So why should anyone give any credence to similar claims about Jesus that were obviously copied from these earlier pagan mystery religions?

This critique, popularized a century ago by German historians, has now returned with a vengeance, becoming one of the most ubiquitous objections to the historical understanding about Jesus. It has spread around the World Wide Web like a computer virus and been forcefully presented in numerous bestselling books, including one that received a prestigious award from a British newspaper.

The "parallels" appear stunning. According to proponents of this "copycat" theory, the pre-Christian god Mithras was born of a virgin in a cave on December 25, had twelve disciples, promised his followers immortality, initiated a communionlike meal, was hailed as the way, the truth, and the life, sacrificed himself for world peace, was buried in a tomb, and was resurrected on the third day.[22] How could Christians possibly explain away such apparent plagiarism?

Were the supernatural qualities of Jesus merely ideas borrowed from ancient mythology and attached to the story of the Nazarene by his overzealous followers in the decades after his ignominious death? Is Jesus no more divine than Zeus? Are the reports of his resurrection no more credible than the fantastical tales of Osiris or Baal? No honest examination of the evidence for Jesus could avoid addressing the alarming theory that the followers of Jesus were nothing more than spiritual plagiarists.

CHALLENGE #5: "Jesus Was an Imposter Who Failed to Fulfill the Messianic Prophecies"

With its multimillion-dollar evangelistic campaign that targeted New York City, the organization Jews for Jesus put the issue squarely on the front burner of public debate in 2006: Is Jesus—or is he not—the Messiah whose coming was foretold in scores of ancient Jewish prophecies?

Counter-missionary organizations in the Jewish community quickly responded by claiming that Jesus never fulfilled those predictions and therefore cannot be the "anointed one" awaited by the Jewish people for millennia. He is, they charge, nothing less than a messianic failure because he never ushered in the world peace foretold by the prophets.

What are the real facts? What's the best case that can be made for Jesus—and Jesus alone—matching the "fingerprint" of the long-anticipated Messiah? And are there any satisfying answers to the sharp critiques that are being passionately argued by contemporary rabbis who reject Jesus as the Jewish Messiah? Without a doubt, these issues call the fundamental mission and credibility of Jesus and the Bible into question, and therefore they cannot in good conscience simply be glossed over.

CHALLENGE #6: "People Should Be Free to Pick and Choose What to Believe about Jesus"

We live in a circus-mirror culture of rampant relativism in which the very concept of truth has become pliable, history is treated with extreme skepticism, and Christianity's claim to being the only way to God is vehemently branded as the height of religious intolerance. For many postmodern people, the "real" Jesus has become whatever each individual wants him to be. Who is to say that anyone's concept of Christ is more valid than someone else's? Wouldn't that smack of the very kind of judgmentalism that Jesus himself deplored?

An increasing number of people are bypassing the dogma of traditional Christianity and creating their own belief system, rejecting tenets that seem hopelessly outdated, and accepting those that they feel are appropriate. The Jesus who emerges is generally kinder and gentler — or at least a lot more broadminded and tolerant — than the rigid and demanding version frequently found in the church. Most often, this customized Christ doesn't use the threat of hell to scare people into submission; rather, he's an affirming and loving companion who sees the good — and even the divine — in each of us.

Is the Jesus I discovered in my initial investigation merely the Jesus for me personally? Or are there objective truths about him that are binding on all people in all cultures? If history is only a matter of subjective interpretation, then can I know anything about him for sure? Is Christianity just one among many equally legitimate pathways to the divine? These questions are more than a product of idle curiosity: their answers could determine whether Jesus of Nazareth is still relevant to this and future generations.

On the Road Again

I sat down for lunch with my wife at a restaurant in Irvine, California, and slid a yellow legal pad over for her to see. The six challenges to Jesus were scrawled across the front page. Leslie glanced over them, squinting at times to make out my nearly illegible handwriting, and then looked up at me. She knew what this meant.

"You're hitting the road again, aren't you?" she asked.

"I have to," I said. "I can't ignore these objections. If any of them is true, it changes everything."

Leslie wasn't surprised. She was aware that I had been wrestling with some of these issues for a while. And after nearly thirty-five years of marriage, she knew that I was someone who had to pursue answers, regardless of the consequences.

My itinerary was already taking shape in my mind: for starters, I would need to book flights to Nova Scotia and Texas. I resolved to put the most probing questions to the most credible scholars I could find. At the conclusion, I was determined to reach whatever verdict was warranted by the hard evidence of history and the cool demands of reason.

Yes, I was looking for opinions, but they had to be backed up with convincing data and airtight logic — no rank speculation, no flights of faith. Like the investigations I undertook at the *Chicago Tribune*, I would have no patience for half-baked claims or unsupported assertions. There was too much hanging in the balance. As the Jonestown victims had chillingly reminded me, my faith is only as good as the one in whom it's invested.

So why don't you come along with me on this investigative adventure? After all, as Jesus himself cautioned, what you believe about him has very real consequences.[23] Let's resolve at the outset to keep an open mind and follow the facts wherever they take us — even if it's to a conclusion that challenges us on the very deepest levels.

In the end, we'll discover together whether the Jesus of historic Christianity manages to emerge intact from the crucible of twenty-first-century skepticism.

"Scholars Are Uncovering a Radically Different Jesus in Ancient Documents Just as Credible as the Four Gospels"

For nineteen hundred years or so the canonical texts of the New Testament were the sole source of historically reliable knowledge concerning Jesus of Nazareth. In 1945, this circumstance changed.

Religion professor Stevan L. Davies[1]

There's a very important historical point here, which is that in the last thirty years we have discovered real Gospels—hundreds of them—that are not the official Gospels, [but] that were part of the discussions in the early church.

Commentator Andrew Sullivan[2]

The rumor mill was churning. A political operative called one of my reporters with a tip that a candidate for Illinois governor had recently been detained by police after allegations that he had abused his wife. If this was true, the irony would be devastating: one of his responsibilities as the state's chief executive would be to oversee a network of shelters for battered women.

Since other news media had been alerted as well, I knew we had only a short period of time to nail down the story. I immediately assigned five reporters to pursue various angles of the investigation. We needed indisputable confirmation—preferably, a written document—before we could publish the story.

The reporters milked their sources. One of them came up with a time frame for the incident. Another got the name of the Chicago suburb where it allegedly took place in a public parking lot. Still, we didn't have enough. The information was too vague and uncorroborated.

Finally, another reporter was able to obtain the key piece of evidence: a police report that described exactly what had happened. But there was a snag. Because no criminal charges had been filed, privacy laws dictated that all names on the report be blacked out. At first glance, it looked like there would be no way to link the candidate to the incident.

As the reporter studied the report more carefully, though, she discovered that the police had inadvertently failed to delete one reference to the person involved. Sure enough, it was the candidate's name. Still, his name was rather common. How could we be sure it was really him? Digging deeper in the report yielded the final clue: the suspect had bragged about being the mayor of a certain suburb—the same position held by the gubernatorial candidate. *Bingo!* A match.

In a dramatic confrontation in the newspaper's conference room, I peppered the candidate with questions about the incident. He steadfastly denied it ever occurred—until I handed him a copy of the police report. Faced with the indisputable evidence, he finally admitted the encounter with police. Within seventy-two hours he had withdrawn from the gubernatorial race.[3]

For both journalists and historians, documents can be invaluable in helping confirm what has transpired. Even so, detective work needs to be done to establish the authenticity and credibility of any written record. Who wrote it? Was this person in a position to know what happened? Was he or she motivated by prejudice or bias? Has the document been kept safe from tampering? How legible is it? Is it corroborated by other external facts? And are there competing documents that might be even more reliable or which might shed a whole new light on the matter?

That last question has come to the forefront in the quest to understand the historical Jesus in recent years. For centuries, scholars investigating what happened in the life of Jesus largely relied on the New Testament, especially Mark, Matthew, and Luke—which are the oldest of the four Gospels and are called the "Synoptics" because of their inter-relationship—as well as the Gospel of John.

In modern times, however, archaeological discoveries have yielded a fascinating crop of other documents from ancient Palestine. Some of them paint a very different portrait of Jesus than the traditional picture found in the Bible, and they throw key theological beliefs into question. But can they really be trusted?

A Different Jesus

In the years since my own investigation into Jesus, the focus on these "alternative gospels," in both academic and popular books, has greatly intensified. In the 1990s, several Jesus Seminar participants and others, led by Robert J. Miller, published *The Complete Gospels*, which juxtaposed the New Testament gospels with sixteen other ancient texts.[4]

"Each of these gospel records offers fresh glimpses into the world of Jesus and his followers," says the book.[5] "All of the ... texts in this volume are witnesses to early Jesus traditions. All of them contain traditions independent of the New Testament gospels."[6]

To me, the implication was clear: these other gospels—with such names as the Gospel of Thomas, the Secret Gospel of Mark, the Gospel of Peter, and the Gospel of Mary—were equal to the biblical accounts in terms of their historical significance and spiritual content. Indeed, said Philip Jenkins, professor of history and religious studies at Pennsylvania State University, "With so many hidden gospels now brought to light, it is now often claimed that the four gospels were simply four among many of roughly equal worth, and the alternative texts gave just as valid a picture of Jesus as the texts we have today."[7]

The case for these other gospels has been bolstered by some scholars who date a few of them to as early as the first century, which is when Jesus' ministry flourished and the four Gospels of the New Testament were written. That would mean they would contain very early—and therefore perhaps historically reliable—material.

For example, Karen L. King, professor of ecclesiastical history at Harvard Divinity School, said the Gospel of Mary may arguably have been written in the late first century.[8] Contrary to the biblical Gospels, in this text Jesus teaches that "salvation is achieved by seeking the true spiritual nature of humanity within oneself and overcoming the entrapping material nature of the body and the world."[9] The disciples Peter and Andrew are depicted as "proud and ignorant men," while the gospel "identifies the true apostolic witness" of Mary Magdalene.[10] In other words, she has the same stature as the other apostles of Jesus.

As for the Gospel of Peter, which includes a bizarre passage about a talking cross and the risen Jesus with his head extending beyond the clouds, scholars such as Arthur J. Dewey, associate professor of Theology at Xavier University in Cincinnati, date its early stage to the middle of the first century.[11]

Then there's the incendiary Secret Gospel of Mark. Award-winning scholar Morton Smith of Columbia University, author of *Jesus the Magician* and other books, reported finding two and a half pages of this formerly unknown gospel in a monastery near Jerusalem in 1958. Scott G. Brown, who based his doctoral dissertation on the gospel, asserted in a 2005 book that it was penned by the same author who wrote the Gospel of Mark and was reserved only for those spiritually mature enough to handle it.[12]

The most shocking claim in that gospel is that Jesus conducted a secret initiation rite with a young man that, according to Smith, may have included "physical union."[13] Specifically, the text says that six days after Jesus raised a wealthy young man from the dead, "in the evening the youth comes to him, wearing a linen cloth over his naked body. And he remained with him that night, for Jesus taught him the mystery of the kingdom of God."[14]

Another explosive text—purportedly written by Jesus himself on papyrus in his own native language of Aramaic—was described by Michael Baigent in his 2006 *New York Times* bestseller *The Jesus Papers*. Directly contradicting what Christianity has taught for two millennia, Jesus explicitly denies that he's the Son of God, clarifying instead that he only embodied God's spirit. According to Baigent, Jesus added that "everyone who felt similarly filled with the 'spirit' was also a 'son of God.'"[15]

The Mystery of Thomas

The darling of liberal scholarship, however, is the Gospel of Thomas, a collection of 114 "hidden" sayings attributed to Jesus. In its 1993 book *The Five Gospels*, the Jesus Seminar granted this text equal status to the New Testament.[16] Thomas's first edition, according to *The Complete Gospels*, was written about AD 50, earlier than any of the biblical Gospels.[17] *The Gnostic Bible*, edited by Willis Barnstone and Marvin Meyer, agrees with the early dating: "A version of this gospel may have been composed, most likely in Greek, as early as the middle of the first century, or somewhat later."[18]

Elaine Pagels, professor of religion at Princeton University and author of *Beyond Belief: The Secret Gospel of Thomas*, told me that she dates Thomas's composition to AD 80 or 90, which would be before many scholars date the Bible's Gospel of John. "The scholars that I know see John and Thomas sharing a common tradition," she said.

Yet the gospels of John and Thomas come to opposing conclusions concerning pivotal theological issues. "John says that we can experience God only through the divine light embodied in Jesus," Pagels said. "But certain passages in Thomas's gospel draw a quite different conclusion: that the divine light Jesus embodied is shared by humanity, since we are all made in the image of God."[19]

The Thomas gospel describes Jesus not as the biblical redeemer, but as a wisdom figure who imparts secret teachings to the disciples who are mature enough to receive them. That's consistent with the Gnostic belief that salvation comes through knowledge, not through Christ's atonement for sin. "The salvation offered in the Gospel of Thomas is clearly at odds with the salvation (by grace through faith) offered in the New Testament," said Ben Witherington III of Asbury Theological Seminary. In the Gnostic view, he said, "a person has to be worthy to receive Jesus' secret wisdom."[20]

Contrary to the Bible, Jesus is quoted in Saying 14 of Thomas as telling his disciples: "If you fast, you will bring sin upon yourselves, and if you pray, you will be condemned, and if you give to charity, you will harm your spirits." He is quoted in Saying 114 as teaching that "every female who makes herself male will enter the kingdom of Heaven." The gospel also quotes Jesus in Saying 7 as offering this inscrutable insight: "Blessings on the lion if a human eats it, making the lion human. Foul is the human if a lion eats it, making the lion human."[21]

"The Gospel of Thomas contains teaching venerated by 'Thomas Christians,' apparently an early group that ... thrived during the first century," says Pagels.[22] "We now begin to see that what we call Christianity ... actually represents only a small selection of specific sources, chosen from among dozens of others.... Why were these other writings excluded and banned as 'heresy'? What made them so dangerous?"[23]

That's a good question. Were these alternative depictions of Jesus censored—even burned—because they dared to deviate from what was becoming the "orthodox" view of him? Was the first century a maelstrom of clashing doctrines and practices—all equally valid—with one dominant viewpoint eventually elbowing its way to prominence and brutally squelching the others?

This is the opinion of some scholars who talk in terms of early "Christianities" rather than Christianity. "With the council of Nicea in 325, the orthodox party solidified its hold on the Christian tradition," says the Jesus Seminar, "and other wings of the Christian movement were choked off."[24]

All of this has profound implications for my personal quest to discover the real Jesus. Is it possible that my earlier conclusions about him have been unduly colored by New Testament accounts that in reality were only one perspective among many? Is the Bible's theology merely the result of one politically connected group repressing other legitimate beliefs?

"We can probably say with some certainty that if some other side had won ... there would have been no doctrine of Christ as both fully divine and human," says agnostic professor Bart Ehrman of the University of North Carolina at Chapel Hill.[25]

Clearly, a lot is at stake. I need to have confidence that the *right* people used the *right* reasoning to choose the *right* documents in the ancient world. I need to know if there was any historical support for these alternative texts seeing Jesus in a different light. Surely the Jesus that emerges from many of these documents looks radically different from the Jesus of Matthew, Mark, Luke, and John. Says Jenkins:

> The hidden gospels have been used to provide scriptural warrant for sweeping new interpretations of Jesus, for interpreting theological statements in a purely symbolic and psychological sense, and for challenging dogmatic or legal rules on the basis of the believer's subjective moral sense. Generally, the hidden gospels offer wonderful news for liberals, feminists, and radicals within the churches, who challenge what they view as outdated institutions and prejudices.[26]

I needed to go wherever the evidence would take me. Knowing there are almost as many opinions as there are experts, I wanted to track down someone who has sterling credentials, who would be respected by both conservatives *and* liberals, and who, most importantly, could back up his insights with solid facts and reasoning.

That meant flying to Nova Scotia and driving to a quaint village to interview a highly regarded historian whose professional endorsers range from the orthodox N. T. Wright to such leftwing scholars as Marcus Borg and even Jesus Seminar cofounder John Dominic Crossan, the now-retired DePaul University professor who claims to have discovered a different Jesus among the once-lost texts of antiquity.

After driving more than an hour from my hotel in Halifax, I rang the doorbell at the colonial-style house of Craig A. Evans in a heavily wooded community near Acadia University, where he serves as a professor of New Testament.

INTERVIEW #1: Craig A. Evans, PhD

Evans came to Acadia University in 2002 after spending more than twenty years as a professor at Trinity Western University, where he directed the graduate programs in biblical studies and founded the Dead Sea Scrolls Institute. He received his bachelor's degree in history and philosophy from Claremont McKenna College, his master of divinity degree from Western Baptist Seminary, and a master's degree and doctorate in biblical studies from Claremont Graduate University, which also has produced numerous members of the Jesus Seminar. In addition, he also has served as a visiting fellow at Princeton Theological Seminary.

He is a prolific writer known for his scholarly precision as well as his ability to pierce the fog of academia with uncharacteristic clarity. He is the author or editor of more than fifty books, including *Noncanonical Writings and New Testament Interpretation; Studying the Historical Jesus; Jesus and His Contemporaries; Eschatology, Messianism, and the Dead Sea Scrolls; Early Christian Interpretation of the Scriptures of Israel; Authenticating the Words of Jesus; The Missing Jesus: Rabbinic Judaism and the New Testament;* and *Ancient Texts for New Testament Studies.* He has lectured at Cambridge, Durham, Oxford, Yale, and other universities, as well as the Field Museum in Chicago and the Canadian Museum of Civilization in Ottawa.

For a decade, Evans served as editor-in-chief of the *Bulletin for Biblical Research,* and he is a member of the Studiorum Novi Testamenti Societas (SNTS), the Institute for Biblical Research, and the International Organization for Septuagint and Cognate Studies. He has been selected chairman of the Society of Biblical Literature's Scripture in Early Judaism and Christianity Section and the SNTS's Gospels and Rabbinic Literature Seminar.

More recently Evans has been expanding his work into the popular arena. He has appeared as an expert on numerous television programs, including *Dateline NBC,* the History Channel, and the BBC, and his excellent book *Fabricating Jesus: How Modern Scholars Distort the Gospels,* was published for a general audience in 2006.

Evans and his wife of thirty-two years, Ginny, opened their front door and invited me in. He was casually dressed in a short-sleeve striped shirt and dark slacks. His graying hair, parted neatly at the side, and his wire-rim glasses gave him a professorial air, while the tone and cadence of his voice sounded vaguely like commentator George Will. As we settled into chairs at his dining room table, I decided to ask him a series of background questions before we plunged into analyzing the legitimacy of the "alternative" gospels.[27]

Kingdom of God, Son of Man

"Why are some scholars coming up with such unusual portraits of Jesus?" I asked, picking up a homemade chocolate-chip cookie from a tray that Ginny set down between us.

Evans thought for a moment. "One reason," he replied, "is many of them lack training in the Semitic background of the New Testament."

"Meaning ..."

"Semitic training deals with Hebrew, Aramaic, Syriac, and various sources written in those languages, such as the Dead Sea Scrolls and early rabbinic writings. Very, very few New Testament scholars go beyond the Hebrew of the Old Testament, which is sort of a 'baby Hebrew.'"

"How does this affect their scholarship?" I asked.

"Here's the rub," he said. "These scholars can read the Greek in which the New Testament is written, but Jesus didn't speak Greek, except perhaps occasionally. Most of his teaching was in Aramaic, and his scriptures were in Hebrew or Aramaic paraphrases. Jesus and his world were very Semitic, yet most New Testament scholars lack adequate training in the very languages and literatures that reflect his world. Since they know Greek, they gravitate toward making comparisons between the Jesus of the Greek Gospels and various Greek philosophies and the Greco-Roman world. It's easy to find parallels if you're not worried about context or nuance."

"So they're reading a Greek influence into Jesus."

"Exactly," came his reply. "With few exceptions, the Jesus Seminar was not known for dealing with the Hebrew, Syriac, Aramaic, rabbinic literature, or the Dead Sea Scrolls. Here's the result: they missed the meaning of Jesus' central proclamation of the kingdom of God."

"Explain what the kingdom of God refers to."

"It's not complicated if you have the Semitic context: Jesus was basically proclaiming the 'rule of God.' He demonstrated that God's rule was truly making itself felt in his ministry through healings and exorcisms. He said in Luke 11:20, 'But if I drive out demons by the finger of God' — that is, the rule of God — 'then the kingdom of God has come upon you.' But the Jesus Seminar studiously avoided that, instead interpreting 'Kingdom of God' in terms of a Greek philosophical concept — and they got it completely wrong.

"They made a similar mistake with the 'Son of Man' title that Jesus repeatedly applied to himself. They didn't know how it was linked to the Son of Man figure in Daniel 7, where there are divine implications. Instead, they pursued a bizarre Greco-Roman understanding, translating 'Son of Man' as 'Son of Adam,' which doesn't clarify anything.

"So if you don't understand Jesus' central proclamation — what the kingdom of God means — and you don't understand Jesus' favorite self-designation — what the Son of Man means — then where are you?" he asked, sounding truly bewildered. "It doesn't surprise me that the Seminar's work is so quirky and so severely criticized by non-Seminar members — probably 90 percent of Gospel scholars around the world."

"So," I interjected, "this is Jesus out of context."

He nodded. "Right. They move Jesus out of his Jewish world and into a Greco-Roman world, turning him into a Western academic who's up in the ivory tower smoking his pipe and — *what do you know!* He's a whole lot like them."

Another example, I mused, of professors finding the Jesus they wanted to find in the first place. "In some ways," I said, "it seems scholars are almost in a competition to see how skeptical they can be."

Evans sighed. "Yes, that's unfortunate," he said. "I don't think that's the appropriate attitude for scholars. If somebody says, 'I believe something is true,' then the right approach should be to reply, 'That's nice, but what are your reasons? What's the evidence? What are your criteria?' That's how the early church began. The women saying Jesus' tomb was empty did not immediately prompt faith. It prompted questions, investigation, and exploration. Some disciples ran to the tomb to confirm it. And I think rather than expressing automatic skepticism, scholars ought to similarly investigate claims with an open mind.

"The problem, though, is there are so many people pursuing doctorates, writing dissertations, pursuing tenure, and trying to get published that there's a tendency to push the facts beyond where they should go. If you're hoping to get on the network news — well, news has got to be *new*. Nobody is going to get excited if you say the traditional view of the Gospels seems correct.

"But if you come up with something outrageous—that Jesus' body was eaten by dogs, for example—then that warrants a headline. Or if you say there's a gospel just as valid as Matthew, Mark, Luke, or John, but it was suppressed in an early Christian power play, well, *that's* news."

Dogmatic Prejudice?

Moving to the issue of the alternative gospels, I asked Evans to set forth the criteria that historians use in determining whether an ancient document is reliable.

"The first question is: When was it written?" he said, leaning back in his chair. "If the document is about Alexander the Great, was it written during the lifetime of those who knew him? Same with the New Testament. There's a huge difference between a gospel written in AD 60—about thirty years after Jesus' ministry—and another document written in AD 150.

"If the Gospel of Mark was written in the 60s—some thirty to thirty-five years after Jesus' ministry—then it was written within the lifetime of numerous people who would have known Jesus and heard him teach. This would have a corrective effect. But if a document is written sixty, eighty, or a hundred years later, then that chain is lost. Although it's not impossible that a document written much, much later could contain authentic material, it's a lot more problematic."

I knew that the dating of the alternative gospels was going to be a major factor in determining whether they can be trusted. Rather than delve deeper into that topic at this point, however, I asked Evans to continue discussing the historical criteria.

"A second issue," he said, "involves a geographic connection. For example, a document written in the Eastern Mediterranean world thirty years after Jesus' ministry is more promising than one written in Spain or France in the middle of the second century.

"A third issue involves the cultural accuracy of the document, in terms of its allusions to contemporary politics or events. This can expose phony documents that claim to have been written earlier than they really were. When we have a writer in the second or third century who's claiming to be recounting something Jesus did, often he doesn't know the correct details. For example, whoever wrote the so-called Gospel of Peter doesn't know Jewish burial traditions, corpse impurity issues, and other matters from Jesus' time. He gets exposed by mistakes that he didn't even realize he had made.

"Then there are motivational questions. Did the writer have an axe to grind? Does he bend over backward to deny something or affirm something that's dubious? These things are often transparent and we can detect them.

"We look at the New Testament documents and, yes, they have an agenda: they're affirming that Jesus is the Messiah, the Son of God. But they also make all kinds of statements that can be evaluated. Are they culturally accurate? Are they true to what we know from other historical sources? Were they written in a time and place that has proximity to Jesus' life? The answers are yes.

"When we get into other gospels, the answers to those questions are almost always no. They're written in a later period of time—too late to be historically reliable. They were written from other places with strange and alien contexts. We find inaccuracies at key points. We can see they're derived from earlier sources. Sometimes there's a philosophy, like Gnosticism, that's being promoted."

A question popped into my mind. "Is this kind of analysis mostly science or art?" I asked.

"It's much more science. It isn't just guesswork and opinion. It's logical," he answered. "When you look at Matthew, Mark, and Luke—also John, but especially the Synoptics—and use the same criteria that you would use in assessing secular historians like Suetonius, Tacitus, or Thucydides, the New Testament Gospels perform very favorably. Actually, these other historians were much further removed from many of the events that they wrote about."

I picked up my notes. "Helmut Koester of Harvard Divinity School says: 'Only dogmatic prejudice can assert that the canonical writings have an exclusive claim to apostolic origin, and thus to historical priority.'[28] Is it mere prejudice on your part," I asked Evans, "that causes you to give priority to the four Gospels of the New Testament?"

"The only way his statement can be true would be if somebody dogmatically asserts it before any evidence is considered," he answered. "If one examines all the evidence fairly and completely, then it's a logical conclusion that the canonical writings have an exclusive claim to being connected to the apostles. For crying out loud," he added with a laugh, "the Gospel of Thomas doesn't! And would anyone claim that the so-called Gospel of Peter—found in the coffin of a monk in the ninth century—really has a connection with Peter? Come on!

"If you had ten documents and you arbitrarily selected four of them and said only they have a connection with the apostles, and you didn't have any reason for saying that— then that would be prejudice, I agree. But if you go through all ten and you discover that you actually do have credible historical evidence for four of them as having some kind of apostolic connection and the others not a chance—then it's not a dogmatic, prejudicial assertion. It's a reasonable and considered conclusion, based on the evidence."

Christianity or Christianities

At this point, I brought up *The Complete Gospels*, in which the Jesus Seminar published sixteen other gospels alongside Matthew, Mark, Luke, and John—suggesting to me that they considered them all equal in terms of their historical validity.

"Some scholars have sought to give these other gospels very early dates of origin," I said to Evans. "This backs up their claim that first-century Christianity featured a broad range of differing doctrines and practices—all equally legitimate—and it was the more powerful orthodox wing that crushed these other valid Christian movements. Is it true that the earliest Christianity was a fluid melting pot of all kinds of different perspectives about Jesus?"

The disdain was apparent on Evans's face. "It's not true at all," he insisted. "This is the product of a modern agenda—a politically correct, multicultural agenda motivated by sympathy for marginalized groups. It's the attitude that says diversity is always good, truth is negotiable, and every opinion is equally valid. The question is: What really did happen in the first century? What's the evidence? What are the facts?"

I jumped in. "What *are* the facts?" I asked.

"Well, the early Christian movement certainly did have disagreements. But there weren't 'Christianities.' There wasn't one Christianity that thought Jesus was the Messiah and another Christianity that didn't; another Christianity that thought he was divine and another Christianity that disagreed; and another Christianity that thought he died on the cross as a payment for sin and another Christianity that scoffed at that. This is nonsense.

"There were no major questions about any of these basic points in the first decades of the Christian movement. The New Testament writings reflect the testimony of the first generation church, which very much depended on the testimony of Jesus' own handpicked disciples. To take second-century diversity and exaggerate it, and then to try to smuggle those controversies into the first century by hypothesizing that there was some earlier version of second-century documents, is just bogus. Real historians laugh at that kind of procedure."

"Still," I objected, "we do see the New Testament talking about controversies in the first century — things like whether converts should be circumcised and so forth."

"Yes, and the New Testament quite honestly discusses disagreements when they occur — issues like circumcision, whether Christians can eat meat sacrificed to idols, those kind of tensions," he conceded. "But that's not what these scholars are claiming. They're trying to smuggle into the first century a mystical, Gnostic understanding of God and the Christian life, even though first century Christians had never heard of these things."

"So the core message of Christianity ...?"

"... Is that Jesus is the Messiah, he's God's Son, he fulfills the scriptures, he died on the cross and thereby saved humanity, he rose from the dead — those core issues were not open for discussion," he said firmly. "If you didn't buy that, you weren't a Christian."

Evans's mention of Gnosticism seemed an apt segue into discussing the most highly touted alternative text: the Gospel of Thomas, whose portrait of Jesus as an imparter of mysterious and secret teachings has intrigued scholars and captivated the public in recent years. The real story behind Thomas, I was soon to learn, was even more fascinating.

DOCUMENT #1: The Gospel of Thomas

"History preserves at least half a dozen references that say there was a gospel purportedly written by Thomas," Evans said in response to my question about the ancient document. "And, by the way, they didn't believe for a minute that this gospel really went back to the disciple Thomas or that it was authentic or early. Nobody was saying, 'Boy, I wish we could find that lost Gospel of Thomas because it's a goodie.' They were saying, 'Somebody cooked this up and it goes by the name of Thomas, but nobody believes that.'"

Hmmmm, I thought to myself. *An interesting start.*

"Then in the 1890s, archaeologists digging in the city dump of ancient Oxyrhynchus, Egypt, found thousands of papyri, including three fragments of the Gospel of Thomas in Greek. Only they didn't know what they were until 1945, when the Nag Hammadi library was discovered at another location in Egypt. Among the thirteen leather-bound codices found in a jar was the Gospel of Thomas in Coptic. That's when scholars realized that the discovery in Oxyrhynchus represented 20 percent of the Thomas Gospel.

"A lot of people assume that the Greek version is earlier than the Coptic version. But now the small number of scholars who have competence in the field believe that may not be true. Instead, Thomas was probably written in Syriac. What's particularly interesting is that most of the material in Thomas parallels Matthew, Mark, Luke, John, and sometimes Paul and other sources. Over half of the New Testament writings are quoted, paralleled, or alluded to in Thomas."

"What does that tell you?" I asked.

"It tells me it's late," he replied. "I'm not aware of a Christian writing prior to AD 150 that references this much of the New Testament. Go to the Epistles of Ignatius, the bishop of Antioch, which were written around AD 110. Nobody doubts their authenticity. They don't quote even half of the New Testament. Then along comes the Gospel of Thomas and it shows familiarity with fourteen or fifteen of the twenty-seven New Testament writings." His eyebrows shot up. "And people want to date it to the middle of the first century? Come on!"

I interrupted. "Elaine Pagels told me that she takes what she called a 'conservative view' of the dating and puts it about AD 80 or 90. Stevan L. Davies says Thomas 'is wholly independent of the New Testament Gospels; most probably it was in existence before they were written. It should be dated AD 50 – 70.'"[29]

"Oh, that's absurd!"

Undeterred, I continued. "John Dominic Crossan says the current text emerged about 60 or 70, but that an earlier edition goes back as far as the 50s.[30] If they're right, that means Thomas has really early material. Are they wrong?"

"They're wrong for several reasons," he said. "Number one, as I explained, Thomas has too much New Testament in it. Not only that, but Thomas doesn't have early, pre-Synoptic material. Thomas has forms that reflect the later developments in Luke or Matthew."

I was confused. "Explain what you mean," I said.

"Matthew and Luke sometimes improve on Mark's grammar and word choice. Mark is not real polished in terms of Greek grammar and style, while Matthew and Luke are much more so. And in the Gospel of Thomas we find these more polished Matthew and Luke forms of the sayings of Jesus. So Thomas isn't referring to the earlier Mark, but to the later Matthew and Luke. We also find references to the special material that's only found in Matthew and only in Luke, both of which scholars think is later, not earlier.

"And Thomas has material from the Gospel of John. How can Thomas be written in the 50s and the 60s but still have Johannine material that doesn't get written down until the 90s? It gets even worse when we find that some of the material that certain scholars think is old and independent actually reflects *Syrian* development."

Again, I asked him to elaborate. "The Gospels are published in the Greek language," he said. "Christianity then spread to all sorts of language groups. Of course, it goes eastward, where people speak a form of Aramaic called Syriac."

"So the Gospels were translated into Syriac?"

"Not immediately. There was a guy named Tatian, a student of Justin Martyr, who created a written harmony of Matthew, Mark, Luke, and John in the year 175. It's called the *Diatessaron*, which means, 'through the four.' What he did was blend all four Gospels together and present it in Syriac. So the first time Syrian-speaking Christians had access to the Gospels was not as separate Matthew, Mark, Luke, and John, but as the blended, harmonized form.

"In blending together the sayings of the four Gospels, Tatian created some new forms, because it was part Matthew, part Luke, and so forth. Here's the clincher: *those distinctive Syrian forms show up in the Gospel of Thomas.*

"What's more, a study by Nicholas Perrin has found that in places the Gospel of Thomas is also acquainted with the order and arrangement of material in the *Diatessaron*. All of this means Thomas must have been written *later* than the *Diatessaron* in 175. Now everything begins to add up. Of course Thomas knows more than half of the New Testament. By the end of the second century, you're in a position to know that much. And Thomas reflects Syrian ideas."

"Such as what?"

Evans replied with a question of his own: "How does the Gospel of Thomas refer to Thomas?"

Feeling a bit like one of his students, I searched my memory. "As Judas Thomas," I offered.

"That's right," he said. "That name is found in the Syrian church —and nowhere else. Also, the Syrian church was very much into ascetics. They did not like wealth. They did not like businessmen and commercialism. That shows up in Thomas. They were into elitism and mysticism. And guess what? That also shows up in Thomas.

"But maybe this is the most interesting evidence. If you read Thomas in Greek or Coptic, it looks like the 114 sayings aren't in any particular order. It appears to be just a random collection of what Jesus supposedly said. But if you translate it into Syriac, something extremely intriguing emerges. Suddenly, you discover more than five hundred Syrian catchwords that link virtually all the 114 sayings in order to help people memorize the gospel.[31] In other words, Saying 2 is followed by Saying 3 because Saying 2 refers to a certain word that's then contained in Saying 3. And Saying 3 has a certain word that leads you into Saying 4. It was a memorization aid.

"So you have distinctive Syrian sayings, you have Thomas called Judas Thomas, you have Syriac catchwords, you have familiarity with more than one-half of the New Testament—what does it all add up to? Everything points to Thomas being written at the end of the second century, no earlier than 175 and probably closer to 200."

I had to admit: that was an extremely impressive case. Still, I knew Thomas supporters would raise arguments to the contrary. "A few scholars point out that there was apparently a collection of Jesus' sayings called Q that was used as a source by Matthew and Luke and was therefore extremely early," I said. "Similarly, the Gospel of Thomas is a collection of sayings—so maybe they're similar genres and therefore Thomas must be early like Q." [32]

Evans rolled his eyes. "Oh, yeah, what a brilliant argument!" he said, his sarcasm in full bloom. "What they don't seem to realize is that at the end of the second century, there was another collection of sayings produced, called the Sentences of Sextus. And by the end of the second century, a collection of sayings of the rabbis was produced. So what is it about collections of sayings that argues for the middle of the first century only? The collections genre was just as popular in Syria at the end of the second century as it was anywhere else in an earlier period."

I tried another approach. "What about the argument that there's an earlier edition of Thomas, with more ancient elements, that's embedded in the text?"

"Obviously, Thomas is depending on some traditions that have been inherited. So, yes, there's some earlier stuff in it," he said. "But when you say there was an earlier Gospel of Thomas—a coherent, whole, discrete unit—now you're claiming something for which you should have evidence. Frankly, there is no such evidence.

"That's when a few scholars turn to what we call 'special pleading.' They're aware of the points I've been making today. They know this evidence embarrasses their theory that Thomas is very early. So they hypothesize a different form of Thomas that they claim was earlier than the one we now have. That is, instead of modifying their theory to fit the evidence, they modify the evidence to fit the theory. Well, I'm sorry —where I come from, when you do history and examine documents, you're not allowed to get away with that. You deal with the evidence that you have."

"Pagels claims: 'The Gospel of Thomas contains teaching venerated by 'Thomas Christians,' apparently an early group that ... thrived during the first century,'" I said.[33] "Do you see any evidence of this stream of Christianity existing in the early days of the faith?"

"No, the 'Thomas Christians' are the Christians of Syria, and they thrived at the end of the second century. Think about this: If 'Thomas Christians' were running around at the end of the first century, how come church fathers writing in the 90s, around 100 and 110, never refer to them? How come they don't appear on the radar until the end of the second century?"

Evans left those questions hanging in the air. There was no need to try to provide an answer.

Jesus According to Thomas

I had to admit: Evans had done a persuasive job in establishing that the Gospel of Thomas dates to the late second century and therefore lacks credibility in its depiction of Jesus. However, I was still interested in how this ancient text portrays him. After all, more and more people are exploring Gnosticism, especially on the Internet, where Davies even maintains a "Gospel of Thomas Homepage."[34]

"How does Jesus in the Gospel of Thomas differ from the Jesus we see in the four Gospels?" I asked Evans.

"Jesus in Thomas teaches a mystical understanding of the good news," he responded. "That is, inner light, inner revelation, freeing oneself from materialism, greed, and the usual worries of life. Some of the material in Thomas is in step with Wisdom teaching, like the book of Proverbs, and even with some of Jesus' teaching. It's just skewed or exaggerated so that it becomes inner, mystical, private, personal, and not very much community or collective. Indeed, some of the mysticism in Thomas is very similar to Tatian's distinctive views, which again argues for lateness, not antiquity.

"There's no longer any interest in this world being redeemed. That, of course, is the Gnostic element. This world is hopeless, it's lost, it will be destroyed, rather than being restored and redeemed. Israel's promises no longer mean anything. In fact, there's a touch of anti-Semitism in Thomas."

"It's a bit anti-women too, isn't it?" I added.

"Yes, it's very politically incorrect the way it concludes," he said. "Simon Peter says, 'Miryam'—or Mary—'should leave us. Females are not worthy of life,' and Jesus answers, 'Look, I shall guide her to make her male, so she too may become a living spirit resembling you males. For every female who makes herself male will enter the kingdom of heaven.' I've actually heard gratuitous assertions that Thomas originally didn't have that conclusion. So there you go: you just redefine the evidence if it doesn't fit your theory."

Interestingly, the Gnostic gospels as a whole don't elevate women in the way that some authors have claimed. As Witherington points out:

> The Gnostic literature is written by those who wish to get beyond human sexual matters, who see such material things as hindrances to the core of a person's true identity. Thus it is not true that women are more affirmed as women in the Gnostic literature than they are in the canonical Gospels. Quite the opposite is the case. The Gnostic literature is all about transcending or ignoring one's material or bodily identity. But the canonical Gospels affirm maleness and femaleness as part of the goodness of God's creation.[35]

"What about salvation in Thomas?" I asked Evans.

"Salvation is not perhaps exactly the way it is in other Gnostic texts, but it's pretty close," he answered. "It comes from self-knowledge, from understanding oneself authentically, and recognizing where one fits into the cosmos, as well as repudiating and not getting caught up with this world. So it's slightly Christian, slightly Old Testament, slightly Gnostic."

"And the resurrection?"

He leaned forward. "That's an interesting question," he said. "Jesus is called the 'living one.' Some wonder if the post-Easter and pre-Easter Jesus are blended together in Thomas. But it doesn't even matter to them—this is the *revealing* Jesus."

"History itself doesn't seem to matter very much to the Gnostics," I observed.

"Yes, that's right," Evans said. "Contrast that with the canonical Gospels. The reason for the Christian movement in the New Testament is that an event of history has taken place. Jesus has become flesh, we have seen him, we have touched him, he died on the cross, and on Sunday morning he was resurrected. But for the Gnostics, Jesus is a revealer — he tells us things and we must internalize and live in light of them. What actually happened becomes less relevant. It isn't the story that counts anymore; it's the thought. It isn't a response of faith in something God has done; it's just knowing what you're supposed to know."

"So the idea of Jesus dying for our sins would not be a . . . ," I said, pausing to let him finish the sentence.

"No, in their view Jesus didn't die for our sins," he said. "He came so that we would have knowledge. How he left doesn't matter."

"The Jesus Seminar elevated the Gospel of Thomas to equal stature with the canonical Gospels in *The Five Gospels*," I observed. "Even if we grant that Thomas was written much later than the New Testament, do you think a legitimate argument can be made that Thomas should have been included in the Bible?"

Evans was adamant. "No, I'm sorry, it cannot," he insisted, becoming more animated as he spoke. "If Thomas is to be included, then why not the *Diatessaron*, because that's its source? Why not any mishmash written by anyone at the end of the second century that takes second- and third-hand materials, blends them together, and creates an inauthentic setting? Would even a Jesus Seminar scholar argue sincerely that the Jesus of Thomas is closer to the historical Jesus of the 20s and 30s than the Jesus we have presented in Mark or Q? I can't believe that!

"What happens is that some radical scholars are hypercritical of the canonical Gospels and shove them to the end of the first century. Then they'll take these alternative gospels and not be critical of them at all. By being naive and gullible, they drag them to the early second century, or they even smuggle them in supposed 'early forms' into the first century. Then they can say all these documents were written at approximately the same time by approximately the same kinds of people in terms of their qualifications. Now you go back to Koester's statement: it's just dogmatism and prejudice to privilege the canonical Gospels.

"If you picture fifteen or twenty gospels as all being part of one soupy gray porridge, then picking out four of them and saying these four are privileged — well, yeah, that does sound rather dogmatic. But that grossly misrepresents the evidence. Matthew, Mark, Luke, and John were earlier than all these other gospels, and they have credible connections with the first generation, apostolic, eyewitness sources. The only way to deny that is to say, well, I don't care what the evidence says, I will instead rely on my own intuition and guesswork and preference. Now, I call *that* dogmatic and prejudiced!"

I was thankful that Evans didn't politely dance around issues the way some scholars do. I decided to ask his opinion about something else Pagels had said to me—suspecting that he would again be direct in his answer.

"Pagels thinks the Gospel of Thomas should be read alongside Mark, which is the public teaching of Jesus, because Thomas 'possibly' preserves Jesus' private teaching," I said. "Would you suggest people use Thomas in this way?"

"I disagree profoundly," came his immediate response. "That's wishful thinking. I don't think there's any hope in the world that this is Jesus' private teaching. Let's put it this way: if anything in the Gospel of Thomas actually goes back to Jesus, it's because it reflects authentic tradition that is already preserved in Matthew, Mark, Luke, and John. Everything distinctive in Thomas turns out to be late second-century Syrian tradition."

Referring to my notes, I read Evans this quote from Jenkins:

> The new portrait of Gnosticism is profoundly attractive for modern seekers, that large constituency interested in spirituality without the trappings of organized religion or dogma. For such an audience, texts like Thomas are so enticing because of their individualistic quality, their portrait of a Jesus who is a wisdom teacher rather than a Redeemer or heavenly Savior.[36]

"Do you think that's true?" I asked.

"We're seeing conflicting graphs these days—there's an increased interest in spirituality and a decreased interest in organized religion," he said. "Well, that makes Thomas attractive. If you are biblically illiterate and don't care about history or what really occurred with Jesus, if you're not interested in the organized church, then Thomas would be interesting. Let's face it: we're in a postmodern era that is interested in oddball, eclectic, in some cases downright spooky aspects of spirituality, and Thomas kind of fits in.

"It's sort of like reading Nostradamus—it's ambiguous, it's vague, it's open to all kinds of interpretation. And Thomas doesn't lay very heavy demands on anyone. You're chastised for being ignorant—well, nobody wants to be ignorant. There isn't any severe rebuke for immorality or injustice—things that the authentic Jesus *does* talk about."

My thoughts went to people who are reading exaggerated claims about Thomas in books and on the Internet. "What about average, everyday Christians?" I said. "What current value does Thomas have for them?"

Evans thought for a moment before answering. "I don't know that Thomas has any value for everyday Christians. If you're looking for the real Jesus, there are far, far better places to go—like the canonical Gospels," he said. "However, I tell my students that if they're curious about documents outside the New Testament, then go ahead and read them. I say, 'You tell me: Should Thomas be right alongside Matthew, Mark, Luke, and John?' Without exception, they come back and say, 'My goodness, what weird stuff. Good grief! Now I think the church chose wisely.'

"Once these documents are carefully studied, fairly and in full context, with no prejudice or no bias, with no axe to grind or special pleading, if you have a historical perspective in mind, then you have to say the early church made very wise choices from the get-go. You don't come up with a Dan Brown conclusion that, boy, somebody really fooled around with the stew; they should have ended up with the gospels of Philip, Thomas, and Mary instead of Matthew, Mark, Luke, and John.

"It's not a photo finish," he declared. "Not even close."

DOCUMENT #2: The Gospel of Peter

Next I turned to the "Gospel of Peter," knowing that when I called it by that title, I was making an assumption that may very well not be correct. "Scholars aren't even sure they've got the 'Gospel of Peter,' are they?" I asked.

"No," he replied. "They're not."

"Then why has it been called by that name?"

"The document was found in the 1880s in Akhmîm, Egypt, in a codex inside the coffin of a Christian monk who died in the ninth century. In this codex was the Apocalypse of Peter, an account of the martyrdom of St. Julian from the Byzantine era, fragments of Greek Enoch, and a gospel fragment without its beginning or end, so there's no title. But because the apostle Peter appears in the text and narrates it, and because it was accompanied by the Apocalypse of Peter when it was found, archaeologists assumed it was the lost Gospel of Peter that the ancient church historian Eusebius and Bishop Serapion had warned was falsely attributed to the apostle."

"They didn't consider it to be reliable?" I asked.

"Oh, heavens, no!" he replied, shaking his head. "It was considered full of errors and false teaching and therefore should not be read in the church."

"So we don't know for sure that this is a copy of that gospel?"

"We don't know that at all."

"What about you?" I asked. "You're apparently pretty skeptical."

"I'm *extremely* skeptical," he said, "because Bishop Serapion says the Gospel of Peter was 'docetic,' which means Jesus only appeared to be physical. In other words, he didn't leave footprints; his feet didn't quite touch the ground. Yet where's the docetism in the Akhmîm fragment?"

I pondered that question. "Some people point to the part that says it was as if Jesus felt no pain during the crucifixion," I observed.

"That's not docetism," Evans insisted. "That's lionizing Jesus by saying that even though he was brutally treated, he didn't lose self-control. He didn't cry out in pain. If the text is understood rightly, it implies he felt the pain but controlled himself."

"Overall," I said, "what does the fragment talk about?"

"It starts with Pilate giving up Jesus to the crowd to be crucified. Then there's this extraordinarily crazy story about the ruling priest spending the night in a cemetery." Evans's eyes got wide. "This writer doesn't know what he's talking about!" he declared. "No ruling priest would do that! Then the stone of Jesus' tomb rolls aside and two angels, whose heads reach all the way to the clouds, go into the tomb and come out helping a third person, whose head goes *above* the clouds. I mean, we have an NBA dream team here!" he added with a chuckle.

"Following them, coming out of the cave, is a cross," he continued. "I mean, this is bizarre! You wonder — how does it ambulate? Is it a pogo stick? Does it have wheels? Then a heavenly voice says, 'Have you preached to them that sleep?' Jesus doesn't answer — the *cross* does! The cross says, 'Yes!' This is extraordinary! You read this and you say, 'I can't believe my eyes.' How can anyone suggest that this account of a talking cross and angels with their heads going to the clouds could really be an early, primitive account about Jesus?"

"But," I insisted, "Crossan does date it very early. He extracts what he calls the 'Cross Gospel' from it and says all four Gospel accounts are based on this. In his book *The Cross That Spoke*, he dates this gospel to as early as AD 50."[37]

Evans shook his head. "Crossan is just about all by himself on that point. Very, very few scholars would say the Akhmîm fragment could be as early as the New Testament Gospels, but I'm not so sure even they would say it's got an early core on which the canonical Gospels depend. Crossan does, but not too many people think that's credible, since it's such a *tour de force* of special pleading.

"The problem is when the Akhmîm fragment is critically studied, it appears to be loosely based on Matthew, and it contains errors that somebody ignorant of first-century political and cultural realities in Palestine would make — like having ruling priests spend the night in the graveyard. They would *not* do that — and anybody writing in the middle of the first century would know that. Obviously, he's ignorant of Jewish burial traditions and rules about corpse impurity. Also, the fragment is anti-Semitic, which would reflect lateness, not earliness. Because who would write a gospel in the 50s?"

"A Jewish person," I ventured.

"That's right. So now we supposedly have an anti-Semitic person writing a document on which the Jewish authors — Matthew, Mark, Luke, and John — would base their accounts?[38] This is absurd! Would they base their accounts on a document that has manifest errors that would be obvious to them? The writer doesn't even know who rules what part of Israel at that time.

"And Jesus' head goes into the clouds? This probably represents embellishment of the Shepherd of Hermes, written between AD 110 and 140, and an addition to Ezra in the mid-second century. What about the cross being buried with Jesus—and talking? This is the stuff of later legend. In the late second century, and on into the third, there were some fantastic ideas that cropped up about Jesus' cross, like going wherever he goes and preceding him into heaven.

"Any fair-minded historical reading of the Akhmîm fragment would say that, given the errors and the coherence with documented late tradition, that this may very well not be the lost Gospel of Peter at all. If it isn't, we could date it in the third century, or even the fourth or fifth centuries. It's little more than a blend of details from the four canonical Gospels, especially from Matthew, embellished with pious imagination, apologetic concerns, and a touch of anti-Semitism.

"Moody Smith of Duke Divinity School put it this way: 'Is it thinkable that the tradition began with the legendary, the mythological, the anti-Jewish, and indeed the fantastic, and moved in the direction of the historically restrained and sober?' "[39]

Evans waited for the question to sink in. "Of course not," he concluded. "That's not how history works. It doesn't move from wild stories of talking crosses and angels with their heads going to the clouds and then progress to the sober accounts of the canonical Gospels."

DOCUMENT #3: The Gospel of Mary

Popularized by Dan Brown's novel *The Da Vinci Code*, the Gospel of Mary has become increasingly fashionable, especially among women who see it as validating female leadership in the church. "What about any historical connection with Mary herself?" I asked Evans.

"Nobody in all seriousness who's a scholar and is competent would say Mary Magdalene composed this gospel that now bears her name."

"Her name was attached to legitimize it?" I asked.

"Sure. And by the way, that's what Gnostics would do. In contrast, the Gospels of Matthew, Mark, and Luke circulated anonymously. Their authority and truth were transparent. Everybody knew this was what Jesus taught, so there wasn't much concern over who wrote it down. But in the second century, they had to force it. So the gospels of the second century and later would attach a first-century name to try to bootstrap their credibility, since they didn't sound like Jesus. They had to compensate by saying, well, Thomas or Peter or Philip or Mary wrote it, so it *must* have credibility."

"You'd date the Gospel of Mary to the second century?"

"Yes, probably between 150 and 200," he replied. "And, frankly, that's not very controversial. Scholars are virtually unanimous about this. There's nothing in it that we can trace back with any confidence to the first century or to the historical Jesus or to the historical Mary."

"What takes place in the gospel?"

"Mary Magdalene tells the disciples about some revelations that Jesus gave her, but Andrew and Peter are skeptical because the teaching is at odds with what Jesus had taught them. Mary is saddened that they'd think she would misrepresent Jesus' words, and she begins to cry. Levi rebukes Peter, defends Mary, and exhorts the disciples to preach the gospel, 'neither setting boundaries nor laying down laws, as the Savior said.' They go forth and that's the end."

"What's the significance of Jesus supposedly being against the setting of boundaries?" I asked.

"It appears to be a reaction to the kind of rules laid down in the pastoral letters. A guy may want to be a bishop, but he must meet certain specified qualifications. Deaconesses likewise must be this and not that. And this Gospel of Mary appears to be something of a protest in the middle of the second century against rules that were probably shutting out eccentric, offbeat teachers, maybe some of whom are women.

"Can you just imagine a woman of a Gnostic orientation who wanted to preach from time to time? The bishop declines permission, maybe appealing to the pastoral letters. So the Gospel of Mary, with a decidedly Gnostic flavor, deals with that particular issue by saying that Jesus told Mary in a revelation not to lay down rules. The gospel defends the right of women to be teachers, perhaps in opposition to the growing institutionalization of Christianity that put some restrictions on women.

"Now, it's just fragmentary enough that we don't know quite the whole story—so you can modernize it, you can make it politically correct, you can feminize it, you can do all kinds of things with it, which some people do. What's clear, though, is that the gospel fits a setting that's no earlier than the mid-second century."

"I hesitate to bring this up, because it's already been thoroughly debunked by so many credible scholars," I said, "but we might as well mention that this gospel does not actually support the now-popular idea that Jesus was married to Mary."[40]

"No legitimate scholar believes they were wed," he replied. "It's the irresponsible, the Dan Browns and Michael Baigents of the world, who use the Gospel of Mary and the Gospel of Philip to try to make that case, but they utterly fail. Those texts are not only unhistorical, but even they don't say they were married. Only the truly gullible — or those advancing their own theological agenda — buy into that."

DOCUMENT #4: The Secret Gospel of Mark

I have investigated a lot of extraordinary cases as a journalist: police framing innocent people, corporate bigwigs knowingly producing dangerous products, and political corruption of all kinds. But as I sat in Evans's dining room, listening in astonishment, he unfolded a bizarre story of academic intrigue that rivaled anything I had ever landed on the front page of the *Chicago Tribune*. On the surface, the Secret Gospel of Mark's homoerotic suggestions were shocking enough; beneath the surface, the story behind the gospel left me shaking my head in bewilderment.

"The story goes like this," Evans began. He took a sip of water and then settled into his chair. "Morton Smith was a professor of Judeo-Christian origins at Columbia University for years. At a meeting of the Society of Biblical Literature in 1960, he announced that two years earlier he had made a historic discovery at the Mar Saba Monastery in the Judean wilderness.

"In the back of a 1646 book was two and a half pages of a letter ostensibly from Clement of Alexandria, who lived in the second century, to someone named Theodore. Smith speculated that a monk copied the letter onto the blank pages at the back of the book to preserve it, maybe because the original papyrus had been crumbling.

"The letter was in Greek, and Smith said it was written with an eighteenth-century hand. Here's what was so interesting: the letter contained two quotes from a previously unknown mystical or secret version of the Gospel of Mark. It describes Jesus raising a young man from the dead, and then later the youth comes to him 'wearing a linen cloth over his naked body' and 'remained with him that night' so that he could be taught 'the mystery of the kingdom of God.' Frankly, the homoerotic suggestion was hard to miss. The letter then ends very abruptly, just after it indicates that something really important was going to be revealed."

"How important was this discovery?" I asked.

"Well, if it really was written by the author of the Gospel of Mark, then it would certainly be significant," Evans said. "Smith later wrote two books analyzing it—one 450-page scholarly treatment published by Harvard University Press, and a more popular edition for a general audience. A few prominent scholars from the Jesus Seminar said Clement's letter could contain an earlier version of Mark than what we have in the New Testament. They made some pretty bold claims about it. But from the beginning there were rumblings that this might be a forgery."

Indeed, the headlines in the *New York Times* at the time of Smith's announcement reflected the brewing controversy. "A New Gospel Ascribed to Mark," said the newspaper on December 30, 1960. The next day came this headline: "Expert Disputes 'Secret Gospel.'"

For a journalist, the next question was obvious: "Why wasn't the document simply examined by experts?"

"Because," Evans said with a grin, "It's gone. *Vanished.* Smith said he left it at the monastery, but today nobody can find it, so it can't be subjected to ink tests and other analysis. But he did photograph it, and after he died in 1991, large color photographs of the text were studied by Stephen Carlson."

Carlson, a well-regarded patent attorney and amateur biblical scholar, thoroughly investigated the case, bringing in handwriting experts and writing *The Gospel Hoax: Morton Smith's Invention of Secret Mark* in 2005.[41]

"What's your opinion about the authenticity of the letter?" I asked.

Evans's answer was dramatic: "I think the clues clearly lead to the conclusion that the letter is a hoax and that Smith is almost certainly the hoaxer."

I sat back in my chair. This was absolutely incredible to contemplate: a prominent professor—lauded by Pagels as having "impeccable ... scholarly credentials"[42]—supposedly falsifying an ancient letter and fooling a lot of other scholars, who formulated their own elaborate theories based on the spurious text.

"Are you saying Smith not only forged the document," I said in amazement, "but that he then wrote a 450-page scholarly book analyzing it?"

"Yes," Evans replied. "It's bizarre. Actually, if you really read his book, you'll find much of it was filler. But I've met people who say, 'I knew Morton Smith, and he was fully capable of doing such a thing.' I do think, though, that the question of his motive is the weakest part of the case. He himself was gay, which was a closely guarded secret in the 1950s. He had been denied tenure at Brown University and may have wanted to demonstrate his intellectual superiority by pulling off something like this."

Evans picked up Carlson's book and searched through it until he came to the quote he was after. "Carlson put it this way," he said, reading:

> [Smith] was denied tenure in 1955 at the university where he started his career. Smith was forty years old and might have been perceived as over-the-hill. A successful hoax could be exactly what Smith needed to prove to himself that he was smarter than his peers and might even jump start his career in the process.[43]

Evans closed the book. "Who knows? I certainly can't divine someone's intentions," he concluded. "But *why* he did it is a rather secondary question. The big issue is *whether* he did, indeed, write the text—and I believe the evidence is compelling that he did."

"Morton the Baldy"

I prodded Evans to elaborate. "What's the evidence?" I asked.

"When experts examined the magnified photos of the text, they could see what they call 'forger's tremor,' where the text isn't really written, but instead it's being drawn by a forger in an attempt to deceive. There are shaky lines, pen lifts in the middle of strokes—all kinds of indications that this was forged. On top of that, when the Greek letters were compared to a sample of Smith's own writing, they found the Clement text had the same unusual way of making the Greek letters *theta* and *lambda* as he did. That's a powerful link.

"Plus, the photos indicated the presence of mildew on the book—something that wouldn't occur in a book from the dry climate where the monastery was located. More likely, the book was from somewhere else—Europe or North America. Also, there was no evidence of this book being in the Mar Saba library prior to Smith's 'discovering' it.

"And here's something strange: the book had 'Smith 65' written on it. Would you, if you were a guest in somebody's library, looking at his rare books, write 'Strobel 65' on the title page? I find that very strange. If it's *your book*, however, you might not hesitate. By the way, a copy of that book back in the 1950s would have cost only a couple of hundred dollars and easily could have been smuggled into the monastery library.

"But one of the most intriguing clues involves another Mar Sara document that had been cataloged by Smith. It's written in the same hand as the Clement letter. But there are two unusual things about it. First, Smith himself dated this sample to the twentieth century, rather than the eighteenth century when the Clement letter was supposedly written. And second, it's signed 'M. Madiotes.'"

The name didn't mean anything to me. "Who's that?"

"Very good question. It sounds like a Greek name, but it turns out it's pseudo-Greek, coming from a root that means 'sphere,' 'cueball,' or 'bald.' Interestingly, Smith was prominently bald for his entire adulthood. So could the name mean 'Morton the Baldy'? Certainly seems possible."

In his book, Carlson said, "It's not uncommon for the hoaxer to plant deliberate mistakes or jokes as clues to the fake's true nature."[44] Secret Mark, he said, "abounds in jokes" that point toward Smith as the hoaxer.[45]

Also intriguing, wrote Carlson, is that Smith's next major work, *Jesus the Magician*, "was careful not to rely on Secret Mark itself," even though it would have seemed appropriate to do so. In fact, he said, "Secret Mark did not become a major factor in his scholarship apart from the books disclosing it to the world."[46]

Evans said this makes perfect sense to him. "After all, Smith considered his other books to be *real* scholarship. He was enough of a scholar that he wasn't going to damage his own work by incorporating into his footnotes and references a work that he knows is phony."

"Anything else?"

"There are a lot of other clues, but one that's particularly damaging is the fact that before he announced the existence of Secret Mark, Smith had earlier written about Mark's mystery of the kingdom of God and forbidden sexual practices—themes that he also finds in Secret Mark, which he just coincidentally happened to have 'discovered.' That's extremely suspicious."[47]

An Episcopalian priest-turned-atheist, Smith has been described as someone who reveled in enraging the establishment, "provoking the conventionally faithful," and painting a portrait of Jesus that was "far from the respectable, rational, middle-class Christianity of most of his readers."[48] His writings claimed Jesus was a magician who used hallucinatory techniques to initiate his closest confidants "into ecstatic visions of heaven ... to share with them his experience of liberation from Jewish law."[49] Wrote Carlson:

> Secret Mark supports not only Smith's love of controversy but also his favorite target. It was written during the 1950s, during an especially oppressive moment in American history when mainline ministers were urging the police to crack down on gay men gathered in public parks. What could be more upsetting to the Establishment in this historical moment than the intimation, revealed in an ancient text by the author of the oldest gospel, that they are crucifying Jesus Christ all over again?[50]

"What does it say about biblical scholarship," I asked Evans, "that many scholars accepted Secret Mark apparently without asking enough critical questions?"

"I think it's an embarrassment," came his reply. "Too many well-publicized scholars are so fond of oddball documents and theories that they were too ready to accept Secret Mark as genuine. In fact, some in the Jesus Seminar were too quick to say, well, yes, there probably was a Secret Mark floating around and, well, yes, it probably is earlier than the canonical Mark.

"And Smith," he added, "had to be laughing."

DOCUMENT #5: The Jesus Papers

I knew I was going to get an earful when I brought up Baigent's recent bestseller *The Jesus Papers*. Scholars uniformly scoff at Baigent's conspiracy theories and poorly supported allegations, which sound convincing to those untrained in ancient history but which quickly collapse upon examination by experts. The coauthor of *Holy Blood, Holy Grail* isn't a historian; his degrees are in psychology and "mysticism and religious experience." Still, I couldn't ignore a book that has received as much media attention—and that has sold as many copies—as *The Jesus Papers*.

"Baigent reports the discovery of two papyrus documents, both written in Aramaic and dated back to the time of Jesus' crucifixion," I said. "The writer calls himself 'the Messiah of the children of Israel,' and he clarifies to the Sanhedrin that he never intended to claim that he was God, but that he merely embodied God's Spirit. Wouldn't you concede that if this is legitimate, it would be a huge discovery?"

"Well, of course. If we were to find something that we had good reason to believe Jesus actually composed, then that would be breathtaking," he said. "But the flimsiness of this entire thing is just ridiculous. Baigent says he met somebody who said that in 1961, while excavating underneath a house in Jerusalem, he found two documents written in Aramaic, which he showed to two famous archaeologists who confirmed their date and authenticity. They dated them to roughly the time that Jesus was put to death.

"Baigent describes how he went into a walk-in safe of an antiquities collector and saw the papyri under glass. He couldn't take a picture of them, of course. He has admitted that he doesn't read Aramaic and said the other guy doesn't either—so how does he know what they say? He's assured that two well-known archaeologists, Yigael Yadin and

Nahman Avigad, have confirmed it. Oh, but did I mention that Yadin and Avigad are dead?

"So we have an author with dubious credibility in the first place; an antiquities dealer who can't be identified; documents that Baigent can't read or produce and for which we have no translation or verification; and two archaeologists who are dead. This is just the dumbest thing."

"Yet," I pointed out, "the book became a bestseller and some people apparently believe it."

"It's astounding," he said, his voice betraying more frustration than amazement. "This is voodoo scholarship. It's just so silly. It's possible that there are some documents under glass that aren't ancient at all and that are spurious or misunderstood. But you have to remember that no papyrus buried in the ground in Jerusalem will survive two thousand years, period. This might happen in the dry sands of the Dead Sea region or Egypt, but it rains in Jerusalem. It's nothing to get two inches of snow in January in Jerusalem. You can't bury papyrus in the moist ground and expect it to still be there, legible, two thousand years later. Any archaeologist will tell you that. So there's nothing to this.

"He's playing on the ignorance of people as well as the desire for a titillating tale of conspiracy, intrigue, and hiding the truth. And it's always the Vatican getting involved—buying off people or pressuring people into silence. Baigent says Pope John XXIII asked the archaeologists to destroy these incriminating documents, but they refused."

Evans's sarcasm hit full stride. "It's astonishing for as active and energetic as the Vatican is when it comes to bribing people and destroying documents that they never are able to cover their tracks," he said, smiling. "Baigent can *always* find out."

DOCUMENT #6: The Gospel of Judas

On April 6, 2006, facing the bright television lights of more than a hundred members of the news media, Evans was among the biblical scholars who announced the discovery and translation of the long-lost Gospel of Judas. The National Geographic Society had recruited Evans to be part of a team to assist with interpreting the codex, which was discovered in the late 1970s and took a circuitous route to end up the focus of intense worldwide interest.

Carbon-14 dating indicates the papyrus dates back to AD 220 to 340, although team members leaned toward 300 and 320. The original gospel, however, was written prior to 180, which is when the church father Irenaeus warned that this "fictitious history" was floating around.[51]

The most sensational claims in the text are that Judas Iscariot was Jesus' greatest disciple, who alone was able to understand Jesus' most profound teaching, and that the two of them conspired to arrange for Jesus' betrayal. "You will exceed them all," Jesus is quoted as telling Judas, "for you will sacrifice the man who clothes me." If true, this would obviously cast Judas and Jesus in a much different light than has traditionally been accepted.

I pulled out a copy of some commentary I had printed out from the Internet. "This person suggests that the Gospel of Judas predates the biblical Gospels and was burned by the church at the Council of Nicea in 325," I said.

Evans was taken aback. "That's just not true," he replied indignantly.

I added, "There was even a crawler along the bottom of a television news program that said: 'The Gospel of Judas was edited out of the Bible in the fourth century.'"

Evans laughed. "Edited out of the Bible? Someone is accepting what Dan Brown says about the Emperor Constantine in the fourth century determining what was in and out of the Bible—which, of course, is pure poppycock."

"Is there anything historical about Jesus and Judas in this document?"

"Probably not. Notice, by the way, that the document calls itself the 'Gospel *of* Judas,' not the 'Gospel *According to* Judas,' as we have in the New Testament Gospels. So whoever wrote this document may have been indicating that Judas should not be understood as the author of the gospel, but rather that this is a gospel *about* Judas. In any event, it's written long after Judas lived. But still, it does have historical significance."

"How so?"

"It tells us Irenaeus knew what he was talking about when he wrote that this gospel existed; so that's another point in favor of his credibility. It tells us something about second-century Gnosticism and perhaps a group called the Cainites, who are a bit mysterious to us. Did they really exist? Maybe."

"What did they believe?"

"They identified with the villains of the Bible," he said. "They believed that the god of this world is evil, and so anyone that he hates must really be a hero. So they would lionize Cain, Esau, the people of Sodom — and naturally Judas fits right in there. Just how positive the portrait of Judas is in this new text remains an open question.

"Of course, our tendency is to demonize Judas, but it's interesting that he carried the money box for Jesus. If you look at the hierarchy in the priestly establishment, you've got the high priest, then number two is the captain of the treasury. He'll be the next high priest, more than likely. And Judas was walking around with the treasury box."

"So he may have been more prominent than we give him credit for?" I asked.

"Yes, exactly. It's interesting too that in the Gospel of John, Jesus says to Judas, 'What you are going to do, do quickly.'[52] The other disciples didn't know what Jesus was talking about. Jesus had apparently made a private arrangement with Judas; we also have other examples of Jesus having a private arrangement with a few disciples.[53] It may be that the Gospel of Judas gives us a greatly developed, unhistorical, and imaginative expansion of this theme."

I said, "You and the other scholars involved with this project have been careful to caution that this gospel doesn't really tell us anything reliable about Jesus or Judas. But I've seen all kinds of wild speculation on the Internet. Does that concern you?"

"When we announced the discovery, I speculated that some popular writers would produce fanciful tales about the 'true story' behind this gospel — and apparently that's happening to some extent," he answered. "Unfortunately, it's a reflection of what we've seen with some of these other gospels. Just because something's on a screen or in a book doesn't mean it's true. I'd caution people to apply the historical tests I mentioned earlier and then make a reasoned judgment instead of being influenced by irresponsible conspiracy theories and other historical nonsense."

Testing the Bible's Four Gospels

I took a moment to assess how far we had come. I had started with the question of whether six "alternative" gospels could tell me anything new about the real Jesus. Contrary to the claims of a few far leftwing scholars, however, all of them failed the tests of historicity. The Gospel of Thomas could tell me something about second-century mysticism and Gnosticism, but nothing about Jesus beyond a few quotes lifted from the New Testament. The Gospel of Peter, with its talking cross and giant Jesus, flunked the credibility test. The gospels of Mary and Judas were written too late to be meaningful. The Secret Gospel of Mark is a hoax and the Jesus Papers are a joke.

All of this brought me back to Matthew, Mark, Luke, and John. How would they fare when subjected to a historian's scrutiny? I asked Evans what he considered to be the best criteria for assessing their reliability.

"One criterion historians use is multiple attestation," he replied. "In other words, when two or three of the Gospels are saying the same thing, independently — as they often do — then this significantly shifts the burden of proof onto somebody who says they're just making it up. There's also the criterion of coherence. Are the Gospels consistent with what we know about the history and culture of Palestine in the 20s and 30s? Actually, they're loaded with details that we've determined are correct thanks to archaeological discoveries.

"Then there's the dating issue. The Synoptics were written within a generation of Jesus' ministry; John is within two generations. That encourages us to see them as reliable because they're written too close to the events to get away with a bunch of lies. And you don't have any counter-gospels that are repudiating or refuting what they say. We have, then, a treasure trove from any historian's point of view. Julius Caesar died in 44 BC, and the historian Suetonius is talking about him in 110–120 AD. That's about 155 to 165 years removed. Tacitus, same thing. The Gospels are much better than that."

"When would you date them?"

"Very cogent arguments have been made for all three Synoptics having been written in the 50s and 60s. Personally, I'd put the first Gospel, Mark, in the 60s. I think Mark had to have been within the shadow of the Jewish-Roman war of 66–70. Jesus says in Mark 13:18, 'Pray that this will not take place in winter.' Well, it didn't. It happened in the summer. This statement makes sense if Mark was published when the war was underway or about to occur. But if it was written in 71 or 72, as some have speculated, that would be an odd statement to leave in place."

I interrupted. "But whether Mark was written in the 50s or 60s, you're still talking very early."

"Absolutely. Jesus died in 30 or 33 AD, and a lot of scholars lean toward 33. That means when Mark's Gospel was composed, some of Jesus' youngest followers and disciples would be in their 50s or 60s. Other people in their 30s and 40s grew up hearing stories about Jesus from firsthand eyewitnesses. There's a density of witness that's very significant. And, of course, don't forget that most of Paul's writings were composed before the Gospels."

Seeking to clarify a key issue, I said: "When you say Mark was written some thirty-five years after Jesus' ministry, you're not suggesting the author had to think back and remember something that happened more than three decades earlier."

"No, there's no one individual who had to try to remember everything. We're not talking about the story of Jesus being remembered by one or two or three people who never see each other. We're talking about whole communities, never smaller than dozens and probably in the hundreds, that got together and had connections, villages filled with Jesus people in Judea and in Galilee and immigrating throughout the Jewish Diaspora—lots of people pooling and sharing their stories. People were meeting frequently, reviewing his teaching, and making it normative for the way they lived. The teaching was being called to mind and talked about all the time."

"Then," I said, "this would protect the story of Jesus from the kind of distortion we see in the children's game of telephone, where people whisper something, one to another, until at the end the original message is garbled?"

Evans nodded. "Unlike the telephone game, this is a community effort," he said. "It's not one guy who tells it to one other guy, who weeks later tells it to one other person, and on and on, so that with the passage of time there would be distortion. This was a living tradition that the community discussed and was constantly remembering, because it was normative, it was precious, they lived by it. The idea that they can't remember what Jesus said, or they get it out of context, or they twist it, or they can't distinguish between what Jesus actually said and an utterance of a charismatic Christian in a church much later — this is condescending."

Glancing at my notebook, I said, "Richard A. Horsley, head of the religion department at the University of Massachusetts, commented recently: 'I think it would be a consensus among the New Testament scholars that none of the four Gospels is reliable, if what we mean by that is that we have an accurate historical report of Jesus.'[54] What's your response?"

"I disagree with Richard completely," Evans retorted.

"So your assessment of their reliability is — what?"

"I would say the Gospels are essentially reliable, and there are lots and lots of other scholars who agree. There's every reason to conclude that the Gospels have fairly and accurately reported the essential elements of Jesus' teachings, life, death, and resurrection. They're early enough, they're rooted into the right streams that go back to Jesus and the original people, there's continuity, there's proximity, there's verification of certain distinct points with archaeology and other documents, and then there's the inner logic. That's what pulls it all together."

"What about the argument that the Gospels are inherently unreliable because they are basically faith documents written to convince people of something?"

"In other words, if you have a motive for writing, then it's suspect?" he asked. "What does that do to the Jesus Seminar publications? There's always a purpose behind anything that's written. Some people will say this is not just historiography for its own sake — but I don't know too much historiography that's written for its own sake anyway. I think that's simply a red herring. Faith and truthful history aren't necessarily at odds."

I issued another challenge. "The Gospels report Jesus doing miraculous things," I said. "To the twenty-first-century mind, doesn't this lead to the conclusion that these writings lack credibility?"

"I say let historians be historians. Look at the sources. They tell us that people in antiquity observed that Jesus could do things far better, far more effectively, far more astoundingly than the scribes could in dealing with healings and exorcisms. In their mind, there was only one way to explain it — it's a miracle. For us to come along and say, 'Unless we can explain it scientifically, metaphysically, and philosophically, we should just reject it,' is high-handed arrogance. Bruce Chilton of Bard College says it's enough for the historian to simply say that the documents tell us this is the way Jesus was perceived by his contemporaries."

"What about the allegation that the reason we don't have any competing gospels from the first century is because they were gathered and burned?"

Evans has little patience for such claims, which he has heard all too often in recent years. "For crying out loud, the Christians had no control over the city. They couldn't command or coerce anyone to burn anything," he said. "The idea that there was some sort of culling process or purging that took place in the first century is really absurd."

"How about the claim we see in *The Da Vinci Code* that Constantine collated the books of the Bible in the fourth century and burned all the alternative gospels?"

"That's just nonsense," he said. "The idea of Constantine telling Christians what ought to be in the Bible and gathering up gospels and burning them — that's fictional material in Dan Brown's book. It isn't legitimate history written by historians who know what they're talking about."

The Identity of Jesus

As we approached the end of our interview, I found myself admiring Evans's passion. He isn't some dry academic. He's bluntly critical of sloppy scholarship and unsubstantiated theories, but at the same time he speaks with heartfelt conviction about the facts that history clearly does support—and that's where I wanted to steer our conversation: if the biblical Gospels contain our best information about the earliest Christian experience, then what do they tell us about the real Jesus?

"There is no question in my mind that Jesus understood himself as being the figure described in Daniel 7 and that he was anointed to proclaim the Good News—the rule of God," Evans began. "He sees himself as one with more than just prophetic authority to proclaim it, but as one who has actually stood before God on his throne and received power and authority to proclaim it.

"He is Israel's Messiah as he defines it, but not as others did. Others saw the Son of David as coming to kill Romans, including the emperor. That was the popular view. Jesus then shocks everyone by saying, no, actually he wants to extend messianic blessings even to the Gentiles.

"So we're on very, very solid footing that Jesus has a messianic self-understanding, but, again, that means more than the fact that he was anointed. Any prophet or priest could claim that. No, the anointing is more than that—there is a divine sense. *He is God's Son.*

"That's the importance of the parable of the wicked vineyard tenants. In that story told by Jesus, the vineyard owner leased his place to tenant farmers, but when the landowner would send servant after servant to collect his share, the tenants would beat or kill them. Finally, the owner sends his 'beloved son,' and they kill him too. When the parable is interpreted in its context, we see that the vineyard owner is God, the tenants represent ancient Israel, and the servants represent prophets. The point is clear: God sent his son. Otherwise, he would just be one more messenger, one more prophet. No—now he has sent his son, and that's Jesus himself.

"So the high priest Caiaphas asked Jesus under oath: 'Are you the Messiah, the Son of God?' Jesus said, 'Yes, I am. You will see the Son of Man'—Daniel 7—'sitting at the right hand of the Mighty One' —Psalm 110—'and coming on the clouds of heaven'—back to Daniel 7. Caiaphas understood what he meant. He was outraged! 'You're going to sit next to God on his chariot throne? Blasphemy,' he said. 'We have no need of further witnesses. You've heard it yourselves. What do you say? He's worthy of death.'

"The scandal of Jesus' answer to Caiaphas, resulting in the crucifixion, is not that Jesus was just claiming to be anointed by God, as some mere messenger of some sort. That could have gotten him a good beating perhaps, especially if he criticized the ruling priest or made threats. But the calls for his execution had to do with him claiming to be God's Son. That's what makes it blasphemous. Not irresponsible, not reckless, not dangerous—it was blasphemous to say, 'I will sit on God's throne.'

"So the evidence, fairly weighed, concludes that Jesus understood himself as the Messiah, the Son of God. From a historian's point of view, that explains why all his followers thought that. I mean, after Easter you didn't have people running around saying, 'Jesus was a prophet.' 'No, actually he was a rabbi.' 'No, he was the Son of God.' All of them believed Jesus was the Messiah and the Son of God—why? Because that's what they believed *before* Easter.

"Easter did not generate that perspective. One of the worst errors in logic on the part of so-called critical scholarship throughout most of the twentieth century was the idea that it was the Easter proclamation that led people to decide Jesus was the Messiah or God's Son. If Jesus had claimed neither of those things, if his disciples had not thought those things prior to Easter, then his postmortem appearances wouldn't have led them to think that.

"Why in the world did they say he's the Messiah and the Son of God? Because that's what they thought *before* Easter—based on his own teachings and his own actions."

Deity *and* Humanity

I intended to wrap up our interview by asking Evans to expand upon his own personal convictions. I anticipated that he would further elaborate on the divinity of Jesus—and yet our discussion ended with an unexpected turn.

"How have your decades of research into the Old and New Testaments affected your own view of Jesus?" I asked.

"Well, it's much more nuanced, but at the end of the day it's a more realistic Jesus. Personally, I think a lot of Christians—even conservative, Bible-believing Christians—are semi-docetic."

That took me off-guard. "What do you mean?"

"In other words," he said, "they halfway believe—without ever giving it any serious thought—what the Docetic Gnostics believed, which is that Jesus actually wasn't real. 'Oh, yes, of course, he's real,' they'll say. But they're not entirely sure how far to go with the incarnation. How *human* was Jesus? For a lot of them, the human side of Jesus is superficial.

"It's almost as though a lot of Christians think of Jesus as God wearing a human mask. He's sort of faking it, pretending to be human. He pretends to perspire, his stomach only appears to gurgle because, of course, he's not really hungry. In fact, he doesn't really need to eat. So Jesus is the bionic Son of God who isn't really human. This is thought to be an exalted Christology, but it's not. Orthodox Christology also embraces fully the humanity of Jesus.

"What I'm saying is that the divine nature of Jesus should never militate against his full humanity. When that part gets lost, you end up with a pretty superficial understanding of Christology. For exam ple, could Jesus read? 'Of course he could read! He's the Son of God!' That's not a good answer. At the age of three days, was Jesus fluent in Hebrew? Could he do quantum physics? Well, then, why does the book of Hebrews talk about him learning and so forth?"

I was listening intently. "So we miss his humanity," I said, half to myself and half to Evans.

"Yeah, we do," he said. "We find ourselves fussing and fuming over the divinity, but we miss the humanity. And from the historic point of view of the early church, that's just as serious an error as, say, the Ebionite direction, which was to deny the divinity."

Wanting him to explain further, I asked, "What is it we miss about his humanity?"

"Well, a big part of the atonement. He dies in our place as a human being who dies in our place. God didn't send an angel," he replied. "And, of course, there's the identification factor. We can identify with him: he was tempted as we are. How was he tempted if he was just God wearing a mask—faking it and pretending to be a human? Again, that's Docetic Gnosticism—Jesus only appeared to be incarnate, only appeared to be human—and a lot of evangelical Christians come pretty close to that."

"Is there something about his human nature you'd want to emphasize?"

Evans reflected for a moment, then replied. "Yes, Jesus' own faith," he said. "He tells his disciples to have faith. Jesus has a huge amount of credibility if we see him as fully human and he actually, as a human, has faith in God. Otherwise, well, that's easy for him to say! Good grief —he's been in heaven, and now he's walking around telling *me* to have faith? But I take the teaching of Jesus' humanness, which is taught clearly in scripture, very seriously."

"Taking everything into consideration," I said, wrapping up our discussion, "when you think about the identity of the real Jesus, where do you come down as an individual?"

"I come down on the side of the church," he said. "Doggone it, bless their bones, I think they figured it out. They avoided errors and pitfalls to the left and to the right. I think the church got it right. Even if you only consider the Synoptics, you find that Jesus saw himself in a relationship with God that is unique. The Son of God is the way that's understood. And then he goes further and demonstrates that he was speaking accurately. If you have any doubts, the Easter event should remove them.

"That's where you always wind up: the Easter event. Otherwise, you have a Moses-like or Elijah-like figure who's able to do astonishing miracles—but so what? Yet the resurrection confirmed who he was. And the resurrection is, of course, very powerfully attested, because you have all classes, men and women, believers, skeptics, and opponents, who encounter the risen Christ and believe in him."

He looked me straight in the eyes. "As I do."

For Further Investigation
More Resources on This Topic

Bock, Darrell L. *The Missing Gospels.* Nashville: Nelson, 2006.

Carlson, Stephen C. *The Gospel Hoax: Morton Smith's Invention of Secret Mark.*
Waco, Tex.: Baylor University Press, 2005.

Evans, Craig A. *Fabricating Jesus: How Modern Scholars Distort the Gospel.*
Downers Grove, Ill.: InterVarsity, 2006.

Jenkins, Philip. *Hidden Gospels: How the Search for Jesus Lost Its Way.* Oxford:
Oxford University Press, 2001.

Witherington, Ben, III. *The Gospel Code.* Downers Grove, Ill.: InterVarsity,
2004.

———. *What Have They Done with Jesus?* San Francisco: HarperSanFrancisco, 2006.

Wright, N. T. *Judas and the Gospel of Jesus.* Grand Rapids, Mich · Baker, 2006.

"The Bible's Portrait of Jesus Can't Be Trusted Because the Church Tampered with the Text"

The more I studied the manuscript tradition of the New Testament, the more I realized just how radically the text had been altered over the years at the hands of scribes.... In some instances, the very meaning of the text is at stake.

Bart D. Ehrman[1]

There is ... an endless record of persistent ideological doctoring of the canonical texts from the earliest dates.

Atheist Richard C. Carrier[2]

When I was a reporter at the *Chicago Tribune*, a college student from a small Midwestern town was hired as a summer intern. Her parents were nervous about her working in such a big and volatile city, so her mother made a habit of regularly calling to check up on her.

One day the phone rang on the intern's desk, and a passing reporter picked up the phone. When the intern's mother asked if she could speak to her daughter, the reporter replied: "Oh, I'm sorry—she's in the morgue."

The shriek through the phone line instantly sensitized the reporter to the fact that not everyone was familiar with newspaper jargon. He wasn't referring to the county morgue, where dead bodies are temporarily stored and autopsied; in journalism lingo, the morgue is the newspaper library where old articles are filed.

The term *morgue* is still in use today, but technology has radically transformed how newspapers handle their archives. When I was at the *Tribune*, librarians would meticulously clip articles from the newspaper, neatly fold them, and file them in yellow envelopes—one each for the topic of the article, every person mentioned in the story, and the name of the reporter. Outside researchers were rarely granted access to the morgue because of concerns about protecting this valuable repository of history.

Today many newspaper archives can be electronically searched through the Internet. In 2006, the *New York Times* announced it was giving its home subscribers free access to every article published in the newspaper since 1851—a treasure trove of historical nuggets that offer on-the-spot accounts of times gone by.[3]

Most historians today don't get to handle the original newspaper clippings on yellowing and brittle newsprint. Instead, they get an electronic copy of the story—one that easily could have been altered by someone intent on rewriting history. For example, the *New York Times*, to its unending embarrassment, was repeatedly scooped by its rival, the *Washington Post*, during the Watergate investigation in the 1970s. What if someone in the *Times*'s library simply doctored the texts of some Watergate articles to make it appear that the *Times* had actually beaten the *Post* to the punch?

When a researcher accessed those altered articles, how would he be able to figure out what had been part of the original stories and what had been added later? There would be numerous clues: later additions would be self-serving to the *Times*. Their writing style may differ subtly from the rest of the story. Instead of fitting into the smooth narrative of the article, they may seem awkwardly out of place. Most importantly, researchers could visit municipal libraries around the country and check micofilm copies of the same *Times* articles. These versions would predate the counterfeit articles, and a comparison would quickly unmask alterations to the electronic copy.

This is roughly analogous to the way scholars try to reconstruct the original text of the New Testament. The earliest papyrus copies have long ago been reduced to dust. Up until the first Greek New Testament was produced on a printing press in the early sixteenth century, scribes would make handwritten copies of New Testament manuscripts. Errors were inevitable in this very human process—so how can we be sure that the text we have today hasn't been altered in significant ways?

Scholars trained in "textual criticism" use a variety of techniques to try to determine the wording of an original text. They meticulously comb through manuscripts in a painstaking search for anomalies. They carefully compare copies of ancient manuscripts from different dates and various regions to see where they agree and where they differ. This was considered a fairly arcane endeavor—until one of the world's leading textual critics, Bart D. Ehrman, penned the first general-interest book on the topic, *Misquoting Jesus*, which exploded onto the bestsellers list in 2006. For months, it was the top religion book in America.

Actually, the book's title is a misnomer. There's almost nothing in its 242 pages about the words of Jesus having been misquoted.[4] The book's underlying message, however, was that readers can't really trust the text of their Bible—and that the common portrait of Jesus gleaned from the New Testament might not be reliable after all.

"We Don't Have the Originals!"

Ehrman's book immediately set off alarm bells among the public. Ehrman, head of the department of religious studies at the University of North Carolina at Chapel Hill, reported that the number of variants, or differences, between various handwritten manuscripts, total between 200,000 and perhaps 400,000—more variants among the manuscripts than there are words in the New Testament![5]

"How does it help us to say that the Bible is the inerrant word of God if in fact we don't have the words that God inerrantly inspired, but only the words copied by the scribes—sometimes correctly but sometimes (many times!) incorrectly?" Ehrman asked. "We don't have the originals! We have only error-ridden copies, and the vast majority of these are centuries removed from the originals and different from them, evidently, in thousands of ways."[6]

Even more troubling, Ehrman said that some scribes through the centuries *intentionally* tampered with the text for theological and other reasons. "In some instances," he said, "the very meaning of the text is at stake, depending on how one resolves a textual problem."[7] For example:

Was Jesus an angry man? Was he completely distraught in the face of death? Did he tell his disciples that they could drink poison without being harmed? Did he let an adulteress off the hook with nothing but a mild warning? Is the doctrine of the Trinity explicitly taught in the New Testament? Is Jesus actually called the "unique God" there? Does the New Testament indicate that even the Son of God himself does not know when the end will come? The questions go on and on....[8]

Many readers were stunned when Ehrman dismissed the authenticity of one of the most beloved passages in the Bible — the moving story of a compassionate Jesus forgiving an adulterous woman. What's more, he said, the ending of the Gospel of Mark, which reports Jesus' post-resurrection appearances, and the Bible's most unambiguous passage describing the Trinity also are later additions that don't really belong in the New Testament.

Ehrman isn't the only scholar questioning the fidelity with which the New Testament has been transmitted. "Even careful copyists make some mistakes, as every proofreader knows. So we will never be able to claim certain knowledge of exactly what the original text of any biblical writing was," wrote members of the Jesus Seminar.[9] Said atheist Richard C. Carrier: "Many of these conflicting readings cannot be explained as mere scribal errors, but are ideological in nature."[10]

Nevertheless, it was Ehrman's book — readable, witty, and seemingly highly credible — that really stoked the controversy. Part of the reason for the book's widespread success was the way Ehrman winsomely recounted how supposed errors in the text of the New Testament launched him on a personal journey from Christianity to agnosticism.

He described having "a bona fide born-again experience" through a Christian student group in high school, later graduating from conservative Moody Bible Institute ("a kind of Christian boot camp") and evangelical Wheaton College, the alma mater of Billy Graham. He came to a turning point while studying at the more liberal Princeton Theological Seminary, where he wrote a paper to offer ways to explain away an apparent discrepancy in the Gospel of Mark. He said he "had to do some pretty fancy exegetical footwork to get around the problem," but he thought his professor, "a good Christian scholar," would appreciate his effort. Instead, the professor simply wrote on the paper: "Maybe Mark just made a mistake."[11]

That comment, Ehrman said, "went straight through me." He concluded, well, yes, perhaps Mark did err—and then "the floodgates opened."[12] Maybe, he said, there were other mistakes in the Bible as well. This eventually resulted in "a seismic change," prompting him to conclude that the Bible "was a human book from beginning to end."[13] Today, he describes himself as a "happy agnostic," who believes that when the end of his life comes, he will "just cease to exist, like the mosquito you swatted yesterday."[14]

The issues he raises in his book are now challenging the faith of others. Here's the text of an email that I received:

> Please help me. I have just read Bart Ehrman's book *Misquoting Jesus*. I was raised in the church and I'm now 26 years old. This book has devastated my faith. I don't want to be kept in the dark; I want to know what really is going on in the Bible and what I should believe, even if it goes against what I've believed since I was a little boy. *Is Ehrman correct?*[15]

That's the question that prompted me to jump on a jet for Dallas to seek out another renowned textual critic whose scholarly credentials rival Ehrman's. At stake was nothing less than whether the New Testament can be trusted to provide a reliable picture of the real Jesus.

INTERVIEW #2: Daniel B. Wallace, PhD

Chilling escapes from death, amazing coincidences, weird twists of fate, oddball occurrences—sooner or later, all reporters get pressed by their editors into writing a short item about some sort of wacky circumstance that belongs in *Ripley's Believe It or Not*. I've covered my share through the years. People read them with wide eyes, then put down the paper and exclaim, "Wow, that's really strange!" These are the type of articles that get forwarded all over the Internet.

Daniel B. Wallace could be one of those stories. How's this for bizarre: Wallace, though he hardly knew the Greek language, taught himself to become a world's leading expert in ancient Greek—and he did it by studying textbooks about Greek that *he himself had written!*

Okay, that calls for an explanation. First, some background: Wallace is a professor of New Testament Studies at Dallas Theological Seminary and one of the world's foremost authorities on textual criticism. The title of his doctoral dissertation suggests how specialized the study of New Testament Greek can be: *The Article with Multiple Substantives Connected by* kai *in the New Testament: Semantics and Significance.* Wallace has done postdoctoral study at Tyndale House, Cambridge, as well as at Tübingen University and the *Institut für Neutestamentliche Textforschung*, both in Germany.

Currently, he's executive director of a new institute for textual criticism, the Center for the Study of New Testament Manuscripts, whose objective is to digitally preserve New Testament manuscripts so scholars and others can examine them via enhancement software on the Internet.[16] Between 2002 and 2006, the center took more than 35,000 high-resolution digital photographs of Greek New Testament manuscripts, including several recently discovered texts.

Wallace has traveled the world so he could personally study ancient manuscripts, visiting the Vatican, Cambridge University, Mt. Sinai, Istanbul, Florence, Berlin, Dresden, Münster, Cologne, Patmos, Jerusalem, and other sites.

He was the senior New Testament editor of the New English Translation of the Bible (NET), which has more explanatory footnotes than any other one-volume Bible translation ever published, and is a member of the prestigious *Studiorum Novi Testamenti Societas.* His articles have appeared in *New Testament Studies, Novum Testamentum, Biblica, Westminster Theological Journal,* and the *Bulletin for Biblical Research.* In addition, he contributed forty articles to *Nelson's Illustrated Bible Dictionary* and has over 150 essays on biblical studies posted on the Biblical Studies Foundation website.[17]

Among the several books he has coauthored is the popular-level *Reinventing Jesus,* in which he critiques Ehrman's *Misquoting Jesus.* But Wallace is most famous among seminarians for his textbook *Greek Grammar beyond the Basics,* which is used by more than two-thirds of the schools that teach intermediate Greek, including Yale Divinity School, Princeton Theological Seminary, and Cambridge University.

It was after Wallace completed this textbook that he was stricken with a crippling bout of viral encephalitis, which confined him to a wheelchair for more than a year and wreaked havoc with his memory. At one point, he had difficulty remembering his wife's name. Eventually, he lost his knowledge of Greek almost completely — which is what prompted him to use his own book and others to actually relearn the difficult ancient language. And that, as radio commentator Paul Harvey likes to say, is the rest of the story.

In the world of textual critics, Wallace's name is one of the few that can be appropriately uttered alongside of Ehrman's. That's what brought me knocking on the door of his suburban Dallas home one Friday evening, which happens to be pizza night in the Wallace household. We sat around his kitchen table, enjoying dinner and a casual conversation, and then adjourned to his office, a two-story dark-wood library with a capacity of six thousand books.

Wallace, with unruly dark gray hair and a graying goatee, couldn't resist showing me his prized possession. Carefully removing a thick volume from the bookshelf, he slowly opened it on his desk. It was one of only 450 modern reproductions of *Codex Vaticanus*, a manuscript dating less than 250 years after the New Testament was written. Some say the original codex was among the fifty Bibles that Emperor Constantine ordered to be produced after the Council of Nicea.

Wallace gently turned the vellum pages to show me the columns of Greek neatly written in uncial (or capital) letters, stealing a glance at my reaction to see if I registered appropriate appreciation for the manuscript's beauty, history, and significance. The truth was that I was awestruck. So detailed was this copy, meticulously handmade at the Vatican, that it even features holes in the pages at the same spots where the actual manuscript is worn through.

We retired to two facing leather chairs for our chat. Wearing a dark green T-shirt, blue jeans, and white socks, and with gold-rimmed glasses perched on his nose, Wallace was animated and focused even as the hour began turning late. He was a fascinating blend: a former California surfer who once prowled the churning waters off Newport

Beach and who now relishes the countless hours he spends in austere monasteries and dusty libraries around Europe and the Middle East, painstakingly photographing ancient manuscripts to preserve them for scholars.

My plan was to steer our discussion to whether we can really trust the description of Jesus found in the texts we've inherited through the centuries—but inevitably, that meant bringing up Ehrman.

Possibility, Probability, Certainty

"One conservative scholar wrote that Ehrman 'has a strong ax to grind, and the fact that he grinds it well in fluid prose makes it all the more beguiling,'"[18] I said. "But doesn't this cut both ways? Scholars who are arguing for the reliability of the New Testament might also be accused of bias."

"You can't interpret the text without certain biases, but we should challenge our biases as much as possible," Wallace replied, leaning back precariously in his swivel chair until it creaked in protest.

"One way to do that is to look for viewpoints that are shared by more than one group of people. The fact is that scholars across the theological spectrum say that in all essentials— not in every particular, but in *all* essentials— our New Testament manuscripts go back to the originals. Ehrman is part of a very small minority of textual critics in what he's saying. Frankly, I don't think he has challenged his biases; instead, I think he has fed them."

"On one level," I observed, "it seems Ehrman has merely told a general audience about the kind of issues that textual critics have grappled with for centuries."

"That's right. He peeled back the curtain on scholarly work, and that revelation alarmed many Christians, who weren't equipped to fully understand the issues," said Wallace. "On another level, though, he tries to create strong doubt as to what the original text said, using more innuendo than substance. Readers end up having far more doubts about what the Bible says than any textual critic today would ever have. I think Ehrman has simply overstated his case. Gordon Fee, the highly respected New Testament scholar, put it this way: 'Unfortunately,

Ehrman too often turns mere *possibility* into *probability*, and probability into *certainty*, where other equally viable reasons for [textual] corruption exist.' "[19]

I looked down at my notes. "How would you answer Robert Funk, who wrote with his Jesus Seminar coauthors: 'Why, if God took such pains to preserve an inerrant text for posterity, did the spirit not provide for the preservation of original copies of the Gospels?' "[20]

Wallace chuckled. "Judging by how the medieval church worshiped all sorts of relics, it's a good thing God didn't do that!" he said. "Enough pieces of Jesus' cross have been found to build the Rose Bowl. What kind of chaos would we have if people claimed to have an original of a particular book? Or if we actually did have the originals intact, what would happen? My guess is that those manuscripts would be venerated but not examined. They would be worshiped but not studied."

Leaning forward in his chair for emphasis, Wallace added: "God doesn't want anyone — or anything — to be worshiped before him. That includes his Word. Frankly, Funk's question strikes me as naive and even arrogant. Who is he to set terms for how God should act? And again, his view presupposes that we can't possibly recover the original. Essentially, scholars do not have to come up with conjecture about what the wording of the original text might be. We have the wording of the original in the manuscripts *somewhere*. Pragmatically, we could say that the wording of the original can be found in the text of our published Greek New Testaments or in their footnotes."

I pointed out that Mark D. Roberts, who holds a doctorate from Harvard in the study of religion, said that even if God did preserve the original copies of the New Testament, skeptics would probably say, "Well, that's great. But this still doesn't prove that what's in them is divinely inspired. The Bible is a human book, whether or not you have the original manuscripts."

"I think Roberts' point is valid," Wallace said. "Even if we did have the originals, skeptics who are philosophically committed to their position would try to explain them away. Many skeptics only appear to be liberals; they're actually a species of fundamentalist. Martin Hengel said that the only difference between a fundamentalist and a radical liberal is their starting presuppositions. Their methods are the same:

they start with where they want to end up and then look at all the evidence selective for their purposes, rather than being open to what the evidence actually reveals."

Inspiration, Inerrancy, Infallibility

I wanted to get some definitions straight at the outset. "The Bible says that all scripture is 'God-breathed,'"[21] I said. "Exactly what do Christians believe was the process by which God created the New Testament?"

"We aren't given a lot regarding the process of inspiration, but we know the Bible wasn't dictated by God," Wallace replied. "Look at the Old Testament: Isaiah has a huge vocabulary and is often considered the Shakespeare of the Hebrew prophets, while Amos was a simple farmer with a much more modest vocabulary. Yet both books were inspired. Obviously, this doesn't mean verbal dictation. God wasn't looking for stenographers but holy men to write his book."

"Then how does inspiration work?" I asked.

"We get some clues from where Matthew quotes the Old Testament, saying, 'This was spoken by the Lord through the prophet.'[22] 'By the Lord' suggests God is the ultimate agent of that prophecy. 'Through the prophet' suggests an intermediate agent who also uses his personality. That means this prophet was not taking dictation from God; instead, God was communicating through visions, dreams, and so forth, and the prophet was putting it in his own words. So the process doesn't coerce the human personality, yet ultimately the result is exactly what God wanted to produce."

Seeking a crisp summary, I said, "Complete this sentence: when Christians say the Bible is *inspired*, they mean that ..."

"... that it's both the Word of God and the words of men. Lewis Sperry Chafer put it well: 'Without violating the authors' personalities, they wrote with their own feelings, literary abilities, and concerns. But in the end, God could say, *That's exactly what I wanted to have written.*'

"Remarkably, the New Testament writers didn't even know they were writing scripture, so obviously God's work was behind the scenes. In the end, I think this is a greater miracle than a Bible coming down from heaven on golden tablets, because the books of the Bible are a collective product that men embraced as their own while ultimately—and often only much later—recognizing that there was another author behind the scenes. It wasn't until one of the final books of the New Testament was written that Peter uses the word *scripture* in referring to Paul's letters."[23]

Wallace stopped for a moment, apparently pondering whether to offer one more remark. "Unfortunately," he said as he continued, "some evangelicals have what one scholar called a 'docetic bibliology.'"

"Hold on!" I said. "You're going to have to define that."

"That means they regard the Bible *only* as divine and not also a human product. Many seminary students start that way. I looked over a student's shoulder while he was translating Greek in a workbook and said, 'That must be from the Gospel of Mark, because the grammar is so bad.' The student was surprised. I said, "Well, yeah, he's one of the worst writers of Greek in the New Testament.' But that doesn't impact inspiration, because we're dealing with what the product *is*, not how it's communicated. If Mark Twain can say 'ain't,' and it's considered good writing, then you can have Mark do the same kind of thing."

"Now, finish this sentence," I said. "When Christians say the Bible is *inerrant*, they mean …"

"They mean a number of things. For some, it's almost a magic-wand approach, where the Bible is treated like a modern scientific and historical textbook that's letter perfect. Some Christians would say, for example, that the words of Jesus are in red letters because that's *exactly* what he said.

"Well, if you compare the same incident in different Gospels, you'll notice some differences in wording. That's fine as long as we're not thinking in terms of quotations being nailed exactly, like a tape recorder. They didn't even have quotation marks in Greek. In ancient historiography, they were concerned with correctly getting the gist of what was said. The other view of inerrancy, on the other end of the spectrum, is to say the Bible is true in what it touches. So we can't treat it like a scientific book or a twenty-first-century historical document."

"How do you define *infallibility*?" I asked.

"My definition of *infallibility* is the Bible is true in what it teaches.

My definition of *inerrancy* is that the Bible is true in what it touches. So infallibility is a more foundational doctrine, which says the Bible is true with reference to faith and practice. Inerrancy is built on that doctrine and it says that the Bible is also true when it comes to dealing with historical issues, but we still have to look at it in light of first-century historical practices.

"So if we were to build a pyramid of bibliology, the broad foundation would be: 'I believe that God has done great acts in history and the Bible has recorded some of those.' On top of that would be: 'The Bible is telling me the truth when it comes to matters of faith and practice.' And on top would be: 'The Bible is true in what it touches.'

"Unfortunately, some have inverted the pyramid and tried to make it stand on its head. Then if you take someone like Ehrman, when a professor tries to kick the legs out from under inerrancy, it's like the whole pyramid falls over. Ehrman ends up throwing out everything. The problem was that he was putting his priorities in the wrong place."

"It was almost as if Ehrman were saying: 'Find me one error and I'll throw out the whole Bible,'" I said. "That's something you hear at some ultraconservative Christian schools."

"Good grief, that's such a shockingly naive approach to take!" Wallace exclaimed. "You've basically turned the Bible into the fourth person of the Trinity, as if it should be worshiped. I've actually had Christians tell me Jesus is called the Word, the Bible is called the Word, and so I worship the Bible. *That's* scary."

The Protective Shell

I knew from Ehrman's own account how finding one apparent discrepancy in the New Testament launched him on a journey toward agnosticism. I wondered what would happen to Wallace in a similar situation. "What if you found an incontrovertible error in the Bible?" I asked. "How would you react?"

He thought for a moment, then replied: "I'd say, well, I guess I have to make some adjustments about what I think about that top level of the pyramid. But it wouldn't affect my foundational view of Christ. I don't start by saying, 'If the Bible has a few mistakes, I have to throw it all out.' That's not a logical position. We don't take that attitude toward Livy, Tacitus, Suetonius, or any other ancient historian's writings. For instance, does the first-century Jewish historian Josephus need to be inerrant before we can affirm that he got *anything* right?

"If we do that to the Bible, we're putting it on a pedestal and just inviting people to try to knock it off. What we need to do with scripture instead is say it's a great witness to the person of Jesus Christ and the acts of God in history. Now, is it more than that? Yes, I think so. But whether it is or not, my salvation is still secure in Christ."

"So it's not necessary for a person to believe in inerrancy to be a Christian?" I asked.

"Personally, I believe in inerrancy," he began. "However, I wouldn't consider inerrancy to be a primary or essential doctrine for saving faith. It's what I call a 'protective shell' doctrine. Picture a concentric circle, with the essential doctrines of Christ and salvation at the core. A little bit further out are some other doctrines until, finally, outside of everything is inerrancy. Inerrancy is intended to protect these inner doctrines. But if inerrancy is not true, does that mean that infallibility is not true? No. It's a non sequitur to say I can't trust the Bible in the minutiae of history, so therefore I can't trust it in matters of faith and practice.

"The question I'm asking is: What must a person believe to be saved? Can you be saved if you don't believe Jesus was raised from the dead or that he's not God in the flesh? I don't think the scriptures allow you that privilege. Can you be saved if you think that the demons in the Gospels were not real? I don't think you're in a good position to say that, but I don't think it impacts your salvation directly. Can you be saved if you don't believe in inerrancy? Yeah.

"Keep in mind that the first Christians didn't even have a New Testament. All they had was the Old Testament and the proclamation of the eyewitnesses to the resurrection. And Christians down through church history have not always believed in inerrancy. It really became a major issue during the Reformation, and especially in the twentieth-century debates between modernism and fundamentalism. So it's possible to be a Christian without holding to inerrancy or even infallibility."

I nodded as he talked to indicate I was following him. "With that concentric-circle approach, then, a supposed error in the New Testament should not be fatal to a person's faith," I said.

"Absolutely," he replied without hesitation. "It might affect inerrancy, which is an outer-shell doctrine, but dismantling that would not affect Christ, who's a core doctrine."

Looking for further clarification, I asked, "Are you saying doctrines like inerrancy and infallibility aren't important?"

"No, not at all," he said. "I'm just saying they're not necessary for salvation. However, they are important — for instance, for spiritual health and growth."

"How so?"

"If you doubt whether the Bible is an authoritative guide for faith and practice, it will inevitably affect your spiritual journey. You might begin questioning passages that are clear in their meaning, but they're too convicting for you, so you reject them. You begin to pick and choose out of the Bible what you want to believe and obey. Thus, infallibility and inerrancy are important for the *health* of the church, but are not essential for the *life* of the church."

"You obviously have a high view of scripture," I observed. "Why?"

"Because Jesus did," he said matter-of-factly.

"How do you know?" I asked.

"One criterion that scholars use for determining authenticity is called 'dissimilarity.' If Jesus said or did something that's dissimilar to the Jews of his day or earlier, then it's considered authentic," he said. "And he's constantly ripping on the Pharisees for adding tradition to scripture and not treating it as ultimately and finally authoritative. When he says that the scripture cannot be broken, he's making a statement about the truth and reliability of scripture.[24]

"The Judeo-Christian scriptures are the only ones in the world that are intended to subject themselves to historical inquiry," Wallace continued. "If God became man in time, space, and history, then he's inviting us to examine the historical evidence for the life of Jesus, the miracles of Jesus, the prophecies of Jesus, the death of Jesus, the resurrection of Jesus.

"The Gospels don't merely say, 'Jesus performed a miracle some-where. I can't recall if there were any eyewitnesses. I don't recall exactly where or when it took place, and I'm not sure if it was a healing miracle or something else. All I know is Jesus is great!' No, they name names, specify places, identify the exact miracles performed, and mention eye-witnesses. When Paul says five hundred people saw the risen Jesus and that most of them were still alive, he meant, 'This is verifiable.' When Jesus was raised from the dead, the rock of the tomb was rolled back, not to let him out, but apparently so the disciples could say, 'The body isn't there.'

"This isn't true of other religions. For instance, you can't scrutinize the teachings of Buddha that way, because they don't connect with his-tory. The Bible claims more. It says it's faith, and it's in the real world. The Bible deserves to be rigorously investigated because the Bible claims to be a historical document. We have to ask the Bible tough questions because that's what Christ not only invites us to do, but requires of us to do."

The Core of the Gospels

Wallace has been subjecting the New Testament's text to scrutiny for decades. "Has your scholarship shaken your belief that the Bible is trustworthy?" I asked.

"No, not at all. But it has caused me to see it in a different light," he said. "For example, I thought when I started out that when I saw the words of Jesus, they must be *exactly* those words that he uttered. But historians of that day were trying to accurately get the gist of what was said.

"For example, it would take you no more than two hours to say all of Jesus' words in the Gospels. Well, that's not a very long time to speak. It takes only fifteen minutes to get through the Sermon on the Mount —but when Jesus delivered his sermons, people were often hungry at the end. I don't think Jesus gave fifteen-minute sermonettes for Chris-tianettes. So the Gospels contain a summary of what he said. And if it's a summary, maybe Matthew used some of his own words to condense it. That doesn't trouble me in the slightest. It's still trustworthy."

"Do you think this idea of inerrancy has been elevated out of proportion to its genuine importance?" I asked.

"At times. Some have made it the litmus test for whether a person is a Christian," Wallace said. "Theologian Carl F. H. Henry argued against this in 1976. He urged young evangelicals to recognize that while inerrancy is important, it's not on the level of certain other crucial truths—and belief in inerrancy shouldn't be used as an excuse not to engage seriously with history. Still, sometimes Christians put a roadblock in front of somebody, saying they can't become a Christian until they believe in inerrancy."

Wallace paused. "May I tell you a story along these lines?" he asked.

"Please," I said.

"Some years ago I met a Muslim girl who was interested in Christianity," he said. "She came to me with six handwritten, single-spaced pages of supposed discrepancies in the Gospels. She had been taught by Muslims that if you can find one error in the Gospels, then you can't believe anything they say. She said to me, 'You're going to have to answer every single one of these before I can believe anything about Christianity.' My response was, 'Don't you think this list proves that the writers didn't conspire and collude when they wrote their Gospels?' She said, 'I've never thought of it that way.'

"I said, 'What you need to do is look at the places where the Gospels do not disagree at all. And what do you find? You find a core message that is revolutionary: Jesus was confessed as the Messiah by his disciples, he performed miracles and healed people, he forgave sins, he prophesied his own death and resurrection, he died on a Roman cross, and he was raised bodily from the dead.

" 'So now, what are you going to do with Jesus? Even if the Gospel writers have differences in their accounts—whether we should really call them discrepancies is a topic for later—then this only adds to their credibility by showing they weren't huddled together in a corner cooking all of this up. Doesn't their agreement on an absolute core of central beliefs suggest that they got the basics right, precisely because they were reporting on the same events?' "

"What happened to her?" I asked.

"Two weeks later, she became a Christian, and now she's a student at Dallas Seminary. My point is this: inerrancy is important, but the gospel is bigger than inerrancy."

Wallace's analysis seemed logical to me. In fact, I was reminded of the way I looked at the Bible when I checked out Christianity for the first time. "When I was an atheist, I set aside the issue of inerrancy and merely treated the New Testament as a set of ancient documents, which it obviously is," I told Wallace. "That way, I could evaluate them as I could any other ancient documents—and, of course, some differences are expected in all such records. Is that a legitimate way to evaluate the New Testament?"

As he was listening, Wallace was sitting back with his arms folded across his chest. "I think it's thoroughly legitimate," he replied. "As one British scholar said, 'We should treat the Bible like any other book in order to show it's not like any other book.' That's better than the opposite position that has become an evangelical mantra: 'Hands off the Bible—we don't want people to find any mistakes in it, because we hold to inerrancy.'"

I brought Wallace back to the apparent discrepancy in Mark 2:26 that essentially wrecked Ehrman's faith. In that passage, Jesus is teaching that the Sabbath was made for people, not vice versa. He cites an incident in the Old Testament where King David and his hungry soldiers ate the showbread in the temple, though this was reserved for the priests to eat. Mark says this happened when Abiathar was the high priest, but 1 Samuel 21:1–6 indicates Abiathar's father, Ahimelech, was priest.

"I'm just curious," I said. "Have you looked at that passage?"

"I wrote a paper for the Evangelical Theological Society that described five possible explanations in dealing with this," he said.[25]

"Did you conclude that one of those explanations was best?" I asked.

"In the end, I didn't have a conclusion," he replied, "but I said whatever you do with this, don't throw out Christ if you're going to question inerrancy. And I think that's fair. Personally, I believe in inerrancy, but I'm not going to die for inerrancy. I will die for Christ. That's where my heart is, because that's where salvation is," he said with conviction.

"The Bible wasn't hanged on the cross; Jesus was."

The Telephone Game — and Snoopy

Some people have likened textual criticism to the children's game of telephone, in which a short message is communicated to an individual by whispering in that person's ear. That person then whispers in the next person's ear and so on for several people. Then the last individual says the message out loud, and inevitably it has become terribly garbled by the time it goes all the way down the chain. The implication is that because textual criticism is like this, people simply can't trust what the New Testament says today. In short, we can't have any confidence that it accurately represents the original.

Wallace, however, said that analogy breaks down at several key points.

"First of all," he said, "rather than having one stream of transmission, we have multiple streams. Now suppose you were to interrogate the last person in, say, three lines. All of them repeat the message they heard in their own line, and that message ultimately goes back to one source. There would certainly be differences in the resultant message, but there also would be similarities. By a little detective work, you could figure out much of what the original message was by comparing the three different reports of it. Of course, you still would have a lot of doubt as to whether you got it right.

"A second difference with the telephone game," he continued, "is that rather than dealing with an *oral* tradition, textual criticism deals with a *written* tradition. Now, if each person in the line wrote down what he heard from the person in front of him, the chances for garbling the message would be remote—and you'd have a pretty boring game!" he added with a smile.

"A third difference is that the textual critic—the person trying to reconstruct what the original message was—does not have to rely on that last person in the chain. He can interrogate several folks who are closer to the original source."

His conclusion? "Putting all this together, the cross-checks among the various streams of transmission, the examination of early generations of copies—often exceedingly early—and the written records rather than oral tradition, make textual criticism quite a bit more exacting and precise than the game of telephone," he said.

There is, however, another game that does demonstrate the effectiveness of textual criticism. Wallace himself has conducted seminars called "The Gospel According to Snoopy" for the past thirty years at universities and other settings. His goal is to demonstrate in a practical way how textual criticism can succeed in reconstructing a missing text.

"In the game, numerous people serve as 'scribes,' who copy out an ancient text on a Friday night," he said. "There are six generations of copies. The scribes all make mistakes, intentionally or unintentionally. In fact, the resultant copies are actually significantly more corrupt than the manuscript copies of the New Testament."

"How corrupt?" I asked.

"For a fifty-word document, they are able to produce hundreds of textual variants," he said. "Then the next morning the rest of the folks at the seminar get to work as textual critics, with the scribes as silent onlookers. But they don't have all the manuscripts to work with. The earliest copies were destroyed or lost. And there are many breaks in the chain. But the textual critics do the best they can with the materials they have.

"After about two hours of work, they come up with what they think the original text said. There are some doubts at almost every turn. But remarkably, even with the doubts, the core idea is hardly changed. Sometimes the doubts have to do with 'too' versus 'also,' or 'shall' versus 'will.' Then, I show the group the original text and we compare the two texts, line by line, word by word."

"How successful are these amateur textual critics?" I asked.

"Altogether, I've conducted this seminar over fifty times in churches, colleges, and seminaries—and we have never missed reconstructing the original text by more than three words. In fact, we were off by three words only once. Often, the group has gotten the original wording exactly right—and the essential message of the original is always intact. Sometimes people break out into spontaneous applause at the end!"

"What's the lesson, then?" I asked.

"It's basically this," he said. "If people who know nothing about textual criticism can reconstruct a text that has become terribly corrupted, then isn't it likely that those who are trained in textual criticism can do the same with the New Testament?"

An Embarrassment of Riches

As Wallace's seminar demonstrates, having a handful of copies can help even amateur sleuths to determine the wording of the missing original text. Scholars trying to reconstruct the text of the New Testament, however, have thousands of manuscripts to work with. The more copies, the easier it is to discern the contents of the original. Given their centrality to textual criticism, I asked Wallace to talk about the quantity and quality of New Testament documents.

"Quite simply, we have more witnesses to the text of the New Testament than to any other ancient Greek or Latin literature. It's really an embarrassment of riches!" he declared.

"Exactly how many copies are in existence?" I asked.

"We have more than 5,700 Greek copies of the New Testament. When I started seminary, there were 4,800, but more and more have been discovered. There are another 10,000 copies in Latin. Then there are versions in other languages—Coptic, Syriac, Armenian, Georgian, and so on. These are estimated to number between 10,000 and 15,000. So right there we've got 25,000 to 30,000 handwritten copies of the New Testament."

"But aren't many of these merely fragments?" I asked.

"A great majority of these manuscripts are complete for the purposes that the scribes intended. For example, some manuscripts were intended just to include the Gospels; others, just Paul's letters. Only sixty Greek manuscripts have the entire New Testament, but that doesn't mean that most manuscripts are fragmentary. Most are complete for the purposes intended," Wallace said.

"Now, if we were to destroy all these manuscripts, would we be left without a witness?" he asked. Without waiting for a response, he said, "Not at all. The ancient church fathers quoted so often from the New Testament that it would be possible to reconstruct almost the entire New Testament from their writings alone. All told, there are more than one *million* quotations of the New Testament in their writings. They date as early as the first century and continue through the thirteenth century, so they're extremely valuable for determining the wording of the New Testament text."

I asked Wallace about the dates of the manuscripts. "About 10 percent of these manuscripts come from the first millennium," he said. "Through the first three centuries, we have nearly fifty manuscripts in Greek alone. Yet remarkably, the additions to the text over fourteen centuries of copying amount to about 2 percent of the total. In other words, the New Testament grew over time, but at less than 2 percent growth per millennium — so banking on its expansion would be a poor investment!

"The quantity and quality of the New Testament manuscripts are unequalled in the ancient Greco-Roman world. The average Greek author has fewer than twenty copies of his works still in existence, and they come from no sooner than five hundred to a thousand years later. If you stacked the copies of his works on top of each other, they would be about four feet tall. Stack up copies of the New Testament and they would reach more than a mile high — and, again, that doesn't include quotations from the church fathers.

"Even the great historians who give us much of our understandings of ancient Roman history are quite incomplete," he added. "Livy, for example, wrote 142 volumes on the history of Rome, but only 35 survive. When you compare the New Testament to the second most copied Greek author, the differences are truly astounding. Homer's *Iliad* and *Odyssey* combined have fewer than 2,400 copies — yet Homer has an eight-hundred-year head start on the New Testament! At bottom, textual criticism for virtually all other ancient literature relies on creative conjectures, or imaginative guesses, at reconstructing the wording of the original. Not so with the New Testament."

Another critical factor is how early manuscripts are dated. Obviously, those closest to the original are the most valued. When I asked Wallace about the dates of New Testament manuscripts, he smiled and started with a story.

"In 1844, F. C. Baur, the father of modern theological liberalism, argued that the Gospel of John was really a synthesis of Peter and Paul's Christianity and it had to be dated after AD 160," he said. "If this were true, then the historical credibility of that Gospel would be very questionable. Baur's best guess was AD 170—but it was based on philosophical presuppositions. Well, as someone once said, 'An ounce of evidence is worth a pound of presumption.'

"In 1934, a papyrologist named Colin H. Roberts was rummaging around in the basement of the John Rylands Library at Manchester University in England. He found a papyrus fragment that was no bigger than the palm of my hand. He read one side and—*oh my gosh!*—this was John 18:31–33. He flipped it over, and it was John 18:37–38.

"Now, you have to understand that finding a Greek New Testament fragment on papyrus is exceedingly rare. We've found somewhere in the neighborhood of 75,000 papyri, and only 117 are from the New Testament. So this finding was just remarkable. Then he sent the fragment to three leading papyrologists in Europe. Each wrote back independently and said, 'This manuscript is not to be dated any later than AD 150 and is as early as AD 100—and I prefer the earlier date.' A fourth expert, Adolph Deissman, said it should be dated to the 90s. So this one scrap of papyrus sent two tons of liberal German scholarship to the flames! An ounce of evidence really is worth a pound of presumption."

"Is that the only fragment from the second century?" I asked.

"Not only isn't it the only one, but in the last five years at least three or four others have also been found from the second century in a museum at Oxford. They were excavated from Oxyrinkchus, Egypt, in 1906, and have been sitting there for nearly a century. They didn't have enough papyrologists to go through all the fragments! To this date we have between ten to fifteen papyri from the second century. That's remarkable—from within a hundred years of when the New Testament was completed. It's absolutely stunning to have that kind of data.

"And even though they're fragmentary, they're not always small. We have, for example, P^{66}, which is from mid-to-late second century and has almost the entirety of John's Gospel. P^{46}, which dates to about AD 200, has got seven of Paul's letters and Hebrews in it. P^{75}, which is late second century to early third century, has John and Luke almost in their entirety. P^{45} is early too—and it has large portions of the four Gospels, so that's a substantial amount of evidence. The earliest manuscripts were on papyrus, and all the papyri together equal about half of the New Testament."

"So we have a really small gap, then, between the actual earliest papyrus and the New Testament documents," I said in summary.

"Right. There's just no comparison to others," he said. "For other great historians, there's a three-hundred-year gap before you get a sliver of a fragment, and then sometimes you have to wait another thousand years before you see something else."

Explaining the Variants

Among Ehrman's disclosures that alarmed readers was that there are somewhere between 200,000 and maybe 400,000 variants between New Testament manuscripts—in fact, more variants than the 138,162 words in the published Greek New Testament. This was old news to textual critics, but it was shocking to the general public. Yet are these variants really significant—and do they jeopardize the message of the Gospels and their depiction of Jesus?

"Tell me about these variants—how are they counted, and how did they come about?" I asked Wallace.

"If there's any manuscript or church father who has a different word in one place, that counts as a textual variant," Wallace explained. "If you have a thousand manuscripts that have, for instance, 'Lord' in John 4:1, and all the rest of the manuscripts have 'Jesus,' that still counts as only one variant. If a single fourteenth-century manuscript misspells a word, that counts as a variant."

"What are the most common variants?" I asked.

"Far and away, the most common are spelling variations, even when the misspelling in Greek makes absolutely no difference in the meaning of the word," he said.

"For example, the most common textual variant involves what's called a 'moveable *nu*.' The Greek letter *nu*—or 'n'—is used at the end of a word when the next word starts with a vowel. It's like in English, where you have an indefinite article—*an* apple or *a* book. It means the same thing. Whether a *nu* appears in these words or not has absolutely no effect on its meaning. Yet they still record all those as textual variants.

"Another example is that every time you see the name *John*, it's either spelled with one or two *n*'s. They have to record that as a textual variant — but how it comes out in English is 'John' every time. It doesn't make any difference. The point is, it's not spelled *Mary*! Somewhere between 70 to 80 percent of all textual variants are spelling differences that can't even be translated into English and have zero impact on meaning."

I did some quick mental math: taking the high estimate of 400,000 New Testament variants, that would mean 280,000 to 320,000 of them would be inconsequential differences in spelling. "Please, continue," I said to Wallace.

"Then you've got nonsense errors, where a scribe was inattentive and makes a mistake that's an obvious no-brainer to spot," he said. "For example, in a manuscript in the Smithsonian Institution, one scribe wrote the word 'and' when he meant to write 'Lord.' The words look somewhat similar in Greek — *kai* versus *kurios*. It was obvious that the word 'and' doesn't fit the context. So in these cases, it's easy to reconstruct the right word.

"There are also variants involving synonyms. Does John 4:3 say, 'When Jesus knew' or 'When the Lord knew'? We're not sure which one goes back to the original, but both words are true. A lot of variants involve the Greek practice of using a definite article with a proper name, which we don't do in English. For example, a manuscript might refer to 'the Mary' or 'the Joseph,' but the scribe might have simply written 'Mary' or 'Joseph.' Again, there's no impact on meaning, but they're all counted as variants.

"On top of that, you've got variants that can't even be translated into English. Greek is a highly inflected language. That means the order of words in Greek isn't as important as it is in English. For example, there are sixteen different ways in Greek to say, 'Jesus loves Paul,' and they would be translated into English the very same way. Still, it counts as a textual variant if there's a difference in the order of words, even if the meaning is unaffected."

Wallace stopped for a moment to consider the situation. "So if we have approximately 200,000 to 400,000 variants among the Greek manuscripts, I'm just shocked that there are so few!" he declared. "What would the potential number be? Tens of *millions*! Part of the reason we have so many variants is because we have so many manuscripts. And we're glad we've got so many manuscripts—it helps us immensely in getting back to the original."

I asked, "How many textual variants really make a difference?"

"Only about one percent of variants are both meaningful, which means they affect the meaning of the text to some degree, and viable, which means they have a decent chance of going back to the original text."

"Still, that's a pretty big number," I said.

"But most of these are not very significant at all," he said.

"Give me an example."

"Okay," he replied. "I'll describe two of the most notorious issues. One involves Romans 5:1. Did Paul say, 'We *have* peace' or '*let us have* peace'? The difference amounts to one letter in the Greek. Scholars are split on this, but the big point is that neither variant is a contradiction of the teachings of scripture.

"Another famous example is 1 John 1:4. The verse says either, 'Thus we are writing these things so that *our* joy may be complete,' or, 'Thus we are writing these things so that *your* joy may be complete.' There's ancient testimony for both readings. So, yes, the meaning is affected, but no foundational beliefs are in jeopardy. Either way, the obvious meaning of the verse is that the writing of this letter brings joy."

It was simply amazing to me that two of the most notorious textual issues are, at bottom, so trivial in their implications.

Intentional Changes

There are a lot of reasons why textual errors occur, many of them involving scribes being inattentive. Ehrman puts a lot of emphasis, however, on scribes who intentionally altered the text as they reproduced it for the next generation of manuscripts. "That makes people very nervous," I said to Wallace.

"Well, he's absolutely correct," Wallace replied. "Sometimes scribes did intentionally change the text."

"What's the most common reason?" I asked.

"They wanted to make the text more explicit. Through the centuries, for example, the church started using sections of scripture for daily readings. These are called lectionaries. About 2,200 of our Greek manuscripts are lectionaries, where they will set forth a year's worth of daily or weekly scripture readings.

"Here's what happened: In the Gospel of Mark, there are eighty-nine verses in a row where the name of Jesus isn't mentioned once. Just pronouns are used, with 'he,' referring to Jesus. Well, if you excerpt a passage for a daily lectionary reading, you can't start with: 'When he was going someplace ...' The reader wouldn't know whom you were referring to. So it was logical for the scribe to replace 'he' with 'Jesus' in order to be more specific in the lectionary. But it's counted as a variant every single time.

"Or here's another example: one lectionary reading says, 'When Jesus was teaching his disciples.' In the original, it doesn't say 'Jesus' or 'his disciples,' but it's clear from the context that this was meant. So the scribes were merely making things explicit in the lectionaries. No meaning is changed whatsoever—yet it's counted as a variant.

"Now, I don't want to give the impression that the scribes didn't ever change the text for theological reasons. They did, and almost always such changes were in the direction of making the New Testament *look* more orthodox. Probably the most common group of such changes are harmonizations between the Gospels. The further we get from the original text, the more the copyists harmonized so as to rid the text of any apparent discrepancies. But such harmonizations are fairly easy to detect."

I interrupted. "Ehrman says: 'It would be wrong ... to say—as people sometimes do—that the changes in our text have no real bearing on what the texts mean or on the theological conclusion that one draws from them.... Just the opposite is the case.'[26] Exactly how many Christian doctrines are jeopardized by textual variants in the New Testament?"

"Ehrman is making the best case he can in *Misquoting Jesus*," Wallace said. "The remarkable thing is you go through his whole book and you say, Where did he actually prove anything? Ehrman didn't prove that *any* doctrine is jeopardized. Let me repeat the basic thesis that has been argued since 1707: *No cardinal or essential doctrine is altered by any textual variant that has plausibility of going back to the original.* The evidence for that has not changed to this day."

"What comes the closest?"

"Mark 9:29 could impact orthopraxy, which is right practice, but not orthodoxy, which is right belief. Here Jesus says you can't cast out a certain kind of demon except by prayer—and some manuscripts add, 'and fasting.' So if 'and fasting' is part of what Jesus said, then here's a textual variant that affects orthopraxy—is it necessary to fast to do certain kinds of exorcisms? But seriously, does my salvation depend on that? Most Christians have never even heard of that verse or will ever perform an exorcism.

"Another orthopraxy issue is 1 Corinthians 14:34–35, where it says let women keep silent in the churches. Ehrman and another scholar I mentioned earlier, Gordon Fee, have argued that those verses are not authentic because the manuscripts either put this after verse 33 or verse 40. And that has caused some scholars to say maybe this wasn't in the original text at all.

"Most New Testament scholars would say, yes, this was in the original text, but it was probably a marginal note that Paul added before that manuscript ever went out the door, and the scribes weren't sure where exactly it should go. I should emphasize that all the manuscripts have the wording in one place or the other. But still, let's say it *isn't* authentic. The role of women in the church has never been a doctrinal point that's necessary for salvation. Of course, I'm not trying to trivialize the role of women in the church. My point is simply that this passage does not alter any essential doctrine.

"Another one would be 1 Corinthians 9:20, where Paul says, 'To those under the law I became like one under the law.' Then there's the line: 'Though I myself am not under the law,' which is omitted in some later manuscripts. So is Paul actually claiming that he's not under the law, or is he not claiming that?

"When you think about it, it doesn't really matter. If he's claiming that he's not under the law—well, we have clear evidence that Christians are no longer under the Old Testament law anyway. But if he's not claiming that here, this doesn't necessarily mean that we are under the law. Even then, it's a stretch to say that this affects a doctrine."

"What's the most interesting example you can give?" I asked.

Wallace's eyes lit up. "Here's a fascinating one," he said. "Everyone knows the number of the beast, right?" he said, motioning for me to answer.

I hesitated, figuring I was being set up. "666," I ventured.

"Well, that's what Revelation 13:18 says. A manuscript from the fifth century, however, has the number as 616. Okay, no big deal, since it was only one manuscript. But five years ago at Oxford they found the earliest manuscript of Revelation chapter 13. It's from the third century — and it also says 616."

"Are you sure?" I asked.

"I was in Oxford and personally examined the manuscript under a microscope to confirm it for myself. No doubt, it says 616. Now, there's no doctrinal statement of the church or any Bible college that says the number of the beast must be 666, but it's interesting, isn't it?"

Interesting, indeed. "Back to your original point then ..."

"My original point is this: no cardinal doctrines are affected by any viable variants."

Beloved, but Inauthentic

It's one of the most beloved stories in the Bible: a woman caught in the act of adultery is brought before Jesus. It's really a trap — the Pharisees knew that she should be stoned to death under the law of Moses, and they wanted to test Jesus.

Jesus bent down and began using his finger to write something in the dirt. Those words aren't recorded, promoting all sorts of speculation through the centuries. Finally, Jesus uttered those often-quoted words, "Let any one of you who is without sin be the first to throw a stone at her." Chastened, the Pharisees walked away one at a time, the oldest ones first. Once they were gone, Jesus said to the adulteress: "Woman, where are they? Has no one condemned you?" She replied, "No one, sir." Then Jesus said: "Then neither do I condemn you. Go now and leave your life of sin."[27]

The only problem with this story is that scholars have known for more than a century that it's not authentic. This was disturbing news, though, to readers of Ehrman's book. Many people seemed to take the loss personally—and they began to ask what else in their Bible can't be trusted.

"This is one of those sad stories, frankly," Wallace said when I asked him about the adultery account. "When you read this passage, you say, 'Oh my gosh, that takes my breath away! I'm just amazed at the love and the grace and the mercy of Jesus and how he could stand up to these Pharisees.' We say, 'I *want* this to be in the Bible.' And that's exactly what the copyists said. They read this as an independent story and ended up putting it in at least half a dozen different locations in John and Luke. It's as if the scribes said, 'I want this to go into my Bible, so I'm going to insert it here or here or here.' "

"So this was a story that came down through time?" I asked.

"Apparently, there were two different stories circulating about a woman who had been caught in some sin and Jesus was merciful to her. More than likely, that much of the story was historically true, but it didn't end up in the scriptures."

"Was it a woman caught in adultery?"

"I don't know."

"Did these Pharisees peel off from the oldest to the youngest?"

"Almost surely that was added later to spice up the story."

"Did Jesus write something on the ground?"

"Almost surely he did, for a variety of reasons," he replied. "My hypothesis is this: These twelve verses look more like Luke's style and vocabulary than John's. Actually, a group of manuscripts put it in Luke instead of John. What did the story look like when Luke had access to it, and why didn't he put it into his Gospel? I don't have the answers yet."

"But it's clear that the story in the Bible is not authentic," I said.

"There's a distinction we need to make," he said. "Is it *literarily* authentic—in other words, did John actually write this story? My answer is an unquestionable no. Is it *historically* authentic? Did it really happen? My answer is a highly qualified yes—something may have happened with Jesus being merciful to a sinner, but the story was originally in a truncated form."

"Why have Bibles continued to include it?" I asked. "Doesn't that simply confuse readers?"

"Evangelicals have followed a tradition of timidity by continuing to include this story because they think Bible readers would freak if it were missing," he said. "Read any Bible translation and you'll find a marginal note that says this is not found in the oldest manuscripts. But often people don't read those. When Ehrman reports in the popular sphere that the story isn't authentic, people think they've been hoodwinked."

I picked up my New International Version of the Bible and flipped to John. Sure enough, there are rules at the top and bottom of the story in order to delineate it, as well as a note in the center of the page that says: "The earliest and most reliable manuscripts and other ancient witnesses do not have John 7:53 – 8:11." But how many people, I wondered, really understand the implications of that note?

"Are Bible publishers misleading people by putting it in?" I asked.

"I would be cautious about saying that," Wallace replied, "but they certainly could do a better job of saying, 'This is not found in the oldest manuscripts, and furthermore the editors of this translation do not believe these words are authentic.' Otherwise you're setting people up for disillusionment if they get this information elsewhere. It's a Chicken Little mentality that says, 'Oh my gosh, I never knew that these precious twelve verses aren't authentic — and what else are you not telling me?' But the fact is publishers *have* told them about it, and it's an exceptional circumstance. There's only one other passage that's even close to that length."

That's the topic I wanted to address next.

Snakes and Tongues

In November 2006, a forty-eight-year-old woman died four hours after she was bitten by a timber rattlesnake during Sunday services in a Kentucky church. She was the seventh such fatality in Kentucky since 1980. In fact, the state felt compelled to pass a law making it a misdemeanor to handle reptiles as part of religious services.[28]

The journalists reporting the woman's death all said that according to the Gospel of Mark, believers in Jesus will be able to handle snakes without harm. None of them, however, noted that this verse—and, in fact, the whole last twelve verses of Mark—were not part of the original Gospel but were added at a later date and are not considered authentic.

This means Mark ends with three women discovering the empty tomb of Jesus and being told by "a young man dressed in a white robe" that Jesus had risen from the dead. "They said nothing to anyone," concludes the Gospel, "because they were afraid." The final twelve verses describe three post-Easter appearances by Jesus and say Christians will be able to pick up snakes without injury, as well as cast out demons, speak in new tongues, and heal the sick.

"How long have scholars known that this longer ending of Mark wasn't part of the original?" I asked.

"Well, *Codex Vaticanus* didn't have it—and we've known about that manuscript since the fifteenth century. And then in 1859 the textual critic Constantin von Tischendorf went to Mount Sinai and brought back *Codex Sinaiticus*. These are our oldest manuscripts for this passage and neither of them has the twelve verses," he said. "They both have so many disagreements with each other that they must go back to a common ancestor that goes very far back—into the second century."

"Where do you think this ending came from?" I asked.

"There are two basic views, but each agrees that the verses aren't authentic. One group says Mark wrote an ending to his Gospel but it was lost."

I could tell by his voice that he was skeptical. "You don't buy that?" I asked.

"This presupposes that Mark was written on a codex rather than a scroll. A page could be lost fairly easily from a codex, because the binding is like a book, but the ending of the Gospel would have been secure on a scroll. The codex, however, wasn't invented until forty or so years after Mark was written.

"I think a far better view is that Mark was writing about the most unique individual who has ever lived, and he wanted to format the ending of his Gospel in a unique way, in which he leaves it open ended. He's essentially saying to readers, 'So what are *you* going to do with Jesus?' "

"Eliminating those twelve verses, then, really has no impact on the doctrine of the resurrection?"

"Not in the slightest. There's still a resurrection in Mark. It's prophesied, the angel attests to it, and the tomb is empty. But you can see why an early scribe would say, 'Oh my gosh, we don't have a resurrection appearance, and this ends with the women being afraid.' I think a scribe in the second century drew essentially on Acts—where Paul gets bitten by a snake and people are speaking in tongues—and he wanted to round out Mark's Gospel so he put on that new ending."

"Why does the Bible still have it?"

"Once it's in the Bible, it's really hard to dislodge it. All Bibles have a note indicating this longer ending isn't in the oldest manuscripts. Some put these verses in smaller type or otherwise bracket it. Of the disputed verses in the Bible, this and the woman caught in adultery are by far the longest passages—and again, they're old news."

There is a third significant passage, however. Ehrman said that "the only passage in the entire Bible that explicitly delineates the doctrine of the Trinity" is found in 1 John 5:7–8 in the King James Version, which says: "For there are three that bear record in heaven, the Father, the Word, and the Holy Ghost: and these three are one."

"Wouldn't you agree that this is inauthentic?" I asked Wallace.

"Absolutely."

"Where did it come from?"

"That actually came from a homily in the eighth century. It was added to a Latin text and wasn't even translated into Greek until 1520. To date we have found a grand total of four manuscripts that have it, all from the sixteenth or seventeenth centuries, plus four others that have it as a marginal note in a later hand. It's obviously inauthentic."

I said, "I got a note from a woman recently who wrote, 'I've got a great verse for you to support the Trinity. And, by the way, you only find it in the King James Version. Take a look; it's there!' So some people still think it's authentic."

Wallace sighed. "We need to do a better job of training the church. The fact that we've been dumbing down the church for so long is just a crime, and now people are panicking when they hear about this sort of thing. You don't even find this in other translations, except perhaps in a footnote."

"Atheist Frank Zindler says that deleting this inauthentic reference 'leaves Christians without biblical proof of the Trinity,'" I observed.[29]

Wallace reacted firmly. "I'm going to be uncharitable here: that's just such a stupid comment, I can hardly believe it," he said. "The Council of Constantinople in AD 381 and Chalcedon in AD 451 emerged with explicit statements affirming the Trinity—obviously, they didn't need this later, inauthentic passage to see it.

"The Bible clearly contains these four truths: the Father is God, Jesus is God, the Holy Spirit is God, and there's only one God," Wallace declared. "And *that's* the Trinity."

An Angry Jesus?

Are there any ways in which our understanding of Jesus is significantly altered by textual variants? In *Misquoting Jesus*, Ehrman presents a few examples, which I decided to test with Wallace. For instance, Ehrman contends that in Mark 1:41, the Gospel incorrectly says Jesus was "filled with compassion" when he healed a leper; actually, said Ehrman, the original text said that Jesus became angry. I asked Wallace about this issue—and I was taken aback by his response.

"I think Ehrman is probably correct about the text," Wallace said.

"Really?" I asked. "That surprises me."

"Well, I've been wrestling with this over the last couple of years, and I think the original text probably did say that Jesus was angry."

I said, "Although he doesn't come out and say it, Ehrman seems to make an implicit argument that if Jesus was angry, he can't be God, because God is love."

That triggered a strong response from Wallace. "Wait a minute—there were only two groups in the ancient world—the Stoics and the one branch of the Pharisees—who felt that anger was always wrong. Everybody else felt that righteous indignation had a place in life—and Jesus was one of them."

"Do you think this change in Mark 1:41 alters our picture of Jesus?"

"It changes how we interpret this one particular verse," he said, "but that doesn't mean we suddenly have a different Jesus."

"Why not?"

"Later in the same Gospel, Mark 3:5 says Jesus responded in anger because he was distressed at the stubborn hearts of the religious leaders who were looking for an excuse to accuse him. In Mark 10:13–16, he gets indignant toward his disciples because they were blocking people from bringing their little children to be blessed by him. Did Jesus express anger and indignation at times? Yes, we've already known that, but this was certainly appropriate on his part."

"But why," I asked, "would he have been angry when he healed the leper?"

"We can hypothesize several reasons. Ehrman summarily dismisses some possibilities out of hand — for instance, that Jesus was angry at the state of the world that's full of disease or that he loves the sick but hates the sickness. But the text is ambiguous, so we don't really know. What we *do* know is that Ehrman fails to back up his claim that Jesus gets angry when anyone questions his authority, ability, or desire to heal. That's simply unsupported unless you twist the text."

I moved on to another claim by Ehrman. Hebrews 2:9 is translated as saying that "by the grace of God [Jesus] might taste death for everyone." But Ehrman maintains that the phrase should read, "apart from God" instead of "by the grace of God."

"According to Ehrman, this affects the interpretation of the entire book," I said. "Do you agree?"

"Again, I think he's overstating his case significantly," replied Wallace. "For one thing, I think 'by the grace of God' is probably correct, although I'll grant that Ehrman may be right that 'apart from God' is the original reading.

"But here's his real agenda: he links that text to Hebrews 5:7, which says that Jesus prayed 'with loud cries and tears.' So Ehrman says Jesus died on the cross 'apart from God' in a screaming, terrified, frightened way, and therefore the underlying implication is he can't be God in the flesh, because God wouldn't be terrified that way."

"And you disagree?"

"I certainly do. Hebrews 5:7 doesn't specify that Jesus was crying out to God *at his death*. It says Jesus offered prayers 'with loud cries and tears ... during the days of Jesus' life on earth.' In fact, the previous verse says he was 'a priest forever, in the order of Melchizedek.' What do priests do? They pray on behalf of other people! So Ehrman is connecting dots that are illegitimate to connect."

Wallace then added one last point to seal his case. "Even if the original text says Jesus died 'apart from God,' this doesn't change anything theologically," he said. "How is this any different from Jesus saying on the cross, 'My God, my God, why have you forsaken me?' It means the same thing. So again, we're not being given a new picture of Jesus."

"That's Just Loony!"

Wallace had brought balance and perspective to the issue of whether the New Testament's text can be trusted. While scholars cannot pin down every single word with absolute confidence, there was no dispute over the fundamentals. As for Jesus, there was nothing that would compel a new perspective on his life, character, miracles, or resurrection.

I glanced at my watch; it was getting late. I had one more issue I wanted to raise, but I didn't relish asking Wallace about it. This wasn't a critique by a reputable scholar, but claims made by three authors whose book has been discredited by historians in so many ways. Still, I believe its widespread popularity—with millions of copies being sold—made it worth addressing.

"Let me ask you about an assertion made in the bestseller *Holy Blood, Holy Grail*," I said.

Wallace rolled his eyes, but I pushed ahead. "The authors claim that in AD 303, Emperor Diocletian destroyed all Christian writings that could be found. That's why there are no New Testament manuscripts prior to the fourth century. Later, Emperor Constantine commissioned new versions of these documents, which allowed the 'custodians of orthodoxy to revise, edit, and rewrite their material as they saw fit.' It was at this point that 'most of the crucial alterations in the New Testament were probably made and Jesus assumed the unique status he has enjoyed ever since.' "[30]

Wallace looked exasperated. "Good grief!" he exclaimed. "That's just loony! Do these authors know *anything* about history at all? Diocletian did not destroy all the Christian manuscripts. He did destroy several, but mostly in the East and South. As far as having no manuscripts prior to the fourth century—well, we have more than four dozen in Greek alone that are prior to the fourth century. And these manuscripts have numerous passages—John 1:1; John 1:18; John 20:28; Titus 2:13; Hebrews 1:8; 2 Peter 1:1—that affirm the deity of Jesus. So it's nonsense to say Jesus' deity wasn't invented until the fourth century when you've already got the evidence in earlier manuscripts.

"Besides, we still have lots and lots of quotations by church fathers prior to the fourth century. Ignatius in about AD 110 calls Jesus 'our God' and then says, 'the blood of God,' referring to Jesus. Where does he get this idea if it wasn't invented for more than two hundred years? And you have a steady march from Ignatius right through the rest of the patristic writers—I mean, you can't make that kind of a claim and be any kind of a responsible historian. No historian would ever even entertain that kind of stupidity."

"Yet apparently millions of people believe it," I said. "What does that do to you as a scholar?"

"It's disturbing that when it comes to the Christian faith, people don't really want—or know how—to investigate the evidence," he replied. "Christians are not being led into proper historical research by their pastors. I have been saying for some time that I don't think the evangelical church has fifty years left of life to it until it repents."

"In what way?"

"First, we have to quit marginalizing scripture," he said. "We can't treat the Bible with kid gloves. We really need to wrestle with the issues, because our faith depends on it. And second, we need to quit turning Jesus into our buddy. He's the sovereign Lord of the universe, and we need to understand that and respond accordingly."

"After years of studying these issues in depth, what has surprised you about the manuscripts you've analyzed?"

"The most remarkable thing to me is the tedium of looking at manuscript after manuscript after manuscript that just don't change," he answered. "Yes, there are differences, but they're so minor. When I teach textual criticism every year, my students spend about a third of their workload transcribing manuscripts—and invariably they marvel at how little the manuscripts deviate.

"Now, I don't want to give a false impression that they don't deviate at all. But the vast majority of differences involve a spelling error or a moveable *nu*. You don't see a line out of the blue where a scribe said, 'Oh, I'm gonna make some kind of bizarre statement here.' So the bottom line to me is how steady the copies of the manuscripts have been over the centuries."

"Do you believe that God has accurately preserved enough for us to know him and his truth?"

"Absolutely. Do we have all the essentials? Yes. Do we have all the particulars? No. But that's the task of a textual critic: to try to get back to the original. I'll spend the rest of my life looking at manuscripts—transcribing them, photographing them, and publishing them. We still won't recover the original wording in every single place. But I hope by the end of my life we'll be a little bit closer—and that's a worthy goal."

Doctor-Father

My interview with Wallace provided strong affirmation that my confidence in the New Testament text was abundantly warranted. Nothing produced by Ehrman even came close to changing the biblical portrait of the real Jesus in any meaningful way.

"When a comparison of the variant readings of the New Testament is made with those of other books which have survived from antiquity, the results are little short of astounding," said biblical expert Norman Geisler, the author or editor of more than fifty books explaining and defending Christianity. "The evidence for the integrity of the New Testament is beyond question."[31]

As I drove away from Wallace's house, my mind flashed back to my interview several years earlier with a scholar who's universally acknowledged as the greatest textual critic of his generation. In fact, Bruce M. Metzger was Ehrman's mentor at Princeton. Ehrman even dedicates *Misquoting Jesus* to him, calling him "Doctor-Father" and saying he "taught me the field and continues to inspire me in my work."[32]

At the time we chatted, Metzger was eighty-three years old. He died in 2007, ten years later. What was fascinating to me was how much his remarks during our interview reflected what Wallace was now telling me years later. For instance, I remember asking Metzger, "So the variations [between manuscripts], when they occur, tend to be minor rather than substantive?"

"Yes, yes, that's correct," Metzger replied, adding: "The more significant variations do not overthrow any doctrine of the church."

Then I recall asking him how his many decades of intensely studying the New Testament's text had affected his personal faith. "Oh," he said, sounding happy to discuss the topic, "it has increased the basis of my personal faith to see the firmness with which these materials have come down to us, with a multiplicity of copies, some of which are very ancient."

"So," I started to say, "scholarship has not diluted your faith—"

He jumped in before I could finish my sentence. "On the contrary," he stressed, "it has built it. I've asked questions all my life, I've dug into the text, I've studied this thoroughly, and today I know with confidence that my trust in Jesus has been well placed."

He paused while his eyes surveyed my face. Then he added, for emphasis, "*Very* well placed."[33]

For Further Investigation
More Resources on This Topic

Geisler, Norman, and William Nix. *From God to Us: How We Got Our Bible.* Chicago: Moody, 1980.

Komoszewski, J. Ed, M. James Sawyer, and Daniel B. Wallace. *Reinventing Jesus.* Grand Rapids, Mich.: Kregel, 2006.

Metzger, Bruce M., and Bart D. Ehrman. *The Text of the New Testament: Its Transmission, Corruption, and Restoration.* 4th ed. New York and Oxford: Oxford University Press, 2005.

Patzia, Arthur G. *The Making of the New Testament.* Downers Grove, Ill.: InterVarsity, 1995.

Wegner, Paul D. *The Journey from Texts to Translations.* Grand Rapids, Mich.: Baker, 1999.

———. *A Student's Guide to Textual Criticism of the Bible.* Downers Grove, Ill.: InterVarsity, 2006.

PART ONE:
"New Explanations Have Refuted Jesus' Resurrection"

Only one conclusion is justified by the evidence: Jesus is dead.
Atheist Richard C. Carrier[1]

Jesus was placed into a common grave, and covered over.... In a very short time only some unmarked bones remained. Even the bones were gone before too long. Nature rather efficiently reclaims its own resources.
Retired Episcopal bishop John Shelby Spong[2]

Outside a Chicago hospital on a humid summer night, a gunshot victim was unloaded from an ambulance and wheeled on a gurney into the emergency room. The teenager gestured toward his abdomen as he was rolled past reporters. "It doesn't even hurt!" he said with a nervous laugh, as if everyone were old friends. "It doesn't even hurt!"

A few hours later, he was dead.

A reporter on the streets of Chicago soon develops more than a passing acquaintance with death. Often the people directly embroiled in an unfolding tragedy—the car accident, the gang fight, the convenience store robbery gone awry—are too bewildered and disoriented to fully comprehend their predicament. But from the detached perspective of the reporter, the grim outcome is much more foreseeable. And when death finally does seize its victims, when their eyes stare blankly, then all hope is gone. They've spoken their last word, they've breathed their last breath, and their time is done—they won't be coming back.

That's why all this talk of Jesus' resurrection seemed so strange to me. It's staggering how quickly the body of a deceased person is reduced to a mere shell. The idea that it could somehow become reanimated, especially after three days, could never quite get past my journalistic skepticism when I was an atheist.

As I documented in *The Case for Christ*, it was my investigation of the historical evidence that eventually convinced me that the resurrection of Jesus really happened.[3] In the succeeding years, however, the resurrection has been subjected to new and more contentious attacks. Do any of these updated objections, I wondered, manage to crack this central pillar of Christianity?

Religious studies professor Bart D. Ehrman of the University of North Carolina at Chapel Hill certainly thinks so. "After years of studying," he said, "I finally came to the conclusion that everything I had previously thought about the historical evidence of the resurrection was absolutely wrong."[4] The graduate of the conservative Moody Bible Institute and the evangelical Wheaton College is now an avowed agnostic.

Skepticism about the resurrection was bolstered by a pre-Easter 2007 television documentary — followed by a popular book — which claimed that the burial site of Jesus and his family had been accidentally uncovered by an Israeli construction crew in 1980. According to the film, the "bone boxes" of "Jesus, son of Joseph," Mary, Joseph, Mary Magdalene, and even "Judah, son of Jesus" were found in the Talpiot Tomb. The discovery threatened to amplify doubts about whether Jesus really had returned from the dead in bodily form.

At the forefront of the most recent challenges to the resurrection have been Muslims, who clearly understand that discrediting the resurrection means nothing less than disproving the truth of Christianity. Muslims interpret the Qur'an as saying that Jesus never actually died on the cross, much less returned from the dead.[5]

A leading Muslim apologist, Shabir Ally, has said that the Messiah was expected to be victorious, and therefore "a crucified Messiah is as self-refuting as a square circle, a four-sided triangle, or a married bachelor."[6] Ayman al-Zawahri, the deputy leader of Al Qaeda, even took time out from excoriating George W. Bush and Pope Benedict XVI in a 2006 videotape to urge all Christians to convert to Islam, which, he said, correctly believes that Jesus was never put to death, never rose from the dead, and was not divine.[7]

Muslims aren't alone. A prominent Hindu leader declared in a 2007 speech that Jesus never died on the cross. "He was only injured and after treatment returned to India where he actually died," insisted K. S. Sudarshan, leader of a nationalist Hindu organization in India.[8]

Atheists, meanwhile, have been mounting ever-more-intense critiques of the resurrection. In 2005, Prometheus Books published an ambitious 545-page anthology called *The Empty Tomb*, in which such skeptics as Michael Martin and Richard Carrier set forth their alternative explanations for the Easter event. The Jesus Seminar's Robert M. Price is emphatic in the introduction: "Jesus," he declared, "is dead."[9]

Reflecting the public's ongoing curiosity about Jesus, two books attacking the resurrection landed on the *New York Times* bestsellers list in 2006. In his book *The Jesus Papers*, Michael Baigent charged that Pontius Pilate didn't want to kill Jesus because Jesus had been urging people to pay their taxes to Rome. "How could Pilate try, let alone condemn, such a man who, on the face of it, was supporting Roman policy?" asked Baigent. "Pilate would himself be charged with dereliction of duty should he proceed with the condemnation of such a supporter."[10]

That's when Pilate hatched a plot, Baigent said. He publicly ordered Jesus crucified to placate the religious authorities who wanted him dead, but at the same time he conspired to ensure that Jesus secretly came down from the cross alive. After all, Baigent said, it's not impossible to survive a crucifixion.[11]

James D. Tabor, who holds a doctorate in biblical studies from the University of Chicago and is currently chair of the department of religious studies at the University of North Carolina at Charlotte, offered his own theory in *The Jesus Dynasty*, a book that New Testament professor Arthur J. Droge said "may very well inaugurate a new phase in the quest for the historical Jesus."[12]

Tabor postulated that Jesus' tomb was empty not due to a resurrection but because Jesus' body had been moved and then interred elsewhere by members of his own family. In a stunning assertion, Tabor even revealed where Jesus might be buried—in Galilee outside the city of Tsfat.[13]

For Tabor, the suggestion of a resurrection could be ruled out from the beginning. "Dead bodies don't rise—not if one is clinically dead —as Jesus surely was," he said. "So if the tomb was empty the historical conclusion is simple—Jesus' body was moved by someone and likely reburied in another location."[14]

A Dropping of Dominoes

While these attacks on the resurrection have been garnering widespread media publicity, Christians have been equally busy producing books to defend the return of Jesus from the dead as being historically credible. N. T. Wright, the Bishop of Durham in England, who has taught at both Cambridge and Oxford universities, offered his 817-page seminal book *The Resurrection of the Son of God* in 2003. His conclusion: "The proposal that Jesus was bodily raised from the dead possesses unrivalled power to explain the historical data at the heart of early Christianity."[15]

At about the same time, Richard Swinburne, a Fellow of the British Academy and professor at Oxford from 1985–2002, published *The Resurrection of God Incarnate*, in which he explored how the character of God and the life of Jesus support the probability of Jesus' return from the dead.

Sometimes the clash between resurrection skeptics and supporters became more direct. Resurrection expert Gary R. Habermas, author of *The Historical Jesus*, and William Lane Craig, who has doctorates from the University of Birmingham in England and the University of Munich, are among the Christian apologists who have clashed with atheists in debates on the issue in recent years.

For example, Habermas and *Skeptic* magazine religion-editor Tim Callahan tangled in a nationally televised encounter on whether the idea of the resurrection has its roots in ancient mythology,[16] but more fascinating was Habermas's give-and-take with the world-renowned philosopher Antony Flew, which resulted in the 2005 book *Resurrected? An Atheist and Theist Dialogue*. This was a reprise of a famous debate between the pair in the 1980s, after which four independent judges declared Habermas the victor and one called the contest a draw. Concluded one previously skeptical judge: "I would think it was time I began to take the resurrection seriously."[17]

Incidentally, I had a rare opportunity in 2006 to conduct a lengthy interview with the eighty-three-year-old Flew about his recently announced decision to abandon atheism because he now believes in a Creator.[18] Though he said he's not a Christian at this point, I pointed out to him that now that he believes in a supernatural Creator, a miraculous event like the resurrection becomes more plausible. He replied, "I'm sure you're right about this, yes."[19]

Craig, author of *Assessing the New Testament Evidence for the Historicity of the Resurrection of Jesus*, debated Ehrman on the resurrection in 2006.[20] Earlier, Craig sparred with New Testament scholar and atheist Gerd Lüdemann, then a visiting professor at Vanderbilt University, who contended: "The risen Christ is the skeleton in the closet of the church. In other words, everybody seems to know that Christ didn't rise, but for some strange reason we decide not to be radical but instead to live within the traditional Christian framework."[21]

That debate spawned the book *Jesus' Resurrection: Fact or Figment?* — a title that cuts to the core of the issue. Does history really support the reality of the resurrection, or have scholars succeeded in establishing that the post-mortem appearances of Jesus are the product of hallucinations, legends, or wishful thinking?

Even skeptics know that a lot is banking on the answer, as I saw in my interview with *Playboy* founder Hugh Hefner. We met in the living room of his opulent Los Angeles mansion, Hefner clad in his trademark pajamas and silk smoking jacket, to discuss matters of faith for a television program. He professed a minimal belief in God, as a word for "the beginning of it all" and the "great unknown," but not in the God of Christianity, which he called "a little too childlike for me."

Then I brought up Jesus' resurrection. "If one had any real evidence that, indeed, Jesus did return from the dead, then that is the beginning of a dropping of a series of dominoes that takes us to all kinds of wonderful things," he told me. "It assures an afterlife and all kinds of things that we would all hope are true."

Even though by his own admission he had never studied the historical evidence for Jesus returning to life, Hefner remained a doubter. "Do I think that Jesus was the Son of God?" he asked. "I don't think that he is any more the Son of God than we are."

That is, unless the resurrection is true. Everything comes down to that. "If Christ has not been raised," said the apostle Paul, "your faith is futile."[22] Nothing is more important in determining the identity of the real Jesus. The cross either unmasked him as a pretender or opened the door to a supernatural resurrection that has irrevocably affirmed his divinity.

I picked up the telephone to call one of the emerging authorities on the resurrection of Jesus, whose provocative books include an imaginary debate on the issue between the apostle Paul and the prophet Muhammad. I invited him over to my house for a chat. Once and for all, I was determined to get to the truth about the most current challenges to this cornerstone doctrine.

INTERVIEW #3: Michael Licona, MA, PhD (Cand.)

Six-foot-three and lanky, Michael Licona was once a second-degree black belt and award-winning instructor in tae kwon do, a modern Korean martial art that is a lethal form of one-on-one combat. While a ruptured disk has sidelined his fighting in the ring, Licona has morphed into a respected and accomplished participant in another kind of mano a mano contest, this time involving intellectual clashes over the historical claims of Christianity.

In recent years, during his extensive travels to university campuses and appearances on national television and radio programs, he has debated such formidable opponents as Shabir Ally, the fierce defender of Islam; atheistic street-fighter Dan Barker; up-and-coming skeptic Richard Carrier; and liberal professor Elaine Pagels of Princeton.

Licona's expertise as a New Testament historian centers on the resurrection of Jesus. His thesis for his master's degree in religious studies dealt with the resurrection, while his dissertation toward a doctorate in New Testament from the University of Pretoria in South Africa uses historical methodologies to assess the evidence for Jesus returning from the dead.

Licona was mentored by Habermas, with whom he coauthored the award-winning 2004 book *The Case for the Resurrection of Jesus.* Historian Paul Maier said the book's response to naturalistic explanations for the resurrection "are the most comprehensive treatment of the subject anywhere."[23] Philosopher J. P. Moreland said the book presented what "may be the most thorough defense of the historicity of the resurrection."[24]

Using his impressive knowledge of Islam, Licona later crafted a fascinating book called *Paul Meets Muhammad: A Christian-Muslim Debate on the Resurrection*, in which he envisions the Christian apostle and the founder of Islam in an intellectual showdown over this key tenet of Christianity. Licona also has been published in the *Review of Biblical Literature* and contributed to *The Big Argument: Twenty-Four Scholars Explore How Science, Archaeology, and Philosophy Have Proven the Existence of God*. He even used the format of a novel, titled *Cross Examined*, to creatively present evidence for the resurrection.

Licona's own faith was sharpened by a period of doubt that he went through at the end of his graduate studies in 1985. His questions about the veracity of Christianity nearly prompted him to jettison the beliefs he had held since the age of ten. Instead, however, his renewed investigation of the evidence for Christianity and a number of other major world religions, as well as his in-depth study of atheism, ended up solidifying his conviction that Christianity rests on a firm historical foundation.

Since 2005, Licona has been the director of apologetics and interfaith evangelism for the North American Mission Board of the Southern Baptist Convention, where he trains leaders, develops resources, and consults on world religions, cults, and apologetics.

Licona stopped by my house near the Santa Ana Mountains, settling into a couch in my family room while I sat down in a couch adjacent to him. California sunshine poured through the windows. He was casually dressed in blue jeans without a belt and a blue button-down shirt with thin white stripes. His brown hair was cropped short, like an athlete's, and he spoke enthusiastically in crisp and complete sentences. Although Licona has a pleasant and friendly demeanor, his eyes appear ever-sharp and observant, seemingly ready to detect any errant thought or lapse in logic.

Before we began, he set up his laptop computer, loaded with sophisticated historical research tools, on the coffee table in front of him — just in case.

The Historian and the Resurrection

I didn't waste any time in launching into my initial line of questions about how historians can investigate an ancient — and supposedly supernatural — event like Jesus returning from the dead.

"Isn't it true that a miracle like the resurrection is actually outside the purview of historians to investigate?" I asked. "Ehrman said: 'Because historians can only establish what probably happened, and a miracle of this nature is highly improbable, the historian cannot say it probably occurred.'"[25]

Licona's eyes didn't break contact with mine. "I'm afraid I totally disagree with him," he said with conviction.

"On what grounds?" I asked.

"If someone says Jesus rose from the dead by natural causes — well, of course, that would be the *least* probable explanation," he replied, dismissing the notion with a wave of his hand. "But nobody is claiming that. Rather, the claim is that *God* raised Jesus from the dead. And if God exists and he wants to raise Jesus from the dead, then I would think that could be the *most* probable explanation. It really comes down to a person's worldview: Is he or she going to allow for the existence of God and the possibility that he could raise someone from the dead?"

I tried a different approach. "Is there any way to compute the probability of the resurrection in mathematical terms?" I asked.

Licona considered the question for a moment. "You'd have to use Bayes' Theorem, which is a complicated mathematical equation that determines probabilities," he said. "But there are problems with that."

"For example?"

"Bayes' Theorem requires that you plug certain background knowledge into the equation, such as the probability that God would *want* to raise Jesus from the dead. I'm sure you'd agree that probabilities like that are inscrutable."

I nodded. "So you can't say with mathematical certainty whether Jesus' resurrection is probable *or* improbable," I observed.

"That's right. Mathematically speaking, Ehrman has no grounds to claim that the resurrection is 'highly improbable.'"

"Then this is really a worldview issue."

"Yes, it is. Even philosopher Antony Flew, when he was an atheist, said the resurrection is enormously more likely if God exists. Frankly, if we look at the totality of the evidence, I think it's certainly more likely than not that God does exist. And if he does, then he could certainly have raised Jesus from the dead."

"But some historians rule out the possibility of the supernatural at the outset," I pointed out. "James Tabor, for instance, says you can't have a virgin birth, so therefore Mary was either raped or had an affair. He says you can't have a resurrection, so there must be some naturalistic explanation for it. Is that legitimate?"

"No, it's not," he shot back, politely but firmly. "Tabor is using not only a methodological naturalism, where you can't consider the supernatural, but he's going further into a metaphysical naturalism, which says this *can't* happen. He says historians have to look at things scientifically and therefore they can't consider the divine. Therefore, he says women cannot conceive children without a natural father. Well, how does he know that? That's metaphysical naturalism, or excluding the supernatural at the outset."

"Yet if a historian allows for the possibility of the miraculous, doesn't that throw history up for grabs?" I asked. "You could invoke a miraculous explanation for all kinds of things that happened in the past."

"No, because you have to apply historical criteria to determine the best explanation for what occurred," Licona said. He quickly thought of an illustration. "For example, Aesop's fables describe animals talking in ancient Greece. Well, did they talk or didn't they?"

I wasn't sure where he was going with this. "Okay," I said, "how would you assess that?"

"Well, when we examine the genre of Aesop's fables, we find that these stories were not meant to be interpreted literally. Besides, there are no credible eyewitness accounts and there's no corroboration from other sources. So the historian would say there's no good evidence that Aesop's fables report actual historical events," he replied.

"But regarding Jesus' resurrection, we find that the Gospels fit into the genre of ancient biographies. We know that ancient biographies were intended to be regarded as history to varying degrees. We've got early accounts that can't be explained away by legendary development, we've got multiple independent sources, we've got eyewitnesses, and we have a degree of corroboration from outsiders. We've also got enemy attestation; that is, affirmation from people like Saul of Tarsus, who was a critic of Christianity until he saw the evidence himself that Jesus had returned from the dead. So weighing the historical criteria, there's no reason to believe Aesop's fables are true, but there are good reasons to believe the resurrection happened."

Licona had made his point, but I wasn't ready yet to delve into the specific evidence for the resurrection. There were still preliminary issues to examine. "What's the standard of proof that historians use in determining the likelihood that the resurrection occurred?" I asked. "Historically speaking, you can't have a hundred-percent certainty, right?"

"All that remains of antiquity are ashes," Licona said. "Philosopher of history Richard Evans of Cambridge says the task of historians is to rake those ashes in order to bring some of them back to life to see what happened in the past. In other words, we have ancient texts, artifacts, and other effects that have come down to us and we try to infer from them what their causes were.

"It's like building a window through which we can peer back into the past. Often the window is blurry, with some spots that are clearer than others. That's why historians of antiquity speak of the probable truth of a theory, rather than absolute certainty. Historical conclusions are like temporary workers waiting to see whether they will one day be awarded a permanent position."

"Then all historical hypotheses are provisional," I observed, more as a summary than a question.

"That's right. New evidence might overturn a theory," came his reply. "For example, when the Titanic sank, some eyewitnesses said it went down intact, whereas others said, no, it split before sinking. Despite the conflicting witnesses, British and American investigations concluded that the Titanic went down intact, based on the preponderance of the evidence at the time. Later, when explorers discovered the sunken Titanic, they found it had indeed broken in two and then sank. That's a good example of why historians need to hold their theories provisionally.

"So again, historians of antiquity don't look for *absolute* certainty; we look for *probable* certainty. When a historian says something occurred, he means that given the evidence at our disposal today, this is the best explanation."

My mind scrolled through several events of ancient history. "Still," I said, "you would concede that some historical matters are far better attested than others."

"Granted, there's a continuum of certainty," he said. "When you have a historical hypothesis that you accept as the best explanation, and it outdistances all competing theories by a significant margin, then we can have more confidence of its truth."

"Like the resurrection?"

He picked up his glass of water and took a sip. "Yes," he said. "In my opinion, that's what we have with the resurrection of Jesus."

The Historian's Three R's

I remain fascinated by the approach historians take in evaluating the evidence that Jesus returned from the dead. "How would a historian begin investigating something like the resurrection?" I asked.

Licona put down his water glass, unbuttoned the cuffs of his shirt, and rolled up his sleeves as if he were getting ready for a lengthy discussion. "You've heard of the three R's of an elementary education: Reading, 'Riting, and 'Rithmetic? Well, there are also three R's for doing good history: Relevant sources, Responsible method, and Restrained results. First, historians must identify all the relevant sources."

"All right," I said. "What would those be in the case of Jesus?"

"There are the New Testament writings; a few secular sources who mention Jesus, such as Josephus, Tacitus, and Pliny the Younger; the apologists, who were early defenders of Christianity; and even the

Gnostic writings. We also want to examine the apostolic fathers, who were the next generation after the apostles."

"Which of the apostolic fathers are the most significant?" I asked.

"Clement of Rome is believed to have been a disciple of the apostle Peter, and Polycarp was probably a disciple of John. So their writings can give us a window into what those apostles taught. That's what makes them particularly valuable," he said. "Then, once all the relevant sources have been identified, we have to apply responsible method. This means assigning the greatest weight to reports that are early, eyewitness, enemy, embarrassing, and corroborated by others."

"And what do you mean by 'restrained results'?"

"This means that historians should not claim more than the evidence warrants. This is where such scholars as John Dominic Crossan and Elaine Pagels get on thin ice. Their imaginations are very good — and I mean that in a positive sense — but I believe their methods are sometimes questionable and their results unrestrained. In the end they may experience some embarrassment because their views are founded upon an early dating for the Gospel of Thomas, and in Crossan's case, the Secret Gospel of Mark. Now it appears Thomas may very well have been written after AD 170 and the Secret Gospel of Mark wasn't actually composed until the twentieth century! What does that do to their revisionist theories, which rely on a much earlier dating of these sources?"

Licona's point was well taken, especially in light of my earlier interview with Craig Evans about "alternative gospels." At the same time, though, I knew that Licona — as well as all conservative scholars — also bring their own prejudices to the discussion.

"What about biases?" I said. "You can't deny that you see the historical evidence through the lenses of your own prejudices."

"Absolutely. Nobody is exempt, including theists, deists, atheists, or whatever — we all have our biases, and there's no way to overcome them," Licona said. He gestured toward me. "Lee, you're trained as a journalist. You know that you can try to minimize your biases, but you can't eliminate them. That's why you have to put certain checks and balances in place. This is what historian Gary Habermas did in creating what's called the 'minimal facts approach' to the resurrection, which he and I wrote about in our book *The Case for the Resurrection of Jesus.*"

"How does this help keep biases in check?"

"Under this approach, we only consider facts that meet two criteria. First, there must be very strong historical evidence supporting them. And secondly, the evidence must be so strong that the vast majority of today's scholars on the subject—including skeptical ones—accept these as historical facts. You're never going to get everyone to agree. There are always people who deny the Holocaust or question whether Jesus ever existed, but they're on the fringe."

"History isn't a vote," I interjected. "Are you saying people should accept these facts just because a lot of scholars do?"

"No, we're saying that this evidence is so good that even skeptical scholars are convinced by it. Let's face it: there's a greater likelihood that a purported historical fact is true when someone accepts it even though they're not in agreement with your metaphysical beliefs. Or let me put it another way: your bias could be leading you to a conclusion. But if the evidence is also leading someone with vastly different beliefs toward the same conclusion, then there's a good chance the conclusion is true. This serves as a check on bias. It's not foolproof, but it's very helpful."

"How do you know what all these scholars believe about the evidence for the resurrection?"

"Habermas has compiled a list of more than 2,200 sources in French, German, and English in which experts have written on the resurrection from 1975 to the present. He has identified minimal facts that are strongly evidenced and which are regarded as historical by the large majority of scholars, including skeptics. We try to come up with the best historical explanation to account for these facts.

"It's like putting together a jigsaw puzzle. Each piece represents a historical fact, and we want to put them together in a way that doesn't leave out any pieces and which doesn't require you to shove or force any of the pieces to make them fit. In the end, the puzzle creates a picture that's based on the best explanation for the facts that we have."

With that background in place, I issued Licona a challenge. "Use only the minimal facts," I said, "and let's see how strong of a case you can build for Jesus rising from the dead."

Licona smiled and moved forward to the edge of the couch. "I thought you'd never ask," he said with a chuckle. "I'll use just five minimal facts—and you can decide for yourself how persuasive the case is."

FACT #1: Jesus Was Killed by Crucifixion

"The first fact is Jesus' crucifixion," he began. "Even an extreme liberal like Crossan says: 'That he was crucified is as sure as anything historical ever can be.'[26] Skeptic James Tabor says, 'I think we need have no doubt that given Jesus' execution by Roman crucifixion he was truly *dead*.'[27] Both Gerd Lüdemann, who's an atheistic New Testament critic, and Bart Ehrman, who's an agnostic, call the crucifixion an indisputable fact. Why? First of all, because all four Gospels report it."

I put up my hand. "Whoa! Hold on!" I insisted. "Are you operating under the assumption that the Bible is the inspired word of God?"

Licona seemed glad I had brought up the issue. "Let me clarify something: for the purposes of examining the evidence, I'm not considering the Bible to be inerrant, inspired, or scripture of any kind," he replied. "I'm simply accepting it for what it unquestionably is—a set of ancient documents that can be subjected to historical scrutiny like any other accounts from antiquity. In other words, regardless of my personal beliefs, I'm not giving the Bible a privileged position in my investigation. I'm applying the same historical standards to it that I would apply to Thucydides or Suetonius."

With that caveat, he went on with his case. "Now, beyond the four Gospels, we also have a number of non-Christian sources that corroborate the crucifixion. For instance, the historian Tacitus said Jesus 'suffered the extreme penalty during the reign of Tiberius.' The Jewish historian Josephus reports that Pilate 'condemned him to be crucified.' Lucian of Samosata, who was a Greek satirist, mentions the crucifixion, and Mara Bar-Serapion, who was a pagan, confirms Jesus was executed. Even the Jewish Talmud reports that 'Yeshu was hanged.'"

"Yeshu? Hanged?"

"Yes, Yeshu is Joshua in Hebrew; the Greek equivalent is translated as Jesus. And in the ancient world to be hung on a tree many times referred to a crucifixion. Galatians 3:13, for example, connects Jesus' crucifixion with the Pentateuch, which says that 'anyone who is hung on a pole is under God's curse.'"[28]

"What were the odds of surviving crucifixion?"

"Extremely small. You saw *The Passion of the Christ*, right? Even though not all of the film was historically accurate, it did depict the extreme brutality of Roman scourging and crucifixion. Witnesses in the ancient world reported victims being so severely whipped that their intestines and veins were laid bare. As I said, Tacitus referred to it as 'the extreme penalty.' Cicero called it 'cruel and disgusting'—so horrendous that he said 'the very word *cross* should be far removed not only from the person of a Roman citizen but from his thoughts, his eyes, and his ears.'"

"Did anyone ever survive it?"

"Interestingly, Josephus does mention three friends who were crucified during the fall of Jerusalem. He doesn't say how long they had been on the cross, but he intervened with the Roman commander Titus, who ordered all three removed immediately and provided the best medical attention Rome had to offer. Still, two of them died. So even under the best of conditions, a victim was unlikely to survive crucifixion. It is very doubtful that Jesus was privy to such conditions. There is no evidence at all that Jesus was removed prematurely or that he was provided any medical attention whatsoever, much less Rome's best."

"We're dealing with a pretty primitive culture," I observed. "Were they competent enough to be sure that Jesus was dead?"

"I'm confident they were. You've got Roman soldiers carrying out executions all the time. It was their job. They were good at it. Besides, death by crucifixion was basically a slow and agonizing demise by asphyxiation, because of the difficulty in breathing created by the victim's position on the cross. And that's something you can't fake.

"Lee, this first fact is as solid as anything in ancient history: Jesus was crucified and died as a result. The scholarly consensus—again, even among those who are skeptical toward the resurrection—is absolutely overwhelming. To deny it would be to take a marginal position that would get you laughed out of the academic world."

With that firmly established, Licona advanced to his next minimal fact.

FACT #2: Jesus' Disciples Believed
That He Rose and Appeared to Them

"The second fact is the disciples' beliefs that Jesus had actually returned from the dead and had appeared to them," Licona said. "There are three strands of evidence for this: Paul's testimony about the disciples; oral traditions that passed through the early church; and the written works of the early church.

"Paul is important because he reports knowing some of the disciples personally, including Peter, James, and John. Acts confirms this.[29] And Paul says in 1 Corinthians 15:11 that whether 'it is I or they, this is what we preach,' referring to the resurrection of Jesus. So in other words, Paul knew the apostles and reports that they claimed—just as he did—that Jesus had returned from the dead.

"Then we have oral tradition. Obviously, people in those days didn't have tape recorders and few people could read, so they relied on verbal transmission for passing along what happened until it was later written down. Scholars have identified several places in which this oral tradition has been copied into the New Testament in the form of creeds, hymns, and sermon summations. This is really significant because the oral tradition must have existed prior to the New Testament writings for the New Testament authors to have included it."

"So it's early."

"Very early, which weighs heavily in its favor, as any historian will tell you. For example, we have creeds that laid out basic doctrines in a form that was easily memorized. One of the earliest and most important creeds was relayed by Paul in his first letter to the Corinthian church, which was written about AD 55. First Corinthians 15:3–7 says: 'For what I received I passed on to you as of first importance: that Christ died for our sins according to the Scriptures, that he was buried, that he was raised on the third day according to the Scriptures, and that he appeared to Peter, and then to the Twelve. After that, he appeared to more than five hundred of the brothers and sisters at the same time, most of whom are still living, though some have fallen asleep. Then he appeared to James, then to all the apostles.'[30]

"Many scholars believe Paul received this creed from Peter and

James while visiting with them in Jerusalem three years after his conversion. That would be within five years of the crucifixion."

Licona's eyes got wide. "Think about that — it's really amazing!" he declared, his voice rising in genuine astonishment. "As one expert said, 'This is the sort of data that historians of antiquity drool over.'[31] Not only is it extremely early, but it was apparently given to Paul by eyewitnesses or others he deemed reliable, which heightens its credibility even more."

"How important is this creed, in your opinion?"

"It's powerful and persuasive," he declared. "Although early dating does not totally rule out the possibility of invention or deceit on the part of Jesus' followers, it is much too early to be the result of legendary development over time, since it can practically be traced to the original disciples of Jesus. In fact, this creed has been one of the most formidable obstacles to critics who try to shoot down the resurrection. It's simply gold for a historian.

"And we've got even more oral tradition — for instance, the New Testament preserves several sermons of the apostles. Actually, these are apparently summaries of the preaching of the apostles, since most of them can be read aloud in five minutes or less. I'm sure the actual sermons lasted a lot longer than that. At a minimum, we can say that the vast majority of historians believe that the early apostolic teachings are enshrined in these sermon summaries in Acts — and they're not at all ambiguous: they declare that Jesus rose bodily from the dead.

"For example, Paul says in Acts 13, which is very similar to what Peter reports in Acts 2: 'Now when David had served God's purpose in his own generation, he fell asleep; he was buried with his ancestors and his body decayed. But the one whom God raised from the dead did not see decay. Therefore, my friends, I want you to know that through Jesus the forgiveness of sins is proclaimed to you.'[32] That's a bold and forthright assertion: David's body decayed, but Jesus' didn't, because he was raised from the dead.

"Finally we have written sources, such as Matthew, Mark, Luke, and John. It's widely accepted, even among skeptical historians, that the Gospels were written in the first century. Even very liberal scholars will concede that we have four biographies written within seventy years of Jesus' life that unambiguously report the disciples' claims that Jesus rose from the dead.

"I think an excellent case can be made for dating the Gospels earlier, but let's go with the more generous estimations. That's still extremely close to the events themselves, especially compared to many other ancient historical writings. Our two best sources on Alexander the Great, for instance, weren't written until at least four hundred years after his life.

"As for Caesar Augustus, who is generally regarded as Rome's greatest emperor, there are five chief sources used by historians to write a history of his adulthood: a very brief funeral inscription, a source written between fifty and a hundred years after his death, and three sources written between a hundred and two hundred years after he died. So it's really remarkable that in the case of Jesus, we have four biographies that even liberals agree were written within thirty-five to sixty-five years after his execution."

My earlier interview with textual critic Daniel B. Wallace came to mind. "You'd admit, though, that the final verses in Mark, which describe the resurrection appearances, were not part of the original text."

"Yes, I believe that's true," he said. "But still, Mark clearly knows of the resurrection appearances of Jesus. Mark predicts the resurrection in five places,[33] and he reports the testimony of the angel to the resurrection, the empty tomb, and the imminent appearance of Jesus in Galilee. In fact, Mark's reference to Peter in Mark 16:7 may be the very same appearance reported in the creed I just mentioned."

Licona paused, then added: "One more thing. Most scholars believe Mark is the earliest Gospel, but we have an even earlier report about the resurrection: the 1 Corinthians 15 creed that I mentioned. This clearly spells out various post-Easter appearances by Jesus—including at one point to five hundred people.

"Then we have the writings of the apostolic fathers, who were said to have known the apostles or were close to others who did. There's a strong likelihood that their writings reflect the teachings of the apostles themselves—and what do they say? That the apostles were dramatically impacted by Jesus' resurrection.

"Consider Clement, for example. The early church father Irenaeus reports that Clement had conversed with the apostles—in fact, Irenaeus commented that he 'might be said to have the preaching of the apostles still echoing, and their traditions before his eyes.' Tertullian, the African church father, said Clement was ordained by Peter himself."

"So what does Clement report about the beliefs of the disciples?" I asked.

"In his letter to the Corinthian church, which was written in the first century, he writes: 'Therefore, having received orders and complete certainty caused by the resurrection of our Lord Jesus Christ and believing in the Word of God, they went with the Holy Spirit's certainty, preaching the good news that the kingdom of God is about to come.'[34]

"Then we have Polycarp. Irenaeus says that Polycarp was 'instructed by the apostles, and conversed with many who had seen Christ,' including John; that he 'recalled their very words'; and that he 'always taught the things which he had learned from the apostles.' Tertullian confirms that John appointed Polycarp as bishop of the church in Smyrna.

"Around AD 110, Polycarp wrote a letter to the Philippian church in which he mentions the resurrection of Jesus no fewer than five times. He was referring to Paul and the other apostles when he said: 'For they did not love the present age, but him who died for our benefit and for our sake was raised by God.'[35]

"So think about the depth of evidence we have in these three categories: Paul, oral tradition, and written reports. In all, we've got nine sources that reflect multiple, very early, and eyewitness testimonies to the disciples' claims that they had seen the risen Jesus. This is something the disciples believed to the core of their being."

"How do you know that?"

"Because we have evidence that the disciples had been transformed to the point where they were willing to endure persecution and even martyrdom. We find this in multiple accounts inside and outside the New Testament.

"Just read through Acts and you'll see how the disciples were willing to suffer for their conviction that Jesus rose from the dead. The church fathers Clement, Polycarp, Ignatius, Tertullian, and Origen—they all confirm this. In fact, we've got at least seven early sources testifying that the disciples willingly suffered in defense of their beliefs—and if we include the martyrdoms of Paul and Jesus' half-brother James, we have eleven sources."

"But," I objected, "people of other faiths have been willing to die for their beliefs through the ages—so what does the martyrdom of the disciples really prove?"

"First, it means that they certainly regarded their beliefs to be true," he said. "They didn't willfully lie about this. Liars make poor martyrs. Second, the disciples didn't just *believe* Jesus rose from the dead, but they knew for a fact whether he did. They were on the scene and able to ascertain for sure that he had been resurrected. So it was for the *truth* of the resurrection that they were willing to die.

"This is totally different than a modern-day Islamic terrorist or others willing to die for their beliefs. These people can only have faith that their beliefs are true, but they aren't in a position to know for sure. The disciples, on the other hand, knew for a *fact* whether the resurrection had truly occurred—and knowing the *truth*, they were willing to die for the belief that they had."

"Then what's the bottom line?" I asked.

"Habermas completed an overview of more than two thousand scholarly sources on the resurrection going back thirty years—and probably no fact was more widely recognized than that the early Christian believers had real experiences that they thought were appearances of the risen Jesus," Licona replied.

"Even the atheist Lüdemann conceded: 'It may be taken as historically certain that Peter and the disciples had experiences after Jesus' death in which Jesus appeared to them as the risen Christ.'[36] Now, he claims this was the result of visions, which I simply don't believe is a credible explanation. But he's conceding that their experiences actually occurred."

Licona reached over to the coffee table and picked up a copy of his book *The Case for the Resurrection of Jesus*, quickly flipping to page 60. "As Paula Fredriksen of Boston University put it—and, again, she's not an evangelical but a very liberal scholar—

I know in their own terms what they saw was the raised Jesus. That's what they say and then all the historic evidence we have afterwards attests to their conviction that that's what they saw. I'm not saying that they really did see the raised Jesus. I wasn't there. I don't know what they saw. *But I do know that as a historian that they must have seen something.*[37]

"In fact, Fredriksen says elsewhere that 'the disciples' conviction that they had seen the risen Christ ... is [part of] historical bedrock, facts known past doubting.'[38] I think that's pretty much undeniable —and I believe the evidence is clear and convincing that what they saw was the return of Jesus from the dead. And we're not done yet—we've got three more minimal facts to consider."

The case for the disciples encountering what they believed to be the risen Jesus did, indeed, seem strong. Still, skeptics have raised some fresh objections in recent years. Rather than sidetrack Licona at this point, however, I decided to wait until he finished describing his five minimal facts. At that point, I could cross-examine him in more depth.

"Go ahead," I said. "What's your third minimal fact?"

FACT #3: The Conversion of the Church Persecutor Paul

"We know from multiple sources that Paul—who was then known as Saul of Tarsus—was an enemy of the church and committed to persecuting the faithful," Licona continued. "But Paul himself says that he was converted to a follower of Jesus because he had personally encountered the resurrected Jesus.[39] So we have Jesus' resurrection attested by friend and foe alike, which is very significant.

"Then we have six ancient sources in addition to Paul—such as Luke, Clement of Rome, Polycarp, Tertullian, Dionysius of Corinth, and Origen—reporting that Paul was willing to suffer continuously and even die for his beliefs. Again, liars make poor martyrs. So we can be confident that Paul not only claimed the risen Jesus appeared to him, but that he really believed it."

I couldn't let this point slip by without at least one brief objection. "People convert to other religions all the time," I said. "What's so special about Paul?"

"When virtually all people convert, it's because they've heard the message of that religion from *secondary* sources—that is, what other people tell them," Licona explained. "Yet that's not the case with Paul. He says he was transformed by a personal encounter with the risen Christ. So his conversion is based in *primary* evidence—Jesus directly appeared to him. That's a big difference.

"You can't claim that Paul was a friend of Jesus who was primed to see a vision of him due to wishful thinking or grief after his crucifixion. Saul was a most unlikely candidate for conversion. His mind-set was to oppose the Christian movement that he believed was following a false Messiah. His radical transformation from persecutor to missionary demands an explanation and I think the best explanation is that he's telling the truth when he says he met the risen Jesus on the road to Damascus.

"He had nothing to gain in this world—except his own suffering and martyrdom—for making this up."

FACT #4: The Conversion of the Skeptic James, Jesus' Half-Brother

"The next minimal fact involves James, the half-brother of Jesus," Licona said.

"Some people might be surprised that Jesus had siblings," I commented.

"Well, the Gospels tell us that Jesus had at least four half-brothers— James, Joseph, Judas, and Simon—as well as half-sisters whose names we don't know.[40] The Jewish historian Josephus, in a section most historians regard as authentic, refers to 'the brother of Jesus who was called the Christ, whose name was James.'"

"Do we know much about James?" I asked.

"In the second century, Hegesippus reports that James was a pious Jew who strictly abided by the Jewish law. But more significantly for our purposes, we also have good evidence that James was not a follower of Jesus during Jesus' lifetime."

"How do you know?"

"Mark and John both report that none of Jesus' brothers believed in him.[41] In fact, John's passage is particularly interesting. It suggests that his brothers had heard about his alleged miracles but didn't believe the reports and were, in a sense, daring their brother to perform them in front of crowds. They were sort of taunting him!"[42]

"Why do you consider the skepticism of Jesus' brothers to be authentic?" I asked.

"Because of the principle of embarrassment," Licona replied. "People are not going to invent a story that's going to be embarrassing or potentially discrediting to them, and it would be particularly humiliating for a first-century rabbi not to have his own family as his followers."

"Do you have any other evidence for their skepticism?"

"At the crucifixion, to whom does Jesus entrust the care of his mother? Not to one of his half-brothers, who would be the natural choice, but to John, who was a believer. Why on earth would he do that? I think the inference is very strong: if James or any of his brothers had been believers, they would have gotten the nod instead. So it's reasonable to conclude that none of them was a believer, and Jesus was more concerned with his mother being entrusted into the hands of a spiritual brother.

"Then, however, the pivotal moment occurs: the ancient creedal material in 1 Corinthians 15 tells us that the risen Jesus appeared to James. Again, this is an extremely early account that has all the earmarks of reliability. In fact, James may have been involved in passing along this creed to Paul, in which case James would be personally endorsing what the creed reports about him.

"As a result of his encounter with the risen Jesus, James doesn't just become a Christian, but he later becomes leader of the Jerusalem church. We know this from Acts and Galatians.[43] Actually, James was so thoroughly convinced of Jesus' Messiahship because of the resurrection that he died as a martyr, as both Christian and non-Christian sources attest.[44]

"So here we have another example of a skeptic who was converted because of a personal encounter with the resurrected Lord and was willing to die for his convictions. In fact, critical scholar Reginald

Fuller said that even if we didn't have the 1 Corinthians 15 account, 'we should have to invent' such a resurrection appearance to account for James' conversion and his elevation to the pastorate of the Jerusalem church, which was the center of ancient Christianity."[45]

Licona paused as if he had finished his point. But something occurred to me as he was telling the story of James. "Makes you wonder why James wasn't a believer during the lifetime of Jesus," I mused. "What did Jesus do or not do that left James skeptical?"

Licona seemed slightly taken aback. "I have to admit, Lee, that has bothered me over the years," he said, his voice taking on a more personal tone. "It still bothers me some, to be honest with you. If the virgin birth really occurred, then how could Jesus' brothers not have believed in him? I'm sure they would have heard it from Mary. Sincerely, I have really struggled with that.

"I mentioned this recently to a friend who is somewhat of a skeptic, and he surprised me by saying, 'It doesn't bother me at all. If I had a brother who was perfect, even if he had been born of a virgin, I'd hate him, and I just wouldn't follow him.' That was interesting to me. But honestly, we don't really know, historically speaking."

I ventured another explanation. "I suppose if you had a brother who was making implicit but very grandiose claims about himself, that might be an embarrassment," I said.

"You know, you're right," Licona replied. "I hadn't thought of the peer pressure of the community in which you live. *This guy thinks he's the Son of God? C'mon! Set your brother straight.* You're going to feel embarrassed."

"In the end, do you think James's conversion is significant evidence for the resurrection?"

"Absolutely, yes, I do," he said. "As resurrection scholar William Lane Craig asks, 'What would it take to convince *you* that your brother is the Lord?' Really, the only thing that could account for that would be what's reported in the early creed: that the crucified Jesus appeared alive to James."

With that, Licona advanced to the last of his minimal facts.

FACT #5: Jesus' Tomb Was Empty

"Although the fifth fact—that the tomb of Jesus was empty—is part of the minimal case for the resurrection, it doesn't enjoy the nearly universal consensus among scholars that the first four do," Licona began. "Still, there's strong evidence in its favor."

"How strong?" I asked.

"Habermas determined that about 75 percent of scholars on the subject regard it as a historical fact. That's quite a large majority. Personally, I think the empty tomb is very well supported if the historical data are assessed without preconceptions. Basically, there are three strands of evidence: the Jerusalem factor, enemy attestation, and the testimony of women."

"Jerusalem factor?" I asked. "What's that?"

"This refers to the fact that Jesus was publicly executed and buried in Jerusalem and then his resurrection was proclaimed in the very same city. In fact, several weeks after the crucifixion, Peter declares to a crowd right there in Jerusalem: 'God has raised this Jesus to life, and we are all witnesses of the fact.'[46] Frankly, it would have been impossible for Christianity to get off the ground in Jerusalem if Jesus' body were still in the tomb. The Roman or Jewish authorities could have simply gone over to his tomb, viewed his corpse, and the misunderstanding would have been over. But there's no indication that this occurred.

"Instead, what we do hear is enemy attestation to the empty tomb. In other words, what were the skeptics saying? That the disciples stole the body. This is reported not only by Matthew, but also by Justin Martyr and Tertullian. Here's the thing: Why would you say someone stole the body if it were still in the tomb? This is an implicit admission that the tomb was empty.

"I've got a twelve-year-old son. If he went into school and said, 'The dog ate my homework,' he would be implicitly admitting he doesn't have his homework to turn in. Likewise, you wouldn't claim that the disciples stole the body if it were still in his tomb. It's an indirect admission that the body was unavailable for display."

"And enemy attestation is strong evidence in the eyes of historians," I commented.

"That's correct. Here, you've got Jesus' opponents conceding his tomb was vacant. There's no way they would have admitted this if it weren't true. On top of that, the idea that the disciples stole the body is a lame explanation. Are we supposed to believe they conspired to steal the body, pulled it off, and then were willing to suffer continuously and even die for what they knew was a lie? That's such an absurd idea that scholars universally reject it today.

"In addition, we have the testimony of women that the tomb was empty. Not only were women the first to discover the vacant grave, but they are mentioned in all four Gospels, whereas male witnesses appear only later and in two of them."

"Why is this important?"

"Because in both first-century Jewish and Roman cultures, women were lowly esteemed and their testimony was considered questionable. They were certainly considered less credible than men. For example, the Jewish Talmud says, 'Sooner let the words of the Law be burnt than delivered to women,' and, 'Any evidence which a woman [gives] is not valid (to offer).' Josephus said, 'But let not the testimony of women be admitted, on account of the levity and boldness of their sex.'

"My point is this: if you were going to concoct a story in an effort to fool others, you would never in that day have hurt your own credibility by saying that women discovered the empty tomb. It would be extremely unlikely that the Gospel writers would invent testimony like this, because they wouldn't get any mileage out of it. In fact, it could hurt them. If they had felt the freedom simply to make things up, surely they'd claim that men — maybe Peter or John or even Joseph of Arimathea — were the first to find the tomb empty."

"So this is another example of the criterion of embarrassment."

"Precisely. The best theory for why the Gospel writers would include such an embarrassing detail is because that's what actually happened and they were committed to recording it accurately, regardless of the credibility problem it created in that culture.

"So when you consider the Jerusalem factor, the enemy attestation, and the testimony of women, there are good historical reasons for concluding Jesus' tomb was empty. William Ward of Oxford University put it this way: 'All the strictly historical evidence we have is in favor [of the empty tomb], and those scholars who reject it ought to recognize that they do so on some other ground than that of scientific history.'"[47]

I interrupted. "Let's put this into context, though: an empty tomb doesn't prove the resurrection."

"Granted, but remember that this is just one of the five minimal facts. And it's entirely congruent with the beliefs of the disciples, Paul, and James that Jesus rose from the dead, since a resurrection implies an empty tomb."

"Okay, I've given you a chance to lay out your mimimal facts," I said. "How would you summarize your case?"

"Let's consider what we have. Shortly after Jesus died from crucifixion, his disciples believed that they saw him risen from the dead. They said he appeared not only to individuals but in several group settings — and the disciples were so convinced and transformed by the experience that they were willing to suffer and even die for their conviction that they had encountered him.

"Then we have two skeptics who regarded Jesus as a false prophet — Paul, the persecutor of the church, and James, who was Jesus' half-brother. They completely changed their opinions 180 degrees after encountering the risen Jesus. Like the disciples, they were willing to endure hardship, persecution, and even death rather than disavow their testimony that Jesus' resurrection occurred.

"Thus we have compelling testimony about the resurrection from friends of Jesus, an enemy of Christianity, and a skeptic. Finally, we have strong historical evidence that Jesus' tomb was empty. In fact, even enemies of Christianity admitted it was vacant. Where did the body go? If you asked the disciples, they'd tell you they personally saw Jesus after he returned to life.

"So we've looked at relevant sources, and we've applied responsible historical methodology. Now we need restrained results. We have to ask ourselves: What's the best explanation for the evidence — the explanation that doesn't leave out any of the facts or strains to make anything fit? My conclusion, based on the evidence, is that Jesus did return from the dead."

"You personally think the case is strong?"

"Oh, absolutely, because it outdistances the competing hypotheses by such a large margin. No other explanation comes close to accounting for all the facts. That makes future disconfirmation unlikely. Historically speaking, I think we've got a cogent and convincing case."

The Rest of the Story

Licona could have presented all kinds of historical evidence for the resurrection, but instead he limited himself only to five facts that are extremely well-attested historically and that the vast majority of scholars — including skeptics — concede are trustworthy. I was impressed that he didn't merely throw around hyperbolic affirmations for the resurrection from conservative Christians who only considered the evidence in favor of their cherished doctrine. Making his case from the lips of liberal and disbelieving scholars served greatly to heighten the credibility of the Easter event. I was reminded of the conclusions of historian N. T. Wright, author of the 741-page *Jesus and the Victory of God* and a visiting professor at Harvard University:

> It is no good falling back on "science" as having disproved the possibility of resurrection. Any real scientist will tell you that science observes what normally happens; the Christian case is precisely that what happened to Jesus is not what normally happens. For my part, as a historian I prefer the elegant, essentially simple solution rather than the one that fails to include all the data: to say that the early Christians believed that Jesus had been bodily raised from the dead, and to account for this belief by saying that they were telling the truth.[48]

As Licona finished his presentation and relaxed back into the couch, I thumbed through the notes attached to a clipboard in my lap. Having studied the most current — and most compelling — objections of Muslims, atheists, and other resurrection doubters, I knew that there was another side to the story. How strong was it? How would Licona respond? Would his evidence emerge unscathed or disintegrate under scrutiny?

"Let's grab some lunch," I suggested as I stood and stretched. "Then we'll see how good your case stands up to cross-examination."

PART TWO:
The Cross-Examination

COL. JESSEP: *You want answers?*
LT. KAFFEE: *I think I'm entitled.*
JESSEP: *You want answers?*
KAFFEE: *I want the truth!*
JESSEP: *You can't handle the truth!*
from the film *A Few Good Men*

Few scenes are as gripping in the movies—or in real life—as the tenacious and effective cross-examination of a witness in a criminal trial. The prosecution may have presented a persuasive case during the first part of the proceedings, but sometimes the persistent questioning of a witness can reverse the entire outcome of a trial.

That's what happened in the Broadway play and subsequent film *A Few Good Men*, in which military attorney Daniel Kaffee was assigned to defend two Marines accused of murdering a problem comrade at Guantanamo Bay Naval Base. Kaffee was trying to prove that his clients were merely following the orders of the ambitious base commander, Colonel Nathan R. Jessep, who had allegedly ordered a "Code Red" against the victim, which is slang for unsanctioned punishment.[1]

In the film's climactic scene, Kaffee (played by Tom Cruise) relentlessly presses Jessep (portrayed by Jack Nicholson) for the truth about what took place. Jessep's anger was clearly mounting. "Did you order the Code Red?" the lawyer demands. "I did the job I was sent to do," barks Jessep. With more intensity, Kaffee repeats: "Did you order the Code Red?" That's when the witness breaks. "You're——right I did!" Jessep shouts back—and his fate is sealed. He is immediately arrested —his career destroyed—but not before he lunges at Kaffee and threatens to kill him.

That's great cinema, but in real life witnesses are rarely badgered into confessing to crimes on the witness stand. Skillful and well-prepared attorneys, however, often succeed in casting doubt on a witness's credibility, poking holes in their opponent's theories, and generating reasonable doubt in the minds of jurors. I learned quickly as the legal-affairs editor of the *Chicago Tribune* never to reach conclusions based on hearing only one side of a case.

So far, New Testament historian Michael Licona had presented seemingly conclusive arguments for Jesus' resurrection by using only five "minimal facts" that are well-evidenced and accepted by the vast majority of critical scholars: Jesus was killed by crucifixion; his disciples believed he rose and appeared to them; the conversion of the church persecutor Paul; the conversion of the skeptic James, who was Jesus' half-brother; and Jesus' empty tomb.

Unchallenged, these facts appear to point convincingly toward the verdict that Jesus returned from the dead and thus authenticated his claim to being the unique Son of God. But what happens when these facts are subjected to cross-examination? How would Licona respond to the alternate theories that have been advanced in the last few years by respected scholars, popular authors, and Internet gadflies? Would "the other side of the story" prompt a far different conclusion: That the resurrection is actually more wishful thinking than historic reality?

Licona and I reconvened in my family room. His eyes seemed to take on a heightened intensity as he watched me shuffle through my list of prepared questions. My plan wasn't to try to provoke, intimidate, or badger him in the style of Tom Cruise's character; rather, I wanted to test his five facts with the most cogent arguments of critics and see whether Licona's answers would really hold up. This wasn't a game of "gotcha"; it was a genuine desire to see how the resurrection would fare against its latest critics.

Since Licona had started his case with the crucifixion of Jesus — confidently declaring that it was "as solid as anything in ancient history" — I decided to begin there too. After all, I mused, the more than one billion Muslims in the world would adamantly dissent from Licona's assertion.

The Qur'an versus the Bible

I picked up my well-worn copy of the Qur'an from the coffee table. "You say Jesus was killed by crucifixion, but on the contrary, Muslims believe Jesus never really died on the cross," I said to Licona. Finding the fourth surah, I read aloud verses 157–58:

> That they said (in boast) "We killed Christ Jesus the son of Mary, the Messenger of Allah"; — but they did not kill him, nor crucified him, but so it was made to appear to them, and those who differ therein are full of doubts, with no (certain) knowledge, but only conjecture to follow, for of a surety they did not kill him; — Nay, Allah raised him up unto Himself; and Allah is Exalted in Power, Wise . . .[2]

I closed the book and continued. "There seem to be two possibilities: either someone was made to look like Jesus and the Romans killed that person, or Jesus was on the cross but Allah made it appear he died when he really didn't. They put him in a tomb, Allah healed him, and he was taken to heaven. Aren't those possible scenarios?"

Licona's posture straightened. "Well, anything is possible with God," Licona said, "but the real question is where does the evidence point? In other words, the question does not concern what God *can do*, but what God *did*. And the Qur'an is not a very credible source when it comes to Jesus."

"You don't believe the Qur'an has good credentials?"

"The Qur'an provides a test for people to verify its divine origin: gather the wisest people in the world and call upon the *jinn*, which are similar to demons but without necessarily all the negative connotations, and try to write a surah, or chapter, that's as good as one in the Qur'an. The implication, of course, is that this can't be done."

"Do you think it can be?"

"I think so, rather easily. One person who speaks Arabic wrote what he calls *The True Furqan*, in which he maintains the style of the Qur'an in Arabic but with a message that's more Christian than Islamic.[3] Some Muslims heard portions of it read and were convinced that it was the Qur'an! One scholar in Arabic dialects told me that some of the classical

Arabic in *The True Furqan* was much more beautiful than anything he had read in the Qur'an. So I guess the test has been passed. For those of us who can't read Arabic—which, by the way, includes about 80 percent of the Muslim world—we can perform a test by comparing the first surah of the Qur'an to Psalm 19 of the Bible."

Licona reached over and picked up my Qur'an to read the first surah out loud:

> In the name of Allah, Most Gracious, Most Merciful.
> Praise be to Allah, the Cherisher and Sustainer of the Worlds;
> Most Gracious, Most Merciful;
> Master of the Day of Judgment.
> You do we worship, and Your aid do we seek.
> Show us the straight way.
> The way of those on whom You have bestowed Your Grace,
> those whose (portion) is not wrath, and who do not go astray.[4]

Closing the Qur'an, he then used his lap-top computer to access Psalm 19 and read it:

> The heavens declare the glory of God;
> the skies proclaim the work of his hands.
> Day after day they pour forth speech;
> night after night they display knowledge.
> There is no speech or language
> where their voice is not heard.
> Their voice goes out into all the earth,
> their words to the ends of the world.
>
> In the heavens he has pitched a tent for the sun,
> which is like a bridegroom coming forth from his pavilion,
> like a champion rejoicing to run his course.
> It rises at one end of the heavens
> and makes its circuit to the other;
> nothing is hidden from its heat.
>
> The law of the LORD is perfect,
> reviving the soul.
> The statutes of the LORD are trustworthy,
> making wise the simple.

The precepts of the LORD are right,
    giving joy to the heart.
The commands of the LORD are radiant,
    giving light to the eyes.
The fear of the LORD is pure,
    enduring forever.
The ordinances of the LORD are sure
    and altogether righteous.
They are more precious than gold,
    than much pure gold;
they are sweeter than honey,
    than honey from the comb.
By them is your servant warned;
    in keeping them there is great reward.

Who can discern his errors?
    Forgive my hidden faults.
Keep your servant also from willful sins;
    may they not rule over me.
Then will I be blameless,
    innocent of great transgression.

May the words of my mouth and the meditation of my heart
    be pleasing in your sight,
    O LORD, my Rock and my Redeemer.

Licona turned to face me. "Both the surah and the psalm talk about the goodness and holiness of God," he said. "But when you read them — well, the psalm seems much more pregnant with meaning and much more beautiful to me. Granted, the Arabic surah has a poetic rhythm; however, so does the Hebrew psalm, which is actually a song."

"But," I pointed out, "Muslims would say you've got to read the surah in Arabic because it's got a particularly beautiful flow in that language."

"I'd reply, 'Can you read Hebrew?'" said Licona. "If not, how do you know that the Arabic is better than the Hebrew song, which has a flowing rhythm similar to the surah? It really comes down to what language sounds best to you, sort of like choosing between McDonalds and Burger King. It's very subjective, don't you think? That's why it's not a good test of the Qur'an's divine nature.

"In contrast, Jesus provided a historical event—his resurrection—as the test by which we can know his message is true. Now, *that's* a good test, because a resurrection isn't going to happen unless God does it."

The Credibility of the Qur'an

I agreed with Licona—the supposed lyrical quality of the Qur'an was unavoidably a subjective test. "That's why you don't believe the Qur'an is credible?" I asked.

"That's only the beginning of the Qur'an's problems when it comes to Jesus," Licona said. "In addition, the Qur'an is fifth-hand testimony at best—the original Qur'an in heaven allegedly coming to us through an angel, then Muhammad, then those who recorded what Muhammad told them, then what was selected by Uthman. Thus, it's quite hypocritical of Muslims when they complain that two of the Gospels, Mark and Luke, weren't written by eyewitnesses. On top of that, you've got the Islamic catch-22."

"The what?"

"Let me explain it," he replied. "We can establish historically that Jesus predicted his own imminent and violent death."

"How so?" I asked.

"We find this reported in Mark, which is the earliest Gospel, and it's multiply attested in different literary forms, which is really strong evidence in the eyes of historians. Also, consider the criterion of embarrassment: A lot of times when Jesus predicts his death, the disciples say, no, this can't happen, or they don't understand. This makes them look like knuckleheads, so it's embarrassing to the disciples who are the leaders of the church to put this in the Gospel. This indicates that this is authentic, because you certainly wouldn't make up something that puts the apostles in a bad light. Consequently, there are good historical reasons for believing Jesus did actually predict his imminent and violent demise."

"Okay, I think that's pretty clear," I said. "But where does the Islamic catch-22 come in?"

"If Jesus did *not* die a violent and imminent death, then that makes him a false prophet. But the Qur'an says that he's a great prophet, and so the Qur'an would be wrong and thus discredited. On the other hand, if Jesus *did* die a violent and imminent death as he predicted, then he is indeed a great prophet—but this would contradict the Qur'an, which says he didn't die on the cross. So either way, the Qur'an is discredited.

"The bottom line is this: unless you're a Muslim who is already committed to the Qur'an, no historian worth his salt would ever place the Qur'an as a more credible source on Jesus over the New Testament, which has four biographies and other writings dated shortly after Jesus and which contains eyewitness testimony. In historical Jesus studies, I don't know of a single scholar who consults the Qur'an as a source on the historical Jesus."

"But you have to admit," I said, "that it would be hard to prove or disprove whether Allah substituted somebody at the last minute on the cross."

"Listen, I could come up with a theory that says we were all created just five minutes ago with food in our stomachs from meals we never ate and memories in our minds of events that never took place. How would you disprove that? But the question is: Where does the evidence point? What seems to be the most rational belief? Again, unless you're a Muslim who already is so predisposed to believing Islamic doctrines that you can't look at the data objectively in any sense, no one would say that the Qur'an is a credible source when it comes to Jesus."

"When I heard a Muslim debate this issue, he took the approach that Jesus was on the cross and Allah made him appear to be dead, even though he wasn't," I said. "Then he claimed Allah healed Jesus."

"That creates another problem," Licona replied. "Wouldn't this make Allah a deceiver? We could understand it if he deceived his enemies who were trying to kill Jesus. But since we can know historically that Jesus' disciples sincerely believed that he had been killed and then his corpse had been transformed into an immortal body, this makes God a deceiver of his followers as well. If Jesus never clarified matters with his disciples, then he deceived them too. Why would you deceive your followers if you knew this was going to spawn a new but false religion? And if God deceived his first-century followers, whom the Qur'an refers to as 'Muslims,' then how can today's Muslims be confident that he is not deceiving them now?"

I found Licona's logic convincing. Simply applying the tools of modern historical scholarship quickly disqualifies the Qur'an as a trustworthy text about Jesus, if for no other reason than the book's late dating. Scholars quibble over a difference of just a few years in the dating of the New Testament, whereas the Qur'an didn't come until *six centuries* after the life of Christ. I also knew, however, that the Qur'an isn't the only book claiming that Jesus didn't die on the cross.

I picked up a copy of the 2006 *New York Times* bestseller *The Jesus Papers* from the couch next to me. Opening it up, I prepared to question Licona about its eye-opening allegations that seek to refute the crucifixion.

Deconstructing Baigent

"Michael Baigent claims in *The Jesus Papers* that although the Jewish Zealots wanted Jesus crucified, Pontius Plate was conflicted because Jesus had been telling people to pay their taxes to Rome," I said, flipping to page 125 and reading to Licona the text that I had highlighted with a yellow marker:

> Pilate was Rome's official representative in Judea, and Rome's main argument with the Jews was that they declined to pay their tax to Caesar. Yet here was a leading Jew—the legitimate king no less —telling his people to pay the tax. How could Pilate try, let alone condemn, such a man who, on the face of it, was supporting Roman policy? Pilate would himself be charged with dereliction of duty should he proceed with the condemnation of such a supporter.[5]

"And so," I continued, "Baigent says Pilate decided to condemn Jesus to placate the Zealots, but he took steps to ensure Jesus would survive so he wouldn't have to report to Rome that he had killed him. After all, Mike, you've already conceded that it's possible to survive a crucifixion, and Baigent speculates that Jesus had been given medication to induce the appearance of death. In fact, the Gospels indicate Jesus died pretty quickly.

"Set aside the issue of Baigent's credibility for a moment," I said. "Let's just deal with the theory he offers. Doesn't this undermine your claim that Jesus died on the cross?"

Licona sighed. "Honestly, Lee, this is just so weak," he said. "First, Baigent claims that aloes or myrrh were used to revive Jesus after his ordeal on the cross. If these common herbs could be used to resuscitate and bring back to health a crucified individual who had been horribly scourged, then why in the world aren't we using them today?" he asked, his tone indignant. "Why aren't hospitals using them? They would be wonder drugs! Come on—that's ridiculous!"

Now he was getting on a roll. "And the idea that Rome would never crucify someone who was supporting them just flies in the face of the facts. Look at Paul—he urged people to obey the governing authorities because God has placed them in charge, yet that didn't stop Rome from executing him!

"Think about it: if Jesus survived the crucifixion, he'd be horribly mutilated and limping. How would that convince the disciples that he's the risen prince of life? That's absurd. Baigent has nothing to back up his wild claims. Look at the writings on the resurrection by legitimate scholars over the past twenty years: only about one in a thousand even suggests it's possible that Jesus survived the crucifixion. There's a tidal wave of scholarship on the other side. This is almost in the category of denying the Holocaust!"

I jumped in. "Baigent claims the Bible itself backs up his theory," I pointed out. "He says that in the Gospel of Mark, when Joseph of Arimathea requests Jesus' body from Pilate, he uses the Greek word *soma*, which denotes a living body. In reply, Pilate uses the word *ptoma* for body, which means a corpse. Says Baigent: 'In other words, the Greek text of Mark's Gospel is making it clear that while Joseph is asking for the living body of Jesus, Pilate grants him what he believes to be the corpse. *Jesus' survival is revealed right there in the actual Gospel account.*'"[6]

Licona shook his head in disbelief. "That's pure rubbish," he said with disdain.

I pointed at him. "Prove it," I said.

"Okay," he said, picking up the challenge. "The truth is that the word *soma* makes no distinction between a living or dead body. In fact, in Acts 9:37, Luke talks about the death of Tabitha. After she dies, he says they washed her *soma*, or her body. Obviously, it's a corpse. In Luke 17:37, it says, 'Where there is a dead body, there the vultures will gather.' Again, the word he uses is *soma*. There's example after example, even in Josephus, of *soma* meaning corpse. So Baigent doesn't know what he's talking about here either.

"What's more, Baigent is ignoring the context in Mark. The Gospel makes it clear that Jesus was dead. Mark 15:37 says Jesus 'breathed his last'; in Mark 15:45, eyewitnesses confirmed Jesus was dead; and in Mark 15:47 – 16:1, Mary Magdalene and the other women watch Jesus being buried and return Sunday morning to anoint him. They surely thought he was dead. So there's nothing at all to support Baigent's claims."

There was no need to go further: Baigent's case would be instantly dismissed by any impartial judge. Licona's first fact — that Jesus was killed by crucifixion — remained unrefuted by any credible counterargument.

Before we moved on, however, I wanted to ask Licona his opinion about popular writers like Baigent, whose authentic-sounding theories often can be confusing to readers unfamiliar with the other side of the story. "Does it bother you that Baigent's book was a bestseller and that thousands of people may believe it's true?" I asked.

"What it shows," said Licona, "is that people are not only credulous toward this sort of nonsense, but Western culture is looking for a justification for an alternative to the traditional view of Christianity."

"Why do you think that's so?"

"There are numerous reasons. Sometimes it's moral issues," came his response. "They don't want to be constrained by the traditional Jesus, who calls them to a life of holiness. One friend of mine finally acknowledged that Jesus rose from the dead, but he still won't become a Christian because he said he wanted to be the master of his own life — that's the exact way he put it. So in many cases — not all — it's a heart issue, not a head issue.

"Some people just don't like what Jesus is demanding of them."

Psychoanalyzing Paul

The next major category of evidence offered by Licona was the appearances of Jesus to the disciples, Paul, and James. Among the most outspoken skeptics on this issue is historian and philosopher Richard Carrier, who holds two master's degrees in ancient history from Columbia University and is pursuing a doctorate there.

The son of "freethinking Methodists" — his mom was a church secretary — Carrier became a philosophical Taoist at age fifteen and an atheist at twenty-one. He has become a popular critic of Christianity on the Internet, and I once moderated a debate between him and a Christian on national television.

Carrier seeks to explain away the supposed appearance of Jesus to Paul by saying this was merely a "revelation" induced by Paul's guilt over persecuting Christians and other psychological factors. Carrier writes:

> I can hypothesize four conjoining factors: guilt at persecuting a people he came to admire; subsequent disgust with fellow persecuting Pharisees; and persuasion (beginning to see what the Christians were seeing in scripture, and to worry about his own salvation); coupled with the right physical circumstances (like heat and fatigue on a long, desolate road), could have induced a convincing ecstatic event — his unconscious mind producing what he really wanted: a reason to believe the Christians were right after all and atone for his treatment of them, and a way to give his life meaning, by relocating himself from the lower, even superfluous periphery of Jewish elite society, to a place of power and purpose.[7]

After reading Carrier's theory to Licona, I asked for his response. "Doesn't this account for Paul's experience on the road to Damascus?" I said.

Licona, who had listened intently as I presented Carrier's argument, clearly didn't see any merit in it. "The question should be: Is this the best explanation?" he said. "I could offer another explanation — that there was a gremlin from Saturn who posed as the risen Jesus and appeared to Paul. That's an explanation, but is it the best? I'd say, no, it's not a very good historical hypothesis — and neither is Carrier's."

"Why not?"

"Because at best it can only account for Paul's belief that he had seen the risen Jesus. It doesn't account for the conversion of the skeptic James, and it doesn't account for the empty tomb. And it doesn't explain the beliefs of the disciples that they had seen the risen Jesus. You've got to account for what changed them to the point where they were willing to suffer continuously and even die for their beliefs that they had seen the risen Jesus. So it's a bad historical hypothesis."

"Do you think that any of the psychological factors mentioned by Carrier could explain Paul's sudden change of mind?"

"Paul himself is crystal clear about why he converted: he says he saw the risen Jesus," Licona replied. "So we have his eyewitness testimony of what happened. On the other hand, what do we have for Carrier's view? There's not a shred of evidence to support it. Paul's writings don't indicate that he converted because he felt guilty or that he secretly admired Christians or that he had a disdain for his fellow Pharisees. This is pure conjecture and speculation on Carrier's part. He's reading things into the text that simply aren't there.

"Besides, there's something else Carrier is forgetting. Luke, who may have been Paul's traveling companion, reports on Paul's conversion in Acts 9, 22, and 26. In all three accounts, it says others were present when Paul encountered Jesus, and they either saw the light or heard the voice but didn't understand it. So this was not merely a subjective experience that occurred in Paul's head. Others were partakers in the experience, which would indicate it's not the product of hallucination or some sort of epiphany."

I jumped in. "Skeptics might object that Luke's accounts contradict each other."

"On the contrary, I think they can be harmonized," he replied, "and don't forget that Luke wrote all three of them. Why would he knowingly write contradictory accounts in the same book? We have to study how the ancients wrote. There might be different things that Luke was trying to emphasize in each of those passages. Frankly, I don't think there are any major tensions between the three accounts that are going to call their credibility in question. What is certainly clear in all three accounts is that there were others with Paul at the time he saw Jesus who noted that phenomena too.

"If you accept what Acts says about Paul's experience, then you can't simply ignore what else Acts reports. For instance, in Acts 13 Paul says David died and was buried and his body decayed but Jesus died and was buried but his body didn't decay. He said God raised Jesus. Thus, Paul believed in the bodily resurrection of the corpse of Jesus."

"Hold on a minute," I said. Licona's emphasis on the *bodily* resurrection of Jesus prompted me to pursue a related line of questioning.

Physical or Spiritual Resurrection?

For years, skeptics and liberal scholars have sought to dilute the impact of the resurrection by attributing it to merely a spiritual experience rather than a physical phenomenon involving the material body of Jesus. For instance, Marcus Borg of the Jesus Seminar said he sees the post-Easter Jesus as "an experiential reality" and not as the "resuscitation" of a corpse.[8]

"Critics cite some of Paul's own words to prove he saw an *immaterial* Jesus who had a *spiritual* resurrection, not a bodily one," I said to Licona.

"In 1 Corinthians 15," I continued, "Paul talks about the resurrection of the dead by saying in verse 44, 'It is sown a *natural* body, it is raised a *spiritual* body.' Verse 50 says, 'I declare to you, brothers and sisters, that flesh and blood cannot inherit the kingdom of God, nor does the perishable inherit the imperishable.' Tabor says Paul equates his own 'sighting' of Jesus, which was 'clearly visionary,' with the other apostles — 'possibly implying that their experiences were much like his.'[9] Do these Corinthian passages indicate Paul's encounter was visionary in nature rather than a bodily, corporeal resurrection?"

Obviously, this was a hot-button issue for Licona. He moved to the edge of the couch and his voice became more animated. "First let's examine this term 'flesh and blood,'" he said. "For the past thirty years, most experts have concluded that this term was an ancient figure of speech, probably a Semitism, that simply meant 'a mortal being.' That's what it means every time it appears in the New Testament, the Septuagint, and throughout the Rabbinic literature. It's kind of like when Americans call a person 'cold blooded,' 'hot-blooded,' or 'red-blooded.' They're not referring to the temperature or color of their blood.

"Now, you can't equate that with what Luke reports Jesus as saying when he appears to the disciples: 'Hey, I'm not a ghost, because ghosts don't have flesh and *bones* as you see that I have.'[10] He said flesh and *bones*, not flesh and *blood*."

"What about the way Paul contrasts the words *natural* and *spiritual*?" I asked.

"I recently analyzed each time these words appeared between the eighth century BC through the third century AD. These words have multiple definitions, but what's really interesting, Lee, is that I never found a single instance in which the Greek word translated 'natural' meant 'material' or 'physical.' Never. Not once.

"It's also important to see how Paul uses these terms elsewhere, especially in the same letter. A few chapters earlier, in 1 Corinthians 2:14–15, referring to spiritual truths, Paul writes that the 'natural' man rejects and cannot understand the things of God, because they are 'spiritually' discerned. But, he adds, 'spiritual' people understand them.

"So when we come to chapter 15, Paul gives a number of differences between our bodies. They're sown in weakness, they're raised in power. They're sown in dishonor, they're raised in glory. They're sown perishable, they're raised imperishable. They're sown *natural*—bodies with all their fleshly and sinful desires and with hearts and lungs — but raised and transformed into a new body with *spiritual* appetites and empowered by God's Spirit. There's no thought about a contrast between physical versus spiritual.

"And here's one other thing: if Paul had meant to draw a comparison between material versus immaterial, he had a better Greek word at his disposal, which he had already used a few chapters earlier with a similar analogy of sowing.[11] He doesn't use that word here, though. That's more evidence that this has nothing to do with material versus immaterial. So to claim that Paul is saying that Christians will have an immaterial body in heaven is no longer sustainable."

I raised a related issue. "Paul says in Galatians 1:16 that God was pleased 'to reveal his Son *in me*.'[12] Doesn't that suggest that Jesus' appearance to Paul was an inward or subjective experience rather than an objective reality?"

Licona frowned. "This is a difficult verse, I admit, because Paul doesn't clarify what he means and the context doesn't help us," Licona replied. "And there's no consensus among experts as to what this means. Some think it's referring to the Damascus Road experience, and he's referring to the inward illumination that coincided with the outward experience of encountering Jesus. Still others translate it as 'to me' instead of 'in me.' The Greek allows this, and this is the way Paul uses the term in 1 Corinthians 14:11. But we really don't know."

"In light of that, how do you employ responsible historical methodology here?" I asked.

"When we come across a passage with an ambiguous meaning, we're required to interpret it according to other passages by the same person that are more clear. So if Paul is referring to a bodily resurrection elsewhere—as he does in at least three other places—then it's irresponsible to translate this passage in a manner that has Paul contradicting himself."

"So Paul is not saying this is merely a spiritual resurrection."

"No, and I think the evidence is so obvious. In 1 Corinthians 15:20, Paul is clear that he regards Jesus' resurrection as a model for our future resurrection. He says in Romans 8:11 that 'he who raised Christ from the dead will *also* give life *to your mortal bodies* because of his Spirit who lives in you.' And he stresses in Philippians 3:21 that the Lord Jesus Christ 'will transform *our lowly bodies* so that they will be like his glorious body.'[13]

"Moreover, in 1 Corinthians 15:53–54, Paul states plainly that in resurrection our present perishable and mortal bodies will 'put on' the imperishable and immortal like a person puts on a sweater over clothing. It's not an abandonment of the body but a further clothing that completely swallows up and transforms. As N. T. Wright shows in his book *The Resurrection of the Son of God*, when Jews talked about resurrection, they were talking about the resurrection of the corpse. This wasn't something that happened just as a vision to Paul.

"One more thing," he said. "We have to keep in mind that Paul's experience came after Jesus' ascension into heaven, so it would make sense that he describes it differently than the disciples, who encountered Jesus before he ascended. Even so, he still believed Jesus rose bodily. He makes that quite apparent."

Hallucinations and Delusions

So far, I felt that Licona had adequately responded to challenges about Jesus' appearance to Paul. But what about the other appearances of Jesus? As for Carrier, his position is quite forthright:

> I believe the best explanation, consistent with both scientific find-ings and the surviving evidence ... is that the first Christians experienced hallucinations of the risen Christ, of one form or another.... In the ancient world, to experience supernatural mani-festations of ghosts, gods and wonders was not only accepted, but often encouraged.[14]

"Doesn't this," I pressed Licona, "neatly account for the appearances of Jesus?"

"First," responded Licona, "I think we can note that ghosts, won-ders, and gods aren't unique to antiquity. People believe in the super-natural today too. In fact, that's probably increasing."

"Maybe that's so," I conceded. "But that doesn't really mean any-thing in terms of what happened in the first century."

"I agree," he said. "Actually, I'd say if all we had was Jesus appearing to Peter, then maybe I'd buy into the hallucination theory."

That admission startled me. "You would?" I asked.

"*Maybe*," Licona stressed. "He's grieving, he's full of anxiety — *maybe*."

That seemed like a significant concession to me. But Licona wasn't finished. "But that's not all we have," he continued. "We've not only got multiple appearances to individuals, but we've got at least three appearances to groups of people. And a group of people isn't going to all hallucinate the same thing at the same time."

"Can you back that up?"

"I lived in Virginia Beach for fourteen years. Half the Navy Seals are stationed there, and I got to know a number of them. To become a Seal, they have to go through 'hell week.' They start Sunday night, and they go through Friday, during which they get maybe three to five hours of sleep the whole time. They're being barked at continually, there's high stress, they're constantly exercising, and inevitably fatigue and sleep deprivation set in.

"About 80 percent of the guys hallucinate due to the lack of sleep. A lot of time they're out on a raft doing an exercise called 'around the world,' where they go out in the ocean, around a buoy, and they come back to shore. They're trying to be first because then they'll be rewarded with rest. It's at this time that many start seeing things.

"One Seal told me he actually believed he saw an octopus come out of the water and wave at him. Another guy believed that a train was coming across the water toward the raft. He'd point to it and the others would say, 'Are you crazy? There are no trains out here in the ocean.' He believed it so strongly that before what he perceived as the train hit him, he rolled into the ocean and they had to retrieve him.

"A Seal told me about another guy who was waving his oars wildly in the air. When he was asked what he was doing, he said, 'I'm trying to hit the dolphins that are jumping over the boat.' I asked the Seal, 'Did you see the dolphins?' He said, 'No.' I said, 'Did anyone else see the dolphins?' He said, 'No, they were busy having their own hallucinations!'

"You see, hallucinations aren't contagious. They're personal. They're like dreams. I couldn't wake up my wife in the middle of the night and say, 'Honey, I'm dreaming of being in Hawaii. Quick, go back to sleep, join me in my dream, and we'll have a free vacation.' You can't do that. Scientists will tell you that hallucinations are the same way.

"We've got three group appearances at least, so the hallucination theory doesn't work. On top of that, hallucinations can't account for the empty tomb. They can't account for the appearance to Paul, because he wasn't grieving—he was occupied with trying to destroy the church. And in the midst of that, he believes he sees the risen Jesus. James was a skeptic; he wasn't in the frame of mind for hallucinations to occur either."

I knew that Licona's analysis of the hallucination theory was solid. According to psychologist Gary Collins, who was a university professor for more than two decades, authored dozens of books on psychology, and was the president of a national association of psychologists and counselors:

> Hallucinations are individual occurrences. By their very nature only one person can see a given hallucination at a time. They certainly aren't something which can be seen by a group of people. Neither is it possible that one person could somehow induce a hallucination in somebody else. Since a hallucination exists only in the subjective, personal sense, it is obvious that others cannot witness it.[15]

I decided to try another approach. "What about the idea that 'group-think' could have taken over in those groups," I asked. "Maybe people were suggestible and perhaps talked into seeing a vision."

"At best, that only would account for the beliefs of the disciples that they had seen the risen Jesus. It would not account for the empty tomb, because then the body should still be in there. It would not account for the conversion of Paul, since it's unlikely an opponent like him would be susceptible to groupthink. Same with the skeptic James. In fact, with the crucifixion of Jesus, James was probably all the more convinced that he was a failed Messiah, because he was hung on the tree and cursed by God."[16]

I wasn't ready to give up yet. "If these weren't technically hallucinations, could these people have been deluded?" I asked. "You know —like Marshall Applewhite of the Church of Venus, who committed suicide with more than three dozen of his followers because they believed a spaceship hiding behind the Comet Hale-Bopp would pick them up."

"You're right—hallucinations and delusions aren't the same," Licona said. "A hallucination is a false perception of something that's not there; a delusion is when someone persists in a belief after receiving conclusive evidence to the contrary. In the case of Applewhite, his followers were delusional. They persisted in their belief that they were seeing a spaceship behind the comet even after astronomers assured them they were actually seeing Mars."

"Well, then," I said, "we could postulate the theory that Peter saw a hallucination of Jesus and then he convinced the other disciples—he deluded them—into believing Jesus had risen from the dead."

"Sorry," came the reply. "That doesn't account for all the facts. For example, it doesn't account for the empty tomb, because the body would still be there, right? And it wouldn't account for the conversion of Paul. Listen—you weren't sucked in by the Church of Venus, were you, Lee? Most people weren't. Paul, who's opposing the church, wasn't going to get sucked into believing Jesus returned from the dead, and neither was James. At best, the delusion theory could only conceivably account for why some of the disciples believed; it doesn't account for most of the facts. So therefore it's not a good historical theory."

Deftly, using evidence and logic, Licona had deflected the biggest objections to the appearances of the risen Jesus that have been promoted by critics in recent years. His "minimal facts"—that Jesus' disciples, the persecutor Paul, and the skeptic James believed they had encountered the risen Jesus—appeared to survive intact.

Still, there was the remaining issue of the burial place of Jesus: Was his tomb empty on the first Easter—and why?

Paul and the Empty Tomb

I began addressing the issue of the empty tomb by recapping to Licona the way that Carrier and Uta Ranke-Heinemann, a professor of the history of religion at the University of Essen in Germany, try to account for it.

"According to Carrier," I said, "Paul didn't believe in an empty tomb, because he believed Jesus had a spiritual body, which is why he never mentions the empty tomb. Later, Mark made up the empty tomb story—for him, it was not historical but symbolic, representing Jesus being freed from his corpse. According to Carrier, Jesus' body was the empty tomb. Then legendary embellishment took over in Matthew, Luke, and John.[17]

"As for Ranke-Heinemann, she says the empty tomb's legendary nature is proven because Paul, 'the most crucial preacher of Christ's resurrection and the earliest New Testament writer besides, says nothing about it. As far as Paul is concerned, it doesn't exist.'"[18] Lüdemann agrees: "If he had known about the empty tomb, he would certainly have referred to it in order to have an additional argument for the resurrection."[19]

With that background, I said to Licona, "You believe the empty tomb is important enough to be included in your five minimal facts, right?"

"That's right," he said.

"Then if it's important in building *your* case for the resurrection, why wouldn't it be equally important for Paul in building *his* case?" I asked. "Why wouldn't Paul have stressed it every bit as much as you did when he was trying to convince others that the resurrection was true?"

Licona looked a little perplexed that this issue was even coming up. "I don't think he had to," came his reply. "It is like when you say a baby died of Sudden Infant Death Syndrome. No one has to speak about an empty crib. It's clearly implied.

"The ancient meaning of resurrection was the bringing back of a corpse to life and transforming it into an immortal body. Imagine saying to Paul, 'If you believed in an empty tomb, why didn't you mention it?' Paul would have said, 'Well, what do you think I meant when I said resurrection? You want me to spell it out for you? Of course, I mean an empty tomb!'

"The New Testament uses two different words for resurrection. One of them means to stand up again. The other means to raise up, and it's used many times of waking up out of a sleep. Well, when you wake up out of a sleep, it's not like you wake up into a new body or into no body at all. When you wake up out of a sleep and stand up again, you're in your body and you stand up using the same body. This is the way it's used when the synagogue ruler's daughter was raised from the dead. She left behind an empty bed, not an empty body."[20]

"Still," I pressed, "why didn't Paul specifically use the words 'empty tomb'?"

For Licona, the answer was all too obvious. "It was unnecessary," he said. "It would be redundant after he said, 'resurrection.'"

"But can you blame people today for wishing Paul had been even more explicit?"

Licona shrugged. "Maybe the skeptics want to have it spelled out for them in the twenty-first century, but Paul was writing this in the first century. They all knew what resurrection meant. To them, Paul was plenty explicit. He's clear in his own letters. Moreover, when Luke reports Paul stating in Acts 13:37 that Jesus' body 'did not see decay,' readers surely understood that his physical body had been raised — and if the body was raised, the tomb was empty. This is early apostolic tradition."

In the end, I had to admit: this made sense to me too.

The "Relocation Hypothesis"

I moved on to another current objection to the empty tomb: the "relocation hypothesis" championed by both Tabor and Jeffery Jay Lowder, whose attacks on the resurrection have proven popular on the Internet.

According to Lowder, "Jesus' body was stored (but not buried) in Joseph's tomb Friday before sunset and moved on Saturday night to a second tomb in the graveyard of the condemned, where Jesus was buried dishonorably."[21] Tabor asserts that someone — probably members of Jesus' own family — removed the body from this "temporary grave" and reburied him elsewhere. He says the post-resurrection appearances were invented to compensate for the original ending of Mark's gospel.[22]

I was curious how Licona would respond. "What's your reaction?" I asked.

"Notice first that this is in contradiction to what Carrier says," he replied. "Carrier says you need to account for the appearances, so Mark invented the empty tomb. Other critics are saying you've got an empty tomb due to reburial, so you've got to account for it by making up the appearances. Apparently, not even the skeptics can agree with each other!"

That was interesting — but it didn't answer the question. "Yes or no?" I said, trying not to sound too impatient. "Does their theory pass muster as a historical hypothesis?"

"No, it doesn't," he answered.

"Why not?"

"Here's the question we have to ask: Does it account for all the facts and do so without straining? At best, even if the reburial hypothesis were true, all it accounts for is the empty tomb. And interestingly, the empty tomb didn't convince any of the disciples—possibly with the exception of John—that Jesus had returned from the dead. It was the appearances of Jesus that convinced them, and the reburial theory can't account for these.

"It's like with David Koresh in the 1990s. He predicted that when he died he would rise from the dead three years later. Well, he didn't. But let's suppose three years after the date of his death at Waco, some Branch Davidians said, 'Hey, Koresh is back to life again.' You go and check for his remains at the coroner's office and they're missing. Would you, as a Christian, abandon your faith and become a Branch Davidian because of that? Of course not. You'd say, "C'mon, the remains were moved, stolen, or misplaced.'

"Think about it: Why did Paul move from skepticism to faith? He said it was the appearances that led to his faith, not his faith that led to the appearances. The same with James. The appearances were the key —and, again, this theory fails to account for them.

"Besides, on a more mundane note, if the family moved the body, don't you think somebody would have said something to straighten out the disciples when they were going around proclaiming a resurrection? And remember: the explanation for the empty tomb that was circulating at the time was that the disciples had stolen the body. If the body had merely been relocated, why didn't somebody in authority point that out so they could squelch the Christian movement in its infancy?"

"What do you think of Tabor's suggestion that he even knows where Jesus is buried—in the north, in Galilee outside the city of Tsfat?" I asked.

A look of exasperation came over Licona's face. "First, this is based on his metaphysical naturalism, which says we know people can't return from the dead and therefore if Jesus' tomb was empty, the body must have been reburied. That's the only logical explanation, according to Tabor. Again, that's a product of his metaphysical assumptions, not because of an open-minded assessment of the historical evidence.

"Second, Tabor gets his information from a sixteenth-century Jewish mystic," he said, his eyebrows raising. "Think about that! If Christians based their theory on what a sixteenth-century Christian reported, we would laugh at that person—and justifiably so. Now, believe me,

I'm not laughing at Tabor—he's certainly a credentialed scholar. But you can't blame people for rejecting his theory. It's just amazing to me that he would disregard the reports of the Gospels, which were all written in the first century, but be credulous of a single source written by a mystic some fifteen hundred years after Jesus."

Licona's analysis reminded me of the words of New Testament scholar Craig A. Evans, whom I had interviewed earlier:

> I find it ironic that Tabor is willing to give credence to the vision of a sixteenth-century mystic and kabbalist, but is not willing to give credence to the vision of the first-century Saul of Tarsus. Saul did not believe Jesus was the Messiah and certainly did not believe that he had been raised from the dead—tomb or no tomb. Saul was hard at work trying to stamp out the new heresy. Then Saul met the risen Messiah. And we know the rest of the story. I'll take Saul's vision any day over [the sixteenth-century mystic's]. I urge Tabor to do the same.[23]

The Jesus Tomb

What about another possibility referenced by Tabor in his book—that the "bone boxes" discovered in the Talpiot Tomb south of the old city of Jerusalem in 1980 once contained the skeletal remains of Jesus and his family?

Hollywood director James Cameron and filmmaker Simcha Jacobovici garnered widespread publicity with their 2007 Discovery Channel documentary in which they said archaeologists had found ossuaries etched with the names "Jesus, son of Joseph," Joseh (or Joseph), Maria (or Mary), Matia (or Matthew), Mariamne Mara (which they claimed was Mary Magdalene), and "Judah, son of Jesus." DNA tests indicated that the individual buried in the Jesus and Mary Magdalene ossuaries were not related through the same mother; the documentary suggested they had been married and had at least one child—Judah.

In his book, however, even Tabor conceded that Amos Kloner, the archaeologist who oversaw the tomb's excavation, said that "the possibility of it being Jesus' family [is] very close to zero," and that Motti

Neiger of the Israeli Antiquities Authority agreed "that chances of these being the actual burials of the holy family are almost nil."[24]

I asked Licona whether any of the original archaeologists concluded that these ossuaries belonged to the biblical Jesus and his family.

"No," came his answer. "They understood that nearly all of the names inscribed on the ossuaries were very common."

"How common?"

"It appears that Mary was the most popular name during the time of Jesus. It's estimated that one out of every four or five women in Jerusalem was named Mary. Joseph was the second most common male name in Jesus' day, with about one out of every seven Jerusalem males being called that. One out of every eleven males was named Jesus, one out of ten was named Judah, and one in every twenty was named Matthew."

"Still," I said, "isn't it significant that ossuaries with the names of Jesus, Joseph, and Mary happened to be found in the same tomb?"

"Well, certainly the potential for significance increases when you place together a specific combination of names, even common ones," he replied. "As Cameron's documentary said, finding the names of John, Paul, and George is no big deal, but when you add Ringo to the pool, you may have something. The problem, of course, is that when you really examine things, there's no equivalent of 'Ringo' in the Talpiot tomb.

"According to calculations by physicist Randy Ingermanson," he continued, "one out of every seventy-nine males in Jerusalem was 'Jesus, son of Joseph.'[25] Hershel Shanks and Ben Witherington III estimate that during the ninety-year period in which ossuaries were used — from 20 BC to AD 70 — there were about 80,000 males in Jerusalem. That means there were approximately 1,000 men named Jesus who had a father named Joseph.[26] Ingermanson then considers the other names in the Talpiot tomb and calculates there were probably eleven men in Jerusalem during that period who fit the profile of the Jesus in the Talpiot tomb.

"So without taking anything else into consideration, there's roughly a one in eleven, or nine percent, chance that the Talpiot tomb contained the biblical Jesus. But there's a whole lot more to consider. In order for Jesus to qualify as one of the eleven, we must see what evidence there is that Jesus was married and had children or was single. And things get significantly worse for the Talpiot theorists when that is considered."

"Is there any evidence that Jesus was, indeed, married to Mary Magdalene?"

"The evidence in the documentary starts with the Acts of Philip, which is where Mary is supposedly first referred to as Mariamne. But the text doesn't actually say 'Mariamne' like the ossuary does; it refers to 'Mariamme.' Mariamme in the Acts of Philip is only identified as the sister of Philip, and there's no hint in the text whatsoever that she's married to Jesus or has a child. In fact, the text seems to demand celibacy. The main character, Philip, tells converts to Christianity to leave their spouses and live a life of sexual abstinence."[27]

"In any event," I said, "nobody thinks the Acts of Philip is historically reliable, do they?"

"The text dates from the fourth century," Licona said. "Even if some of its traditions go back to the second century, that's still long after the canonical Gospels. In their book *The Jesus Family Tomb*, Jacobovici and Charles Pellegrino cite both the Gospel of Philip and the Gospel of Mary as suggesting that Jesus may have been romantically involved with Mary Magdalene, but these writings post-date the New Testament. No widely respected scholar holds that they contain any historically reliable information about Jesus or his followers. On top of that, these texts don't even claim that Jesus and Mary were married or had a child."

"Is there any evidence that Jesus was single?"

"Absolutely!" he declared. "Even though there's no obvious reason why the Messiah needed to be single, our four earliest biographies of Jesus, written within seventy years of his life, present him that way. And Paul didn't mention Jesus as having been married when it certainly would have been to his advantage to do so."

"For instance ...," I prompted him.

"When writing to the church in Corinth, he affirms he has the right to have a Christian wife accompany him, like the rest of the apostles, the Lord's brothers, and Peter.[28] If Jesus had been married, surely Paul would have added his name as his primary example. Paul's silence is a deafening shout pertaining to Jesus' marital status."

"Do you believe the ossuary labeled 'Mariamne Mara' belongs to Mary Magdalene?"

"It's extremely unlikely, since Mary Magdalene doesn't appear to have been referred to anywhere as 'Mariamne.' In addition, while 'Mara' could possibly mean 'the great' or 'Lord,' it could easily be short for 'Martha.' Without a Mary Magdalene in the Talpiot tomb, Cameron's proposal collapses—in short, there's no 'Ringo.'"

I asked, "How about the DNA evidence that Cameron presented?"

"Something the team neglected to mention is that even though there were ten ossuaries discovered in the tomb back in 1980, as many as thirty-five were buried there. So this tomb probably included extended family members. Mariamne could just as likely have been Jesus' cousin, aunt, grandmother on his father's side, half-sister from a previous marriage of his father, niece, or daughter-in-law."

"So what's your conclusion about the Jesus tomb?" I asked.

"Cameron's opening words in *The Jesus Family Tomb* provide a hint about what we can expect throughout the book: 'What if Jesus didn't exist at all? Today many experts are saying exactly that.'[29] Well, that's ridiculous. It merely shows how out of touch Cameron is with scholarship.

"Sure, there are some self-proclaimed experts on the Internet who claim Jesus never existed, but these aren't scholars with academic credentials. Only a very small handful of legitimate scholars, such as the skeptic Robert Price, suggest they wouldn't be surprised if Jesus never existed, but even Price falls short of asserting Jesus never lived.

"The arguments that the Talpiot tomb contained the remains of the biblical Jesus are extremely weak. And besides, don't forget all the persuasive affirmative evidence that I've already cited for Jesus rising from the dead."

Indeed, Cameron's documentary sparked an onslaught of criticism from knowledgeable scholars. "Almost no one agrees that the name Mariamne refers to Mary Magdalene, or that Mara means 'Lady' or 'Master,' as though it were a title of honor," Evans told me in an email. "It is, rather, an abbreviation of Martha, which is attested in other inscriptions." Given its Greek form, he said the etching on the ossuary could very well be read as: "Mariamne's (daughter) Mara (or

Martha)." Others translate it as: "[Ossuary] of Mariamne (who is also called) Mara."

As far as the DNA is concerned, Evans said, "Ossuaries often contained more than one skeleton in them, so there is some question whether the tested bone fragments actually match the names inscribed on the ossuaries."

Historian Paul Maier was blunt in describing the Jesus Tomb: "This is merely naked hype, baseless sensationalism, and nothing less than a media fraud."[30] In the end, the public seemed to agree. A Zogby poll showed that among those with or without knowledge of the documentary, there was absolutely no difference in the percentage who believe in the bodily resurrection of Jesus.[31]

Producing Jesus' Body

One way Christians often defend the empty tomb is to say that if the grave still contained Jesus' body, then the authorities could have paraded it down Main Street in Jerusalem and thus killed the incipient Christian movement. In fact, Licona had used a similar argument.

But is that really true? After all, the disciples' public proclamation about the resurrection came some seven weeks after the crucifixion, when Peter declared to a crowd of several thousand people in Jerusalem: "God has raised this Jesus to life, and we are all witnesses of it."[32]

Price suggests the disciples were "shrewd enough" to wait this long so that "disconfirmation had become impossible." He said that after fifty days "it would have been moot to produce the remains of Jesus."[33] Agreed Lowder: "The body would have been far too decomposed to be identified without modern forensics."[34]

Licona was incredulous. "Price thinks the disciples were being *shrewd* to wait until the corpse was unrecognizable?" he asked. "They were laying their lives on the line! Why would they plot and scheme this way so their reward would be continual suffering, even to the point of death? That doesn't add up."

"What about recognizing the body?" I asked.

"I talked to three coroners from Louisiana, Virginia, and California about whether a body would be recognizable after fifty days. All agreed that even in a humid climate, you would still be able to recognize a body somewhat — at least in stature, the hair, and possibly the wounds.

"Now, had you been able to go back to Jesus' tomb after fifty days and seen a severely decomposed body of the same stature as Jesus and with the same hair, and possibly note wounds consistent with scourging and crucifixion, enough doubt would have been put into enough minds that subsequent Christian apologists would have had to address why there was a great exodus of believers at that point. But we have no record of any such thing.

"In other words, if the authorities had claimed this was Jesus, then the burden of proof would have shifted. The onus would have been on the disciples to disprove it. Nobody needed to see all his facial features; merely producing a severely decomposed body from the right tomb and with the right stature and hair type would have put the disciples on the defensive. Their movement would have been greatly undermined. But of course, there's absolutely no historical evidence to suggest this happened."

"A Divine Miracle"

Try as they might, the skeptics still couldn't put Jesus' body back in his tomb. Time after time, what sounded like a knockout objection had been successfully overcome by Licona's explanations.

Challenge the post-Easter appearances of Jesus and you've still got the empty tomb. Theorize that Jesus' body was moved to an undisclosed location and you're still faced with the appearances that revolutionized the disciples, Paul, and James. The hallucination theory might work with Peter, but not Paul, James, or groups of people. Alternate scenarios that seemed credible from a distance unraveled at an alarming rate when examined up close.

The five minimal facts — themselves just a skeleton of an even more robust case that could have been made for the resurrection by using the broader Gospel accounts — remained intact. "The rational man," said Craig, "can hardly now be blamed if he infers that at the tomb of Jesus on that early Easter morning a divine miracle has occurred."[35]

I drained the remainder of my glass of water and settled deeper into the couch. Licona and I had talked for a long time; the sun had shifted so it was no longer flooding the room. He had answered the historical questions well, but there were still a couple of other issues I wanted to cover.

"How would you respond to Carrier when he makes this observation: 'Why on earth would a God, who wanted to save all mankind, only appear to a few hundred, most unnamed, people and then give up? Wouldn't it be much more efficient and effective ... to bypass the apostolate and just appear to everyone?' "[36]

Licona's eyes narrowed as he thought. "That's not really a historical issue," he said.

"I know—but what do you think?"

Licona deliberated a little longer. "Whatever reason God had for doing it that way, it worked," he said finally. "Nearly a third of the world today claims to be Christian. And I think it's just like the Christian God to use the weak to trump the strong, and the fools to shame the wise. It would be just like that God to take the few and the obscure to influence the masses. Now, because of that, the world has been turned upside down."

"What about you personally?" I asked. "Are you at the point where you never doubt anymore?"

Licona's reply was candid. "Yeah, I still have periods when I experience some doubt—in a way, that's my personality," he said. "Sometimes I still wonder, 'Am I looking at these arguments as objectively as I can?' I'm always trying to neutralize my biases. When someone raises an objection, most of the time I'm not trying to think of a refutation. I'm trying to understand and internalize the argument—to grant its full weight. I try to feel it as the person who holds it feels it. And that will cause some doubts, because I'm sort of experiencing what they're experiencing."

"What do you do then?"

"I look at the data. I try to apply responsible historical methodology," he said. "And I always come back to the resurrection."

Over and over, Michael Licona ultimately finds it convincing: a very real event of history that validates the divinity of the real Jesus.

Bridging the Gap

"Nonsense."

More than any other word, that sums up Lüdemann's assessment of the bodily resurrection of Jesus. To this spiritually skeptical professor at the University of Göttingen in Germany, it's outside the realm of possibility. "If you say that Jesus rose from the dead biologically, you would have to presuppose that a decaying corpse—which is already cold and without blood in its brain—could be made alive again," he said. "I think that is nonsense."[37]

Surely it's not something an elite scientist could embrace—especially one who's also a physician and thoroughly acquainted with human anatomy. Yet the reality of the resurrection, which transformed skeptics like Paul and James in the first century, continues to radically redirect lives today—even of tough-minded scientists.

For example, few researchers in America have achieved the professional acclaim of Francis S. Collins. As a medical doctor with a doctorate in chemistry, he was appointed by President Clinton to head the Human Genome Project, which successfully decoded the three billion genes of human DNA. He also has helped discover the genetic anomalies that lead to cystic fibrosis, neurofibromatosis, and Huntington's disease. I've had the pleasure of exchanging emails with him from time to time.

For much of his early life, Collins was an atheist, looking at Jesus as "a myth, a fairy tale, a superhero in a 'just-so' bedtime story." Then the faith of some of his desperately ill patients prompted him to investigate spiritual issues. Eventually, it was the universal existence of right and wrong—the Moral Law—that led him to believe in an "infinitely good and holy" God—and which, in contrast, brought him face-to-face with his own failings, selfishness, and pride.

Turning to history, he was amazed at the evidence for Jesus of Nazareth. The four Gospels, he found, were written within decades of Jesus' death. They were clearly rooted in the testimony of eyewitnesses. They had been passed through the centuries with great fidelity. And, of course, they describe Jesus rising bodily from the dead.

Can a rational scientist believe in such "nonsense"? This was, conceded Collins, "difficult stuff." In the end, though, came this epiphany: "If Christ really was the Son of God, as He explicitly claimed, then surely of all those who had ever walked the earth, He could suspend the laws of nature if He needed to do so to achieve a more important purpose."

For Collins, this was more than just a historical curiosity. "The crucifixion and resurrection also provided something else," he said in his 2006 bestseller *The Language of God*.

"My desire to draw close to God was blocked by my own pride and sinfulness, which in turn was an inevitable consequence of my own selfish desire to be in control," he said. "Now the crucifixion and resurrection emerged as the compelling solution to the gap that yawned between God and myself, a gap that could now be bridged by the person of Jesus Christ."[38]

That is what the real—and resurrected—Jesus does.

For Further Investigation
More Resources on This Topic

Bowman, Robert M., Jr., and J. Ed Komoszewsi. *Putting Jesus in His Place: The Case for the Deity of Christ*. Grand Rapids, Mich.: Kregel, 2007.

Copan, Paul, and Ronald K. Tacelli, eds. *Jesus' Resurrection: Fact or Figment?* Downers Grove, Ill.: InterVarsity, 2000.

Habermas, Gary R., and Antony G. N. Flew. *Resurrected? An Atheist and Theist Dialogue*. Lanham, Md.: Rowman & Littlefield, 2005.

————, and Michael R. Licona. *The Case for the Resurrection of Jesus*. Grand Rapids, Mich.: Kregel, 2004.

Licona, Michael R. *Paul Meets Muhammad: A Christian-Muslim Debate on the Resurrection*. Grand Rapids, Mich.: Baker Books, 2006.

Strobel, Lee. *The Case for Christ*. Grand Rapids, Mich.: Zondervan, 1998.

Swinburne, Richard. *The Resurrection of God Incarnate*. Oxford: Oxford Press, 2003.

Wright, N. T. *The Resurrection of the Son of God*. Minneapolis: Fortress, 2003.

"Christianity's Beliefs about Jesus Were Copied from Pagan Religions"

Why should we consider the stories of Osiris, Dionysus, Adonis, Attis, Mithras, and the other Pagan Mystery saviors as fables, yet come across essentially the same story told in a Jewish context and believe it to be the biography of a carpenter from Bethlehem?

Timothy Freke and Peter Gandy, *The Jesus Mysteries*[1]

There is nothing the Jesus of the Gospels either said or did ... that cannot be shown to have originated thousands of years before, in Egyptian Mystery rites and other sacred liturgies.

Tom Harpur, *The Pagan Christ*[2]

As a young reporter at the *Chicago Tribune*, I watched in sympathy as a heartbreaking spectacle unfolded in the newsroom. The editor received an anonymous envelope containing a recent column by an up-and-coming *Tribune* writer, as well as a photocopy of an article written eight years earlier by Pete Hamill of the *New York Post* and reprinted in a collection of his works.

The theme and substantial parts of the language were virtually identical, resulting in a charge of plagiarism—a humiliating and career-stunting allegation that led to the reporter's suspension for a month without pay. Subsequent disclosure of another impropriety resulted in the writer's resignation. It was painful to see a colleague's promising career derailed, but as the *Tribune*'s editor said at the time, "We condemn deception in others; we cannot accept it among our own without penalty."

Through the years, allegations of plagiarism have vexed lots of journalists, scholars, politicians, and students — even a young Helen Keller.[3] It's a serious and escalating problem at universities. Today's ready access to the Internet has made cut-and-paste plagiarism much easier for students who are facing imminent deadlines for term papers, prompting entrepreneurs to create Web-based resources that help professors detect previously published passages.

Technically, it's not a crime to commit plagiarism, but it can be a serious civil offense to claim another person's words or literary concepts as his or her own.[4] Most of the time, though, the penalties are informal but nevertheless devastating: an embarrassing loss of credibility.

In an analogous way, a wave of recent books has claimed that Christianity's key tenets about Jesus — including his virgin birth and resurrection — are not historical but rather were plagiarized from earlier "mystery religions" that flourished in the Mediterranean world. The allegation that Christianity is merely a "copycat" religion, recycling elements from ancient mythology, has decimated its credibility to many people.

"Nothing in Christianity is original" is among the most famous lines in one of publishing's greatest success stories, *The Da Vinci Code*. The book charges that everything of importance in Christianity, from communion to Jesus' birthday to Sunday worship, was "taken directly from earlier pagan mystery religions."[5]

Indeed, even those claims aren't original. More than a century ago, scholars published books and articles pointing out similarities between the life of Jesus as recorded in the Gospels and mythological gods like Mithras, Osiris, Adonis, and Dionysus. Popular books and Internet sites have elaborated on these themes in recent years, making this issue one of the most damaging current objections to the historicity of Jesus.

"Christianity began as a cult with almost wholly Pagan origins and motivations in the first century," said former Anglican priest Tom Harpur.[6] "Christianity in its final orthodoxy was simply a reissuing of an ancient wisdom in a literalized and highly exclusivist form. The result was a kind of plagiarism, but in a badly warped and weakened edition."[7]

A book called *The Jesus Mysteries*, which promoted similar themes, was named Book of the Year by London's *Daily Telegraph* in 1999. "The story of Jesus and the teachings he gives in the New Testament are prefigured by the myths and teachings of the ancient Pagan mysteries," said the authors, Timothy Freke and Peter Gandy.[8] They added:

> Each mystery religion taught its own version of the myth of the dying and resurrecting Godman, who was known by different names in different places. In Egypt, where the mysteries began, he was Osiris. In Greece he becomes Dionysus, in Asia Minor he is known as Attis, in Syria he is Adonis, in Persia he is Mithras, in Alexandria he is Serapis, to name a few.[9]

In his book *Those Incredible Christians*, Hugh J. Schonfield said, "Christians remained related under the skin to the devotees of Adonis and Osiris, Dionysus and Mithras."[10] Philosopher John H. Randall maintained that, thanks to the apostle Paul, Christianity "became a mystical system of redemption, much like the cult of Isis, and the other sacramental or mystery religions of the day."[11]

At first blush, the parallels between the story of Jesus and the myths of ancient gods appear to be striking. For instance, writers have said that the pre-Christian god Mithras was born of a virgin in a cave on December 25, was considered a great traveling teacher, had twelve disciples, promised his followers immortality, sacrificed himself for world peace, was buried in a tomb and rose again three days later, instituted a Eucharist or "Lord's Supper," and was considered the Logos, redeemer, Messiah, and "the way, the truth, and the life."[12] Sound familiar?

"The traditional history of Christianity cannot convincingly explain why the Jesus story is so similar to ancient Pagan myths," Freke and Gandy said.[13] They believe, however, that they have the answer. "Christianity," they declared, "was a heretical product of Paganism!"[14]

Said Harpur: "Not one single doctrine, rite, tenet, or usage in Christianity was in reality a fresh contribution to the world."[15] He went on to say:

> The only difference — and it was quite radical — between the Jesus story of the New Testament and the many ancient myths ... is that nobody among the ancients, prior to the full-fledged Christian movement, believed for one moment that any of the events in their dramas were in any way historical.... In Christianity, however,

the myth was eventually literalized. Jesus was historicized.... The Church converted a whole mass of romantic legends or myths into so-called history, a multiplication of "fictitious stories." What emerged was in many ways a cult of ignorance.[16]

If these allegations are true, then the so-called "real Jesus" has no more authority than an imaginary "sun god" worshiped by primitive tribes millennia ago. If his life, teachings, and resurrection are merely echoes of mythological characters, then there would be no good reason to follow, worship, or rely on him. He becomes as impotent as the make-believe Zeus, as irrelevant as the long-forgotten Mithras.

But are these charges accurate? I decided to focus initially on the allegation that Jesus' resurrection—the pivotal event that Christians say confirmed his deity—was essentially plagiarized from earlier pagan stories. Among those giving credence to that theory is *Skeptic* magazine religion editor Tim Callahan. "The possible influences on the Jews that might have produced a belief in resurrection are the myriad fertility cults among all the peoples of the ancient world," he said.[17]

My first step was to raise the issue with historian and resurrection expert Michael Licona, coauthor of the award-winning book *The Case for the Resurrection of Jesus* and the authority I questioned earlier on challenges to Jesus rising from the dead.

A Nearly Universal Consensus

"Why," I asked Licona, "should the story of Jesus' resurrection have any more credibility than pagan stories of dying and rising gods—such as Osiris, Adonis, Attis, and Marduk—that are so obviously mythological?"

Licona was well-versed on this controversy. "First of all, it's important to understand that these claims don't in any way negate the good historical evidence we have for Jesus' resurrection, which I spelled out in our earlier discussion," he pointed out. "You can't dismiss the resurrection unless you can refute its solid core of supporting evidence."[18] I agreed that was an important caveat to keep in mind—and one which "copycat" theorists typically forget.

"Second, T. N. D. Mettinger—a senior Swedish scholar, professor at Lund University, and member of the Royal Academy of Letters, History, and Antiquities of Stockholm—wrote one of the most recent academic treatments of dying and rising gods in antiquity. He admits in his book *The Riddle of Resurrection* that the consensus among modern scholars—*nearly universal*—is that there were no dying and rising gods that preceded Christianity. They all post-dated the first century."

Obviously, that timing is absolutely crucial: Christianity couldn't have borrowed the idea of the resurrection if myths about dying and rising gods weren't even circulating when Christianity was birthed in the first century AD.

"Then Mettinger said he was going to take exception to that nearly universal scholarly conviction," Licona continued. "He takes a decidedly minority position and claims that there are at least three and possibly as many as five dying and rising gods that predate Christianity. But the key question is this: Are there any actual parallels between these myths and Jesus' resurrection?"

"What did Mettinger conclude?" I asked.

"In the end, after combing through all these accounts and critically analyzing them, Mettinger adds that none of these serve as parallels to Jesus. *None* of them," Licona emphasized.

"They are far different from the reports of Jesus rising from the dead. They occurred in the unspecified and distant past and were usually related to the seasonal life-and-death cycle of vegetation. In contrast, Jesus' resurrection isn't repeated, isn't related to changes in the seasons, and was sincerely believed to be an actual event by those who lived in the same generation of the historical Jesus. In addition, Mettinger concludes that 'there is no evidence for the death of the dying and rising gods as vicarious suffering for sins.'"[19]

I later obtained Mettinger's book to double-check Licona's account of his research. Sure enough, Mettinger caps his study with this stunning statement: "There is, as far as I am aware, no *prima facie* evidence that the death and resurrection of Jesus is a mythological construct, drawing on the myths and rites of the dying and rising gods of the surrounding world."[20]

In short, this leading scholar's analysis is a sharp rebuke to popular-level authors and Internet bloggers who make grand claims about the pagan origins of Jesus' return from the dead. Ultimately, Mettinger affirmed, "The death and resurrection of Jesus retains its unique character in the history of religions."[21]

Bowling in Heaven

Mettinger's assessment was extremely significant, but I wanted to dig deeper into the mythology. "Do I understand correctly that these ancient myths were used to try to explain why things died in the fall and came back in the spring?" I asked.

"Yes, things like that," Licona replied. "When I was a kid, I asked my mom, 'What's thunder?' She said, 'It's angels bowling in heaven.' Obviously, that's just a story. Similarly, in ancient Canaan, a kid would ask his mom, 'Why does the rain stop in the summer?' And his mom would tell him the story of Baal."

"Is this one of the myths that Mettinger thinks predates Christianity?" I asked.

"That's right. In one of the more popular stories, Baal is the storm god in heaven. He's responsible for the rain. His nemesis is Mot, who's in the netherworld. One day Mot and Baal are trash-talking each other. Mot says, 'You think you're so tough, Baal? You leave behind your clouds and lightning bolts and wind and rain and come on down here — I'll show you who your daddy is.' So Baal leaves everything behind and goes to the underworld — where Mot swallows him. How do we know this? It stopped raining!

"Later, Baal's mother goes down and tells Mot, 'Let my son go!' Mot says, 'No!' So she brutalizes him until he finally says, 'Okay, mercy! Go away and I'll let him go!' She leaves the netherworld, and a couple of months later, Baal's dad says, 'Our son's alive.' How does he know? It's raining again!

"This is like my mom trying to explain thunder to me as a child. They talked about this every year: Baal died and Baal came back. Nobody ever saw it. There were no eyewitnesses. It supposedly occurred in the gray, distant, undated past. It was a fable to explain why there's no rain in the summer — and nothing more. Now, does that sound anything like the resurrection of Jesus? Absolutely not! It's totally different. Jesus' resurrection is supported by strong historical data that is by far best explained by him returning from the dead."

That's just one myth, I thought to myself. There were still others to consider. "How about the other fables that are commonly mentioned?" I asked.

"Attis? This myth is older than Christianity but the first report we have of a resurrection of Attis comes long after the first century. Adonis is more than a hundred years after Jesus. There's no clear account in antiquity of Marduk even dying—and so a resurrection is even less clear. Some scholars say Tammuz is an account of a dying and rising god—but that's disputed, and besides, it's not a good parallel since there are no reports of an appearance or an empty tomb and this myth was tied to the changing of the seasons."

"What about Osiris?"

"Osiris is interesting," he said, smiling. "The most popular account says Osiris's brother killed him, chopped him into fourteen pieces, and scattered them around the world. Well, the goddess Isis feels compassion for Osiris, so she looks for his body parts to give him a proper burial. She only finds thirteen of them, puts them back together, and Osiris is buried. But he doesn't come back to this world; he's given the status of god of the netherworld—a gloomy, shadowy place of semiconsciousness. As a friend of mine says, 'This isn't a resurrection, it's a zombification!' This is no parallel to Jesus' resurrection, for which there is strong historical support."

I spotted an apparent flaw in Licona's reasoning: one of Christianity's earliest apologists, or defenders of the faith, was Justin Martyr, who lived from about AD 100 to 164. In a letter he wrote in about 150, he discussed several parallels between Christianity and the rising gods of pagan religions. I pointed this out to Licona and asked, "Isn't that evidence that Christians recognized that Jesus' resurrection was merely a form of mythology?"

Licona was quite familiar with Justin's writings. "First, we have to look at why Justin was writing this. The Romans were severely persecuting Christians, and Justin was telling the emperor, 'Look, you don't persecute people who worship other gods who are similar, so why persecute

Christians?' Basically, he's trying to use some arguments to defuse the Roman attacks on the church.

"But look at the parallels he gives. He has to strain to make them. He talks about the sons of Jupiter: Aesculapius was struck by lightning and went to heaven; Bacchus, Hercules, and others rode to heaven on the horse Pegasus. He describes Ariadne and others who 'have been declared to be set among the stars.' He even mentions that when the emperor Augustus was cremated, someone in the crowd swore that he saw his spirit ascending through the flames.

"These aren't resurrections! I know of no highly respected scholar today who suggests that these vague fables are parallels to the resurrection of Jesus. We only hear this claim from the hyper-skeptical community on the Internet and popular books that are marketed to people who lack the background to analyze the facts critically."

Licona's answers had quickly deflated many of the claims I had heard and read about Jesus' resurrection having been plagiarized from antiquity. I still had questions, however, about the broader implications of the "copycat" allegations. I decided to seek out a leading scholar of ancient history who also is an expert on Mithraism, a "mystery religion" that was once a major rival to Christianity—and, some charge, the source of many beliefs that Christians took and applied to Jesus.

My trip to picturesque Oxford, Ohio, was almost cancelled because of torrential winter rains. Local rivers were swelling toward flood stage. But I managed to arrive on one of the last flights of the day. The next morning, using an umbrella to shield me, I knocked on the door of an immaculate green house where Edwin Yamauchi lives with Kimie, his wife of forty-four years.

INTERVIEW #4: Edwin M. Yamauchi, PhD

With a doctorate in Mediterranean studies from Brandeis University, and having taught at Miami University of Ohio for more than thirty-five years, Edwin Yamauchi has been called "a scholar's scholar."[22] As one admiring colleague put it, he has "dug archaeologically, taught brilliantly, read voraciously, researched meticulously, and published endlessly."[23]

Yamauchi has studied twenty-two languages, including Akkadian, Aramaic, Greek, Hebrew, Chinese, Comanche, Coptic, Egyptian, Mandaic, Syriac, and Ugaritic. He has received eight fellowships from Brandeis, Rutgers, and elsewhere; delivered eighty-eight papers on Mithraism, Gnosticism, and other topics at scholarly societies; published nearly two hundred articles and reviews in professional journals; lectured at more than a hundred colleges and universities, including Cornell, Princeton, Temple, Yale, and the University of Chicago; and participated in archaeological expeditions, including the first excavation of the Herodian temple in Jerusalem.

Yamauchi's seventeen books include the 578-page authoritative tome *Persia and the Bible*, which includes his findings on Mithraism, as well as *Greece and Babylon, Gnostic Ethics and Mandaean Origins, The Stones and the Scriptures, Pre-Christian Gnosticism, The Archaeology of the New Testament, The World of the First Christians*, and *Africa and the Bible*. In 1975 he was invited to deliver a paper at the Second International Congress of Mithraic Studies in Tehran, a conference hosted by the then-empress of Iran.

Born into a Japanese Buddhist family but a Christian since 1952, Yamauchi has a sterling reputation in the academic world. One book called him "a scholar known for his extreme care and sober judgment with historical texts."[24] Award-winning historian Paul Maier said Yamauchi wields "crystal logic and hard, potent evidence," adding:

> No one in the academic world today can better sniff out sensationalism in place of sense, excesses beyond the evidence, and speculation instead of scholarship. Whatever historical or theological fad might come along — and *so* many have! — one brilliant article by Yamauchi supplies the evidence to skewer any bloated pretensions against the cause of truth.[25]

That's exactly what I needed for this topic, where so many voices of questionable credibility are making such serious claims. And that's why I interviewed him for my earlier book, *The Case for Christ*, about the evidence for Jesus in ancient sources outside the Bible.[26] At the time, I found him to be unassuming, soft-spoken, thorough, and highly credible. He was not as loquacious as some scholars I've questioned, but his statements tended to be heavy with meaning.

He and Kimie greeted me at the door before she departed to do some volunteer work in the community. Although recently retired from Miami University, Yamauchi continues to teach a few history courses there. Now on the cusp of seventy years of age, the bespectacled scholar was spry and focused, his hair highlighted with silver.

He walked me down into his basement, much of which was a warren of bookshelves, and we sat at a small table on which I saw stacks of papers. I immediately knew what they were. I had let Yamauchi know in advance the topics I wanted to cover, because I was aware of his penchant to back up his own opinions with scholarly articles by other experts. I could see he was ready for me.

The Mystery Religions

"Maybe you could start by giving me some background on the mystery religions," I began as we claimed chairs on adjacent sides of the table. "When were they popular? What traits did they have in common?"

"The so-called 'mystery religions' were a variety of religious movements from the eastern Mediterranean that flourished in the early Roman Empire," he replied, sipping from a cup of coffee. "They offered salvation in a tight-knit community. They were called mystery religions because those who were initiated into them were sworn to secrecy. They had sacred rites, often a common meal, and a special sanctuary."[27]

"What was the oldest of them?" I asked.

"That would be the Eleusinian cult of Demeter, which was already established in the Archaic Age of Greece, which would be from 800 to 500 BC. The latest, and certainly the most popular in the later Roman Empire, was the mysteries of Mithras, who started as a Persian god. There were also the mysteries of Cybele and Attis, which were restricted to non-Romans until the middle or late first century."

"Were some of these religions tied to the vegetation cycle?" I asked, thinking back to Licona's comments.

"Oh, yes, many of them were," he confirmed.

Trying to narrow the topic a bit, I asked, "Who popularized the

idea that Jesus' resurrection was derived from the worship of dying and
rising fertility gods?"

"In the scholarly world, these comparisons were promoted by a
group of scholars called the *Religionsgeschichtliche schule*," he said, the
German rolling off his tongue. "That's the so-called History of Religions School, which flourished at the end of the nineteenth and into the
early twentieth centuries. The seminal work by Richard Reitzenstein
was published in German in 1910 but not translated into English until
1978.[28] He thought the sacrifice of Christ aligned itself with the killing
of a bull by Mithras. Carsten Colpe and others severely criticized the
anachronistic use of sources by these scholars.

"On the popular level, Sir James Frazer gathered a mass of parallels
in his multivolume work called *The Golden Bough*, which was published
in 1906," Yamauchi continued. "He discussed Osiris of Egypt, Adonis
of Syria, Attis of Asia Minor, and Tammuz of Mesopotamia, and concluded there was a common rising and dying fertility god. Unfortunately, much of his work was based on a misreading of the evidence, but
nevertheless this helped introduce these ideas to popular culture. Later,
in the 1930s, three influential French scholars claimed that Christianity
was influenced by the Hellenistic mystery religions."

Yamauchi picked up a copy of an article he had written and scanned
it for a quote. "One of those scholars," he added, "said Christ was 'a
savior-god, after the manner of an Osiris, an Attis, a Mithras.... Like
Adonis, Osiris, and Attis, he died a violent death, and like them he
returned to life.'"[29]

I glanced at my notes. "Albert Schweitzer said that popular writers made the mistake of taking various fragments of information and
manufacturing 'a kind of universal Mystery-religion which never actually existed, least of all in Paul's day.'[30] Do you agree?"

"Yes, there was a widespread view that there was a general, common
mystery religion, but upon a closer examination of the sources, nobody
believes that any longer," he replied. "These were quite different beliefs.
In fact, by the mid-twentieth century, scholars had established that the
sources used in these writings were far from satisfactory and the parallels were much too superficial. It was pretty much of a closed issue in

the scholarly community, but it seems to have been revived in recent years among writers on a popular level—sort of like Frankenstein."

Yamauchi's comments reminded me of the words of the late scholar Ronald H. Nash, the highly respected professor with a doctorate from Syracuse University and author of more than thirty books, who said in *The Gospel and the Greeks*:

> During a period of time running roughly from about 1890 to 1940, scholars often alleged that primitive Christianity had been heavily influenced by Platonism, Stoicism, the pagan mystery religions, or other movements in the Hellenistic world.[31] Largely as a result of a series of scholarly books and articles written in rebuttal, allegations of early Christianity's dependence on its Hellenistic environment began to appear much less frequently in the publications of Bible scholars and classical scholars. Today most Bible scholars regard the question as a dead issue.[32]

Nash went on to lament the revival of these discredited theories. He said that a few current textbooks, as well as more popular publications, were "repeating claims and arguments that should have been laid to rest decades ago," circulating "one-sided and misinformed arguments," and ignoring "the weighty scholarly opinion" that has already been published to refute their assertions.[33] "Efforts to undermine the uniqueness of the Christian revelation via claims of a pagan religious influence collapse quickly once a full account of the information is available," he insisted.[34]

That was precisely what I was determined to investigate as I turned my interview with Yamauchi to issues involving the most commonly cited mystery religion: Mithraism.

Mithraism and Christianity

To make sure we were on the same page, I asked Yamauchi to provide an overview of Mithraic beliefs. He took a drink of coffee before launching into his reply.

"Mithraism was a late Roman mystery religion that was popular among soldiers and merchants, and which became a chief rival to Christianity in the second century and later," he said. "The initiates were all men, though one of my students, Jonathan David, recently published a paper arguing that some women may have been involved.[35] The participants met in a cavelike structure called a *mithraeum*, which had as its cult statue Mithras stabbing a bull, the so-called *tauroctony.*"

"How much information about Mithraism exists?"

"There are relatively few texts from the Mithraists themselves. We have some graffiti and inscriptions, as well as descriptions of the religion from its opponents, including neo-Platonists and Christians. Much of what has been circulated on Mithraism has been based on the theories of a Belgium scholar named Franz Cumont. He was the leading scholar on Mithraism in his day, and he published his famous work, *Mysteries of Mithras*, in 1903. His work led to speculation by the History of Religions School that Mithraism had influenced nascent Christianity. Much of what Cumont suggested, however, turned out to be quite unfounded. In the 1970s, scholars at the Second Mythraic Congress in Tehran came to criticize Cumont."

Yamauchi dug out a large photograph from the papers on the desk, showing a crowd of scholars at the Congress posing with the Empress of Iran on the front steps of a stately building. I surveyed the faces and quickly picked out Yamauchi in the front row.

"The Congress produced two volumes of papers. A scholar named Richard Gordon from England and others concluded that Cumont's theory was not supported by the evidence and, in fact, Cumont's interpretations have now been analyzed and rejected on all major points.[36] Contrary to what Cumont believed, even though Mithras was a Persian god who was attested as early as the fourteenth century BC, we have almost no evidence of Mithraism in the sense of a mystery religion in the West until very late — too late to have influenced the beginnings of Christianity."

That was a critically important assessment that would seem to rule out the "copycat" theory. Seeking further clarification, I asked Yamauchi for details concerning when the Mithraic mysteries were introduced in the West. He took another sip of coffee and then answered.

"The first public recognition of the Mithras in Rome was the state visit of Tiridates, the king of Armenia, in AD 66. It's said that he addressed Nero by saying, 'And I have come to thee, my god, to worship thee as I do Mithras.' There is also a reference earlier to some pirates in Cilicia who were worshipers of Mithras, but," he noted, "this is *not* the same as Mithraism as a mystery religion."

Settling back into his seat, he continued. "Mithraism as a mystery religion cannot be attested before about AD 90, which is about the time we see a Mithraic motif in a poem by Statius. No mithraea [or Mithraic temples] have been found at Pompeii, which was destroyed by the eruption of Vesuvius in AD 79. The earliest Mithraic inscription in the West is a statue of a prefect under the emperor Trajan in AD 101. It's now in the British Museum.

"The earliest mithraea are dated to the early second century. There are a handful of inscriptions that date to the early second century, but the vast majority of texts are dated after AD 140. Most of what we have as evidence of Mithraism comes in the second, third, and fourth centuries AD. That's basically what's wrong with the theories about Mithraism influencing the beginnings of Christianity."

"The timing is wrong," I observed.

"That's correct," he said, picking up a copy of his hefty *Persia and the Bible* and leafing through it until he found a reference to Gordon, the senior fellow at the University of East Anglia who has published extensively on history and archaeology. "Gordon dates the establishment of the Mithraic mysteries to the reign of Hadrian, which was AD 117–138, or Antoninus Pius, which would be from 138 to 161," Yamauchi said. "Specifically, Gordon said, 'It is therefore reasonable to argue that Western Mithraism did not exist until the mid-second century, at least in a developed sense.' "[37]

Then he picked up a photocopy of an article from a scholarly journal called *Mithras*, published by the Society for Mithraic Studies in the aftermath of the 1974 Iranian conclave of scholars. He read the words of E. J. Yarnold of Oxford University: "The fervor with which historians used to detect wholesale Christian borrowings from the Mithraic and other mysteries has now died down."[38]

Yamauchi looked up at me. "As Ronald Nash and so many other knowledgeable scholars have concluded, the dating disproves that Christianity borrowed its tenets from Mithraism," he said. Indeed, Nash is emphatic: "The flowering of Mithraism occurred after the close of the New Testament canon, too late for it to have influenced the development of first-century Christianity."[39]

Yamauchi loaded me down with copies of academic articles and books by highly regarded scholars who back up that claim. Manfred Clauss, professor of ancient history at Free University in Berlin, said in *The Roman Cult of Mithras* that it does not make sense to interpret the Mithraic mysteries "as a fore-runner of Christianity."[40] In his book *Mithraism and Christianity*, published by Cambridge University Press, L. Patterson concluded there is "no direct connection between the two religions either in origin or development."[41]

Gary Lease, professor of religious studies at the University of California at Santa Cruz and long-time executive secretary of the North American Association for the Study of Religion, noted in an academic article that such eminent scholars as Adolf von Harnack, Arthur Darby Nock, S. G. F. Brandon, William R. Halliday, and Ernst Benz "have seen little evidence to support claims of such influence and mutual borrowing" between Mithraism and Christianity.[42]

Lease, who earned his doctorate at the University of Munich and later occupied its renowned Romano Guardini Chair for Theory of Culture and Religion, added:

> After almost 100 years of unremitting labor, the conclusion appears inescapable that neither Mithraism nor Christianity proved to be an obvious and direct influence upon the other in the development and demise or survival of either religion. Their beliefs and practices are well accounted for by their most obvious origins and there is no need to explain one in terms of the other.[43]

The weight of the evidence was heavy: the claim that Christianity borrowed its central ideas from Mithraism has been thoroughly demolished by a close examination of the dates for when it took root in the West. But what about the numerous parallels between Mithraism and Christianity that popular writers, including novelist Dan Brown, have touted as evidence of Christianity's plagiarism? I was anxious to see how Yamauchi would handle those specific charges.

Mithras versus Jesus

I pulled out a list of parallels between Jesus and Mithras. "First, popular writers claim that Mithras was born of a virgin," I said. "Is that true that this was what Mithraism taught?"

Yamauchi looked pained. "No, that's definitely *not* true," he insisted. "He was born out of a rock."

"A rock?"

"Yes, the rock birth is commonly depicted in Mithraic reliefs," he explained. "Mithras emerges fully grown and naked except for a Phrygian cap, and he's holding a dagger and torch. In some variations, flames shoot out from the rock, or he's holding a globe in his hand."

I chuckled. "So unless the rock is considered a virgin, this parallel with Jesus evaporates," I said.

"Entirely correct," he said.

"And that means he wasn't born in a cave, which some writers claim is a second parallel to Christianity."

"Well, it is true that Mithraic sanctuaries were designed to look like caves," Yamauchi said. "Gary Lease discusses that in his chapter on Mithraism and Christianity."

I later examined Lease's work. He makes the important observation that nowhere in the New Testament is Jesus described as having been born in a cave. This idea is first mentioned in the letter of Barnabas at the beginning of the second century.

Justin Martyr said in the second century that Mithras's cave was a demoniacal imitation of the tradition that Jesus was born in a cave. Lease pointed out, however, that scholar Ernst Benz "has shown conclusively that this Christian tradition does not come from a dependency on Mithraism, but rather from an ages old tradition in Palestine itself of holy shrines in caves." Concluded Lease: "There is no doubt that the Christian tradition does not stem from the Mithraic account."[44]

Returning to my list, I said to Yamauchi: "The third supposed parallel with Jesus is that Mithras was born on December 25."

"Again, that's not a parallel," he replied.

"Why not?"

"Because we don't know the date Jesus was born," he said. "The earliest date celebrated by Christians was January 6—in fact, it's still celebrated by many churches in the East. Of course, December 25 is very close to the winter solstice. This was the date chosen by the emperor Aurelian for the dedication of his temple to Sol Invictus, the god called the 'Unconquerable Sun.' Mithras was closely associated with Sol Invictus; sometimes they're depicted shaking hands. This is apparently how Mithras became associated with December 25."

"When did that date become Christmas for Christians?"

"That seems to be in 336, a year before the death of Constantine, the first Roman emperor to embrace Christianity. We know that before his conversion, he worshiped Sol Invictus. We know for sure that Constantine made Sunday, or the Lord's Day, an official holiday, even though Christians had already been observing it as the day on which Jesus was resurrected. So it's conceivable Constantine also may have appropriated December 25 for the birthday of Christ. We know that Christian emperors and popes suggested that instead of simply banning pagan ceremonies that they appropriate them for Christianity."[45]

"What about the fourth parallel that Mithras was a great traveler or master with twelve disciples?"

"No—he was a god, not a teacher," Yamauchi replied, sounding a bit impatient.

"The fifth parallel is that his followers were promised immortality."

"Well, that can be inferred, but certainly that was the hope of most followers of any religion," he said. "So that's not surprising."

"How about the sixth claim, which says that Mithras sacrificed himself for world peace?"

Yamauchi sighed. "That's reading Christian theology into what's not there. He didn't sacrifice himself—he killed a bull."

"The seventh parallel—and one of the most important—is that Mithras was buried in a tomb and rose after three days," I said. "Is there any truth to that?"

"We don't know anything about the death of Mithras," Yamauchi said firmly. "We have a lot of monuments, but we have almost no textual evidence, because this was a secret religion. But I know of no references to a supposed death and resurrection." Indeed, Richard Gordon declared in his book *Image and Value in the Greco-Roman*

World that there is "no death of Mithras"—and thus, there cannot be a resurrection.[46]

I went on, though I had a feeling I could guess his replies. "Eight, Mithras was considered the Good Shepherd, the Way, the Truth, and the Life, the Logos, the Redeemer, the Savior."

"No, again that's reading Christian theology into this."

"Ninth, there was a sacramental meal in Mithraism that paralleled the Lord's Supper."

"Common meals are found in almost all religious communities," he replied. "What is noteworthy is that the Christian apologists Justin Martyr and Tertullian point out the similarities to the Lord's Supper, but they wrote in the second century, long after the Lord's Supper was instituted in Christianity. They claimed the Mithraic meal was a satanic imitation. Clearly, the Christian meal was based on the Passover, not on a mystery religion."

Yamauchi referred me to Clauss's book *The Roman Cult of Mithras*. "This earthly meal is a ritual reproduction of the celebration of his victory [over the bull] which Mithras performed with the sun-god before their joint ascension in the Sun's chariot," he said.[47] "The ritual meal was probably simply a component of regular common meals. Such meals have always been an essential part of religious assembly; eating and drinking together creates community and renders visible the fact that those who take part are members of one and the same group."[48]

Oxford's Yarnold said that Cumont's systematic description of Mithraic liturgy in Christian terms—particularly referring to the Mithraic meal as communion—"is now seen to be misleading, not to say mischievous."[49]

Lease agrees there is no connection between the Christian and Mithraic ceremonies. "Nothing in any of the sources we have leads to a viable theory that the origin of the Christian meal is to be found in Mithraism, nor for that matter may one derive the Mithraic meal from the Christian."[50]

He noted that the Christian sacrament "is centered in the Jewish tradition of the Passover feast and the specifically historical recollection of Jesus's last acts," while the Mithraic feast "has its origins in Mazdean [that is, Persian] ceremonies."[51] He concluded: "There is simply no need to link these two events together in terms of derivation or direct influence."[52]

I tossed my list of now-discredited parallels on the table. Amazingly, despite so many writers who have tried to discredit Christianity with such charges of plagiarism, the allegations merely evaporated under scrutiny. Still, one related issue remained: whether a gory Mithraic ritual was the source for the apostle Paul's teaching of redemption through the blood of Jesus.

The Blood of Bulls

Following the lead of Reitzenstein, French theologian Alfred Loisy, who died in 1940, believed that a Mithraic rite called the *taurobolium* was the basis for the Christian belief that people are saved "through the blood" of Jesus. He specifically linked this ritual to Paul's imagery in Romans 6, where the apostle talks about "all of us who were baptized into Christ Jesus were baptized into his death."[53]

To bolster his thesis, Loisy presented evidence of a taurobolic inscription that says *in aeternum renatus* — or "reborn for eternity" — which he said parallels the Christian concept of spiritual rebirth.[54]

I asked Yamauchi to describe the taurobolium, which he had written about in *Persia and the Bible.*

"This rite was practiced by Mithraists only in exceptional cases. It was associated almost entirely with the cult of Attis, which was another mystery religion," he said. "In its developed form, the initiate was placed in a pit and a bull was slaughtered on a grate above him, drenching him in the bull's blood."

He paused before adding a bit of understatement: "It was a very vivid rite."

This, of course, seemed totally alien to the practices of the Jewish sacrificial system and its foreshadowing of Jesus' death as "the Lamb of God, who takes away the sin of the world."[55]

Yamauchi continued. "Again, the dating of practices like this are the Achilles' heel of these comparative studies — they don't pay attention to the dates of the sources and they're used anachronistically."

"When was the taurobolium instituted?" I asked.

"This rite is reported in the second century AD," he said, gesturing toward a quote from Swiss scholar Günter Wagner in an article Yamauchi had written:

The taurobolium of the Attis cult is first attested in the time of Antoninus Pius or AD 160. As far as we can see at present it only became a personal consecration at the beginning of the third century AD. The idea of a rebirth through the instrumentality of the taurobolium only emerges in isolated instances towards the end of the fourth century AD.[56]

"So there's no way this rite could have influenced Christianity's theology about redemption," Yamauchi stressed.

"What about the inscription that mentions being 'reborn for eternity'?" I asked.

"Ah, that's an interesting tale," he said with a small grin. "It turns out the *renatus* inscription was dated after AD 375. There's another inscription from about the same time period that says this rite was only efficacious for twenty years. Bruce Metzger from Princeton suggested this may be an example of Christianity influencing Mithraism. That is, Christianity promised its adherents eternal life, and so perhaps in response the efficacy of the blood bath was raised in the Mithraic cult from twenty years to eternity."[57]

One by one, the grandiose claims that Christianity copied itself after Mithraism had been convincingly swept away by solid scholarship. It was staggering to me that writers could so irresponsibly — or maliciously — make claims about parallels that simply are not accurate.

"Do you see any evidence that Christianity borrowed *any* of its beliefs from Mithraism?" I asked Yamauchi.

"Not really," he said. "They were rivals in the second century and later. Sometimes a Mithraic temple was right next to a Christian sanctuary in Rome. When Christianity became the official religion, sometimes the Christians destroyed the mithraeum."

"In his book *The Mysteries of Mithras*, Payam Nabarz quotes a historian he identifies as Joseph Renan as saying, 'If Christianity had been checked in its growth by some deadly disease, the world would have become Mithraic,'" I said. "Do you think that's true?"

Yamauchi shook his head. "First of all, he has the name wrong. It's *Ernest* Renan, an anti-Catholic French scholar who wrote a sensationalistic work called *Vie de Jesus,* or *Life of Jesus,* in 1863 — one of the works Albert Schweitzer criticized in his famous indictment of biographies of Jesus by liberal scholars."

Yamauchi provided additional background that further discredited Renan, pointing to comments by Stephen Neill and Tom Wright in a book published by Oxford University Press: "Renan confuses rhetoric with profundity.... Professing to work as an historian, he does not pursue with the needed seriousness the historical problems of the life of Jesus."[58]

"Needless to say," continued Yamauchi, "Renan's work, published nearly 150 years ago, has no value as a source. He knew very little about Mithraism, and besides, we know a lot more about it today. Yet this is a quote that's commonly used by people who don't understand the context. It's simply far-fetched."

I consulted my notes for another quotation I'd read. "In his book, Nabarz claims: 'The assimilation of Mithraism by its rival Christianity resulted in the early decline and loss of true meaning in both religions. The peace-loving message of Christianity, as taught by Christ, was diminished and replaced by the warrior mind-set of Mithraism.'"

Yamauchi wasn't buying it. "Nabarz is a practicing Dervish and Druid who's a member of the Golden Dawn Occult Society and a revivalist of the Temple of Mithras. Though he has a PhD from Oxford, it's in science. He lacks credibility as a historian of Christianity," Yamauchi said.

"There's no evidence of Mithraism influencing first-century Christianity. Far from assimilating Mithraism, the church fathers — from Justin Martyr to Tertullian — denounced Mithraism as a satanic imitation. Some scholars have suggested Christianity may have consciously or unconsciously borrowed minor practices much later, which could be true. This has no impact on Christianity's foundational beliefs, however."

Along those lines, Yarnold suggests Mithraism may have influenced a fourth-century Christian practice of having converts renounce Satan in a special ceremony that's no longer practiced. But Yarnold warned against reading too much into the scant remnants of Mithraism. "The modern Mithraic scholar," he said, "is often seduced by apparent lack of evidence to grasp at straws which offer little or no support to his argument."[59]

The Usual Suspects

I turned our conversation to the issue of whether any other gods in antiquity might have provided the prototype for the resurrection stories about Jesus. Essentially, I wanted to see whether Yamauchi would agree with what Licona told me about the matter.

Yamauchi went down the list of the "usual suspects" who appear in popular literature. "First of all," he said, "there's no resurrection of Marduk or Dionysus. There is a resurrection that had been alleged for Tammuz, a fertility god of Mesopotamia, known in Sumerian as Dumuzi, but it turns out there was no real resurrection."

I was confused. "What do you mean?"

"His resurrection by the goddess Inanna-Ishtar had been assumed even though the end of the texts about the myth were missing. Then in 1960, S. N. Kramer published a newly discovered poem that proves that Inanna didn't rescue Damuzi from the underworld but sent him there as her substitute.[60] There's also an obscure and fragmentary text indicating Dumuzi might have had his sister take his place in the underworld for six months of the year.[61] Again, this is tied to the seasons and the vegetation cycles. It's not a resurrection."[62]

"And Adonis?" I asked.

"Tammuz was identified by later writers with Adonis, who was loved by Aphrodite. The worship of Adonis was never very important and was restricted to women. Pierre Lambrechts has shown that there are no indications of a resurrection in the early information we have about Adonis. While there are four texts that speak of his resurrection, they date from the second to the fourth centuries AD — long after Jesus."[63]

"What about Cybele and Attis?" I asked.

"Attis was a young man who was loved by Cybele, also known as the Great Mother goddess. Attis was unfaithful, so Cybele drove him mad; he castrated himself and died. That's why the priests of Cybele were eunuchs," Yamauchi noted. "But Lambrechts has demonstrated that the supposed 'resurrection' of Attis doesn't appear until after AD 150—more than a century later than Jesus."[64]

Again, this myth is tied to the vegetation cycle. "Many worshipers of Cybele believed that an annual rehearsal of the Attis myth was a way of guaranteeing a good crop," Nash said.[65] He pointed out that "Cybele could only preserve Attis's dead body. Beyond this, there is mention of the body's hair continuing to grow, along with some movement of his little finger. In some versions of the myth, Attis's return to life took the form of his being changed into an evergreen tree."[66]

I brought up the topic of Osiris, whose body was cut into fourteen pieces and then reassembled—minus one part—by his sister Isis, as Licona described earlier.

"Actually," said Yamauchi, "there also was an earlier incident where his brother Seth murders Osiris and sinks his coffin in the Nile. It's after Isis revives him that the dismemberment occurs."

"Do these accounts pre-date Christianity?"

"They're found in Plutarch, who wrote in the second century AD, but they seem consistent with statements made in early Egyptian texts —so, yes. It's misleading, however, to equate the Egyptian concept of the afterlife with a resurrection in the Christian tradition. The Egyptians believed that to attain immortality, the body had to be mummified, nourishment had to be provided, and magical spells had to be used. The Egyptian concept didn't entail rising from the dead; instead, separate entities of the individual's personality—called the *Ba* and the *Ka*—hover around his body."

"So this isn't a resurrection?"

"Not in the same sense that Jesus was resurrected," he emphasized. "Osiris was brought to life but he's the king of the underworld."[67]

Metzger agrees. "Whether this can be rightly called a resurrection is questionable, especially since, according to Plutarch, it was the pious desire of devotees to be buried in the same ground where, according to local tradition, the body of Osiris was still lying."[68]

French scholar Roland de Vaux, who was director of the École Biblique in Jerusalem, said Osiris "will never again come among the living and will reign only over the dead." He concluded that "this revived god is in reality a 'mummy' god."[69] Wagner concurred. "Osiris knew no resurrection, but was resuscitated to be a ruler of the Netherworld," he said.[70]

The contrast with Jesus, said Yamauchi, couldn't be more stark. "All of these myths are repetitive, symbolic representations of the death and rebirth of vegetation. These are not historical figures, and none of their deaths were intended to provide salvation," he pointed out. "In the case of Jesus, even non-Christian authorities, like Josephus and Tacitus, report that he died under Pontius Pilate in the reign of Tiberius. The reports of his resurrection are quite early and are rooted in eyewitness accounts.

"They have the ring of reality," he stressed, "not the ethereal qualities of myth."

Claims of Other Virgin Births

Matthew, a follower of Jesus, and Luke, a first-century physician who said he "carefully investigated everything" about Jesus "from the beginning,"[71] both report that Jesus was born to a virgin. It's an extraordinarily improbable claim — *unless* the resurrection of Jesus is true, in which case his divinity was convincingly established and a virgin birth becomes not only believable but inexorably logical.

One of the most popular objections to Jesus, however, is that his virgin birth was not historical but was stolen from earlier mythology and therefore is as fanciful as the outlandish stories about Zeus or Perseus.

"The notion that Jesus had no human father because he was the Son of God ... was originally a pagan notion," said Robert J. Miller, associate professor of religion at Juniata College.[72] "Gentiles in a pagan culture expect a man whose life embodied divinity to have a divine father and a human mother. The virgin birth thus corresponds to what Gentile Christians expected in a biography of Jesus."[73]

Walter E. Bundy, who started writing about the synoptic gospels in 1919 and taught at DePauw University, agreed that "the idea of a supernatural or virgin birth is pagan" and that "it must have found its way into the story of Jesus through Gentile-Christian channels."[74]

Similarly, skeptic Tom Flynn wrote in *Free Inquiry* magazine that if Jesus were a man "just remarkable enough to trigger the myth-making machinery of his time," then it would be expected that "such formulaic and derivative claims" like the virgin birth should result.[75]

I asked Yamauchi for his assessment. "The idea of the virgin birth of Jesus is distinctive because it's based on ancient prophecy, specifically the Septuagint translation of Isaiah 7:14," he began in response. "As you know, Isaiah uses the Hebrew word *'almah*, which means a 'young woman' would give birth, and the Septuagint makes her virginity more explicit by using the Greek word *parthenos*, which specifically means 'virgin.' Of course, it should be said that a young maiden in those days was assumed to be a virgin; we can't necessarily say that in our contemporary society."[76]

"What about the parallels that are often cited between Jesus' virgin birth and mythological gods?" I asked.

"Some of these supposed parallels break down upon close examination," he said. "Some of those that are often cited — like Zeus, for example — are anthropomorphic gods who lust after human women, which is decidedly different from Jesus' story. The mythological offspring are half gods and half men and their lives begin at conception, as opposed to Jesus, who is fully God and fully man and who is eternal but came into this world through the incarnation. Also, the Gospels put Jesus in a historical context, unlike the mythological gods. On top of that, even if a story of an extraordinary birth in mythology predates Christianity, that doesn't mean Christians appropriated it."

That last point is also made by Robert Gromacki, a professor at Cedarville University, in his 2002 book *The Virgin Birth*:

> This is a perfect example of the logical fallacy *post hoc ergo propter hoc* ("after this, therefore, because of this"). Plato wrote about the existence of God long before Paul authored his epistles, but the latter was in no way dependent upon the Greek philosopher. The argument of pagan derivation assumes too much in the way of parallelism and overlooks the radical differences.[77]

I pulled out a list of the most commonly mentioned parallels to the Jesus account. "What about Dionysus, the god of wine and fertility who's also known as Bacchus?" I asked. "He's frequently cited as being the product of a virgin birth."

"No, there's no evidence of a virgin birth for Dionysus," Yamauchi said. "As the story goes, Zeus, disguised as a human, fell in love with the princess Semelê, the daughter of Cadmus, and she became pregnant. Hera, who was Zeus's queen, arranged to have her burned to a crisp, but Zeus rescued the fetus and sewed him into his own thigh until Dionysus was born. So this is not a virgin birth in any sense."[78]

"What about the story of Zeus impregnating Danaë through a shower of gold and her giving birth to Perseus?" I asked.

"There are many stories about Zeus and his liaisons with human women. Here's the big difference: The Jewish God—Yahweh—could be anthropomorphic, but these were metaphors not to be taken literally, whereas in Greek mythology, the anthropomorphism was taken quite literally. The gods were very human—they lusted after mortal women. That's the focus of these myths. Although Yahweh is sometimes expressed in human imagery, he is utterly unlike human beings. So these parallels break down on a very fundamental level. You're talking about two very different concepts of God."[79]

The prominent scholar J. Gresham Machen, who taught New Testament at Princeton Theological Seminary for twenty-three years, makes a similar point in his magnum opus, *The Virgin Birth of Christ*:

> Zeus may have union with Danaë not in human form, but in a shower of gold, but all the same the union is a satisfaction of his lust for the human maid. Everywhere it is the love of the god for the mortal woman, and not merely the exclusion of a human father of the child, which stands in the forefront of interest.... Could anything be more utterly remote from the representation in Matthew and Luke than these stories of the amours of Zeus?[80]

Machen also notes that Christian apologist Justin Martyr, writing in the middle of the second century, argues that Jesus has a virgin birth "in common" with Perseus. Some have cited Justin's writings as evidence that the two are, indeed, linked. Machen points out, however:

> We should never forget that the appeal of Justin Martyr and Ori-

gen to the pagan stories of divine begetting is an *argumentum ad hominem*. *"You* hold," Justin and Origen say in effect to their pagan opponents, "that the virgin birth of Christ is unbelievable; well, is it any more unbelievable than the stories that you yourselves believe?" ... When Justin ... refers to the birth of Perseus as a birth from (or through) a virgin, he is going beyond what the pagan sources contained. There seems to be no clear evidence that pagan sources used the word "virgin" as referring to the mothers of heroes, mythical or historical, who were represented as being begotten by the gods.[81]

Claims about extraordinary births of mythological gods were one thing, but quite another are the allegations that certain pre-Christian *historical* figures— from Buddha to Alexander the Great—are the products of virginal births. I planned to pursue these parallels next.

Other Reports from History

My first question along these lines involved the conception of Alexander the Great. Several stories swirl around his birth, and some writers have claimed he was immaculately conceived.

"There's no question that Alexander's mother was Olympias and his father was Philip of Macedon," Yamauchi explained. "It was only as Philip's son that Alexander inherited the throne when his father was assassinated in 336 BC. The story about Olympias being impregnated by Zeus according to her dream was later propaganda designed to support Alexander's demand for worship."

Indeed, there's a report by Plutarch that Olympias explicitly rejected the story of Alexander's conception by Zeus, saying in reference to Zeus's wife, "Will not Alexander cease slandering me to Hera?"[82] Actually, said historian Peter Green, "The truth of the matter is that we have surprisingly little direct evidence about Alexander's childhood from any source, and what does exist is of very limited historical value."[83]

Yamauchi continued. "Buddha's birth is often called virginal, but that's not accurate either," he said. "Sources for the life of Buddha do not appear in written form until five centuries after his death, so they're not very reliable historically. According to legend, Buddha's mother dreamed that he entered her in the form of a white elephant—fully formed! In addition, she had been married for many years prior to this, so she certainly wasn't a virgin.[84]

"The later sources for Buddha, coming five hundred to fifteen hundred years after his life, exaggerate the supernatural elements of his life. It's even possible that some of the supposed parallels to the life of Jesus may have been borrowed from Christianity."[85]

As an aside, his reference to Buddha reminded me of a figure tied to another Eastern religion. "Some authors mention the Hindu god Krishna as having been born of a virgin," I said.

Yamauchi quickly dispatched that claim. "That's not accurate," he replied. "Krishna was born to a mother who already had seven previous sons, as even his followers readily concede."[86]

"What about Zoroaster?"

"Zoroaster lived before 1000 BC, according to Mary Boyce, or in the sixth century BC, according to other scholars," Yamauchi said. "The idea that his mother conceived him by drinking the sacred haoma drink appears in the Denkard, which dates to the ninth century AD. That's an extremely long time later—and far after Jesus."

"What's your opinion, then, of this allegation that the virgin birth of Jesus was copied from these other stories?"

"No, there are too many differences," he said. "I don't think anyone can make a convincing case that the virgin birth of Jesus—which was reported quite soon after the fact and in documents that are sober in their reporting—was derived from any pagan or other sources."

Raymond E. Brown agrees. One of America's premier New Testament scholars, he taught at Union Theological Seminary in New York for twenty-three years and was awarded honorary degrees from two dozen universities in the U.S. and abroad.

He stressed that the supposed virgin-birth parallels "consistently involve a type of *hieros gamos* where a divine male, in human or other form, impregnates a woman, either through normal sexual intercourse or through some substitute form of penetration. They are not really similar to the non-sexual virginal conception that is at the core of the infancy narratives, a conception where there is no male deity or element to impregnate Mary."[87]

His conclusion was that "no search for parallels has given us a truly satisfactory explanation of how early Christians happened upon the idea of a virginal conception unless, of course, that is what really took place."[88]

Even Thomas Boslooper, a liberal professor who wrote a book on the virgin birth although he rejected its historicity, nevertheless scoffed at the suggestion that it was derived from pagan myths. I found his scathing conclusion to be astute:

> Contemporary writers invariably use only secondary sources to verify such claims. The scholars whose judgment they accept rarely produced or quoted the primary sources. The literature of the old German *Religiongeschichtliche schule*, which produced this conclusion and which has become the authority for contemporary scholars who wish to perpetrate the notion that the virgin birth in the New Testament has a non-Christian source, is characterized by brief word, phrase, and sentence quotations that have been lifted out of context or incorrectly translated and used to support preconceived theories. Sweeping generalizations based on questionable evidence have become dogmatic conclusions that cannot be substantiated on the basis of careful investigation.[89]

In the end, allegations about Christianity stealing its belief about the virgin birth fared no better than the claims that it copied Jesus' resurrection from dying and rising gods in antiquity. In the words of the University of Chicago's renowned historian of religion, Mircea Eliade: "There is no reason to suppose that primitive Christianity was influenced by the Hellenistic mysteries."[90]

Efficiently and authoritatively, Yamauchi had dismantled the plagiarism case that has been hyped by so many critics of Christianity. With Boslooper's blunt critique in mind, I decided to wrap up my interview by asking about ways that unsuspecting readers can protect themselves from fiction masquerading as fact.

Will Truth Win Out?

My final line of questions triggered a strong response from Yamauchi. "Do you find that people are writing on these topics of mystery religions who lack the appropriate academic background and are often sloppy in the way they make generalizations?" I asked him.

"Very much so," he said sternly. "They don't have the languages, they don't study the original sources, they don't pay attention to the dates, and they frequently quote ideas that were popular in the nineteenth and twentieth centuries but have already been refuted. Reputable and careful scholars like Carsten Colpe of Germany, Günter Wagner of Switzerland, and Bruce Metzger of the United States have pointed out that, number one, the evidence for these supposed parallels is often very late, and number two, there are too many generalizations being made.

"People see parallels and then jump to conclusions that one religion influenced another. Of course there are going to be some parallels — most religions talk about some sort of salvation, practice certain rituals, or have a common meal. But that doesn't mean there is dependence.

"Christianity is quite distinct in that it rose from a Jewish background, which is monotheistic, and it centers around a historical figure who was put to death in a barbaric manner, which is attested in non-Christian sources. Jesus' followers were eyewitnesses in the first generation. Paul was converted by encountering the risen Christ and had access to eyewitnesses such as Peter and James. Christianity flourished and expanded in spite of persecution from the Roman authorities. It was a new message of love and God's intervention in the world, and it incorporated all people, including slaves and women, the educated and noneducated — unlike Mithraism, which was confined primarily to soldiers.

"So this new message was universal, yet it was rooted in an ancient tradition, fulfilling prophecies that had been foretold for many centuries. And it was exclusivistic. It wasn't comfortable, as were the polytheistic pagan religions, in being eclectic or syncretistic — that is, enfolding beliefs and practices from other religions. That's why, in fact, Christianity was persecuted. The mystery religions were inclusive — you could worship the emperor and you could still adhere to more than one of these at the same time."

"Do you think that in this age of the Internet, where half-truths and misinformation keep getting recycled, scholars are doomed to forever be responding to overblown claims that have long been answered?"

"Yes, unfortunately, probably so," he said, his tone resigned.

"Do you think in the end the truth will win out?"

"For some people," he answered. "For others—they're looking for what they want to find."

I wanted some guidance for those interested in pursuing the truth. "What advice would you give to people looking for reliable information?"

Yamauchi put down his cup of coffee. "First, be careful of articles on the web. Even though the Internet is a quick and convenient source of information, it also perpetuates outdated and disproved theories," he said. "Also check the credentials of the authors. Do they have the training and depth of knowledge to write authoritatively on these issues? And be sure to check the dates of sources that are quoted. Are they relying on anachronistic claims or discredited scholars? And finally, be aware of the biases of many modern authors, who may clearly have an axe to grind."

All of that made sense. At the same time, however, I was feeling a rising sense of indignation toward writers who either purposefully or carelessly confuse readers by making sweeping "copycat" allegations that sow unwarranted seeds of skepticism towards the real Jesus.

Many of their claims are so outlandish—like the author who likened the sinking of Osiris's coffin in the Nile to the Christian rite of baptism—that they would be laughable if the damage they wrought wasn't so serious.[91] Yet in many cases, people are believing them—a great illustration of the old saying that falsehood can make a trip around the world before truth can even get its boots on.

I thanked Yamauchi for his help in setting the record straight. Battling the rain and wind again, I climbed into my rental car and began the long trek to the Cincinnati airport. The whole time, however, I couldn't shake the frustration I felt over the proliferation of misleading information that has confused so many people. It was the same emotion that launched Nash on a crusade to expose the illegitimacy of the "copycat" argument prior to his untimely death in 2006.

The Tide of Scholarship

Ronald Nash, the author of such books as *Faith and Reason* and *The Meaning of History*, took truth seriously. He was a plain-talking professor with little patience for scholars or popular writers who took intellectual shortcuts or twisted the facts to support their own preconceived beliefs.

His students quickly learned what it meant when Nash would mockingly sway his hips from side to side while quoting from a book. "It meant he believed what he was reading aloud was at best ridiculous and at worst heretical," said a colleague. For Nash, he said, truth was more than an ideological parlor game: real lives were at stake.[92]

So Nash was understandably intolerant of books that repeated worn-out Christian "copycat" claims that had been thoroughly answered decades ago. Offended by the blatant misrepresentations, sloppy logic, and trumped-up "parallels," he sat down to write *The Gospel and the Greeks* as an antidote in 1992. When the onslaught didn't stop, he updated his book in 2003.

With facts, logic, and clarity, he counters the "careless language," "massive amounts of oversimplification and attention to detail," and "flights of fancy" found in so many "greatly overstated" works on the topic.[93]

"It is clear that the liberal arguments exhibit astoundingly bad scholarship. Indeed, this conclusion may be too generous," he said with characteristic candor.[94] His passion bleeds through the pages:

> Which mystery gods actually experienced a resurrection from the dead? Certainly no early texts refer to any resurrection of Attis. Attempts to link the worship of Adonis to a resurrection are equally weak. Nor is the case for a resurrection of Osiris any stronger.... And of course no claim can be made that Mithras was a dying and rising god. French scholar André Boulanger concluded: "The

conception that the god dies and is resurrected in order to lead
his faithful to eternal life is represented in *no* Hellenistic mystery
religion."[95]

Nash summarized seven succinct arguments against Christian
dependence on the mystery religions.[96] First, "copycat" proponents
often illogically assume that just because two things exist side by side,
one of them must have caused the other. Second, many alleged similarities are exaggerated or fabricated. Writers frequently use language borrowed from Christianity to describe pagan rituals, then marvel at the
"parallels" they've discovered. Third, the chronology is wrong. Writers
cite beliefs and practices that postdate the first century in an attempt to
argue that they influenced the first-century formation of Christianity.
Just because a cult had a belief or practice in the third or fourth century
AD doesn't mean it had the same belief or practice in the first century.

Fourth, Paul would never have consciously borrowed from pagan
religions; in fact, he warned against this very thing.[97] Fifth, early Christianity was exclusivistic; any hint of syncretism in the New Testament
would have caused immediate controversy. Sixth, unlike the mystery
religions, Christianity is grounded in actual historical events. And seventh, what few parallels remain could reflect a Christian influence on
pagan beliefs and practices. Pagan attempts to counter the growing
influence of Christianity by imitating it are clearly apparent.[98]

One thing was for sure. "The tide of scholarly opinion has turned
dramatically against attempts to make early Christianity dependent
on the so-called dying and rising gods of Hellenistic paganism," said
Nash.[99]

Two millennia ago, the apostle Peter was equally unambiguous:
The accounts about Jesus in the pages of the New Testament weren't
distilled from fanciful stories about mythological deities. Peter wasn't
reporting rumors or speculation, and he certainly wasn't trusting his
future to the likes of Zeus or Osiris. He was only interested in the *real*
Jesus.

"We did not follow cleverly devised stories when we told you about
the coming of our Lord Jesus Christ in power," he declared, "but we
were eyewitnesses of his majesty."[100]

For Further Investigation
More Resources on This Topic

Komoszewski, J. Ed, M. James Sawyer, and Daniel B. Wallace. *Reinventing Jesus*. Grand Rapids, Mich.: Kregel, 2006.

Machen, J. Gresham. *The Virgin Birth of Christ*. Grand Rapids, Mich.: Baker, 1965, reprint of Harper & Row edition, 1930.

Mettinger, Tryggve N. D. *The Riddle of Resurrection*. Stockholm: Almqvist & Wiksell, 2001.

Metzger, Bruce. *Historical and Literary Studies: Pagan, Jewish and Christian*. Grand Rapids, Mich.: Eerdmans, 1968.

Nash, Ronald H. *The Gospel and the Greeks*. 2nd ed. Phillipsburg, N.J.: P & R Publishing, 2003.

Wagner, Günter. *Pauline Baptism and the Pagan Mysteries*. Edinburgh: Oliver and Boyd, 1967.

Yamauchi, Edwin M. *Persia and the Bible*. Grand Rapids, Mich.: Baker, 1996.

"Jesus Was an Imposter Who Failed to Fulfill the Messianic Prophecies"

There's no such thing as a Jew for Jesus. It's like saying a black man is for the KKK. You can't be a table and a chair. You're either a Jew or a Gentile.

Comedian and rabbi Jackie Mason[1]

I have a special love for Jesus because he is the fulfillment of the prophecies to my people, the Jews.

Christian scholar Paul Feinberg[2]

The response has been volcanic."

For the leader of an organization with such an incendiary name, David Brickner of Jews for Jesus is soft-spoken and mild-mannered — and if anything, his assessment of what occurred in New York City during the summer of 2006 might actually be an understatement.

In a month-long evangelistic campaign, Brickner led two hundred missionaries through all five boroughs of the city that has the largest Jewish population outside of Israel. They mailed 80,000 Yiddish copies of the *Jesus* film to Hasidic homes, distributed a million tracts, and plastered advertisements in subway stations and newspapers.

"We're saying Jesus is the Messiah of Israel," said Brickner. "What could be more Jewish?"[3]

Volcanic? To say the least, the reaction was emotional for many. "Jews for Jesus Hit Town and Find a Tough Crowd," said a headline in the *New York Times*.[4] Letters to newspapers decried the group's "insidiousness" and "invitation to betray."[5] Though much of the response came in the form of quiet indignation, one incensed commuter did

punch an evangelist in the mouth, and copies of the *Jesus* film were publicly burned.[6] Jewish comedian Jackie Mason sued over his image being
used in a pamphlet.[7] In opposing the campaign, a "counter-missionary"
organization called Jews for Judaism stationed its own volunteers close
to Brickner's evangelists and even staffed a toll-free hotline for family
members wanting to bring back a relative who decided to follow Jesus.

"Someone is trying to get you to betray not just your religion, but
your parents and your grandparents," warned David Berger, professor of
religion at Brooklyn College.[8] Scott Hillman, head of Jews for Judaism's
countereffort, said, "Judaism has been around for 3,500 years. Surely
we have an answer for any question they could raise."[9]

In his own understatement, Rabbi Joshua Waxman wrote: "Jews for
Jesus push a lot of people's buttons." For him, the issues are straightforward: "Couldn't you be Jewish and believe in Jesus? The answer is
no."[10]

One conviction that unites many Jewish and Christian scholars is
that the Tanakh, known by Christians as the Old Testament, does foretell the coming of the Messiah. "Belief in the coming of the Messiah has
always been a fundamental part of Judaism," said Rabbi Aryeh Kaplan.
"Thus, for example, [Jewish philosopher] Maimonides counts the belief
in the Messiah as one of the thirteen cardinal principles of Judaism. It
is a concept that is repeated again and again throughout the length and
breadth of Jewish literature."[11]

Maimonides, whose writings are foundational to Orthodox Judaism, said in the twelfth century, "I firmly believe, in complete faith,
in the coming of the Messiah, and although he may tarry, I daily wait
for his coming."[12] Today, Orthodox Jews, and among them especially
Hasidic Jews, particularly emphasize messianism.[13]

The big controversy is whether Jesus of Nazareth is the one who fulfilled the ancient prophecies and thus fits the fingerprint of this much-
anticipated Messiah, a word that means "anointed one." The Greek
word for Messiah is *christos*, or Christ, the term that has been firmly
affixed to Jesus' name throughout history. "To call Jesus the Christ,
therefore, is to make a theological claim — that he is the Messiah long
expected by the Jews," said Stephen Prothero, chair of the religion
department at Boston University.[14]

Since the Bible doesn't explicitly label verses as being messianic, scholars must pore over the context of various passages to determine which ones deal with the coming of the Messiah. In his *Encyclopedia of Biblical Prophecy*, J. Barton Payne digs out 127 personal messianic predictions in 3,348 verses of the Old Testament.[15] In addition, there are 456 Old Testament passages cited in some 558 rabbinic writings that refer to the Messiah and the messianic times.[16]

If these predictions really did come true in Jesus of Nazareth, the implications are enormous for everyone, not just those with a Jewish background. First, this would confirm the supernatural nature of the Bible, since the odds of fulfilling so many ancient prophecies by mere chance would be mathematically prohibitive. "The Bible is the only book in the world that has precise, specific predictions that were made hundreds of years in advance and that were literally fulfilled," said eminent Christian apologist Norman Geisler.[17] That would mean that the Bible has credentials that are absent from the Qur'an of Islam, the *Upanishads* and *Bhagavad-Gita* of Vedanta Hinduism, the Book of Mormon, and all other religious texts.

Second, if Jesus — and only Jesus — fulfilled these ancient forecasts, then this would be a definitive affirmation of his identity as the one sent by God to be the Savior of Israel and the world. Of course, the reverse is equally significant. Jesus said in Luke 24:44: "Everything must be fulfilled that is written about me in the Law of Moses, the Prophets and the Psalms." When a Samaritan woman said to him, "I know that Messiah is coming," Jesus replied: "I, the one speaking to you — I am he."[18] Having made these unambiguous claims, if he then fails to match the prophetic portrait, Jesus would be an imposter worthy of rejection and disdain — a false prophet who should be rejected by Jews and Gentiles alike.

Obviously, these matters are critical to all spiritual seekers, regardless of their religious background. Nothing less than the trustworthiness of the Bible and the identity and credibility of Jesus are at issue. So it's not surprising that disputes over the prophecies have raged for centuries from university classrooms to scholarly books — and to the sweltering subways of New York City, where dueling ads clashed over whether Jesus should be embraced by Jews searching for their Messiah.

Few religious topics engender as much passion. I once moderated a debate in which a respected rabbi angrily denounced Brickner as being "a spiritual Nazi" for trying to convince Jews to follow Jesus. And as the number of messianic Jews increases in both the U.S. and Israel—with estimates ranging from 120,000 to twice that figure and higher—the dispute continues to grow.[19] Indeed, both sides seem to have become more adamant in the last few years.

Could Jesus really have been the Christ? What happens when emotions subside and the evidence is systematically examined? How strong is the case for Jesus the Messiah—and can it withstand the most potent objections of those who deny that he was described in prophecies dating back hundreds of years before his birth in Bethlehem?

"Everything Christians Claim ... Is False"

Attacks on the idea that the messianic prophecies culminated in Jesus have proliferated over the last three hundred years. By 1793 the German biblical scholar J. G. Eichhorn, considered the father of modern higher criticism, felt the confidence to declare: "The last three decades have erased the Messiah from the Old Testament."[20] Thus, said Old Testament professor Walter C. Kaiser Jr. of Gordon-Conwell Theological Seminary, "the eighteenth century began the long debate, which has continued to this very hour, about the apologetic 'argument from prophecy' for the Messiah."[21]

The debate has been most vociferous on the popular level, particularly the Internet, often in response to evangelistic initiatives from Jewish followers of Jesus. "Everything Christians claim for Jesus as the Jewish Messiah is false," insisted prominent Orthodox Rabbi Pinchas Stolper in a book subtitled *A Jewish Response to Missionaries.*[22]

A "counter-missionary survival guide," published by Jews for Judaism, said Christians "may claim that there are over three hundred biblical 'proofs' for their position. A careful examination of these passages —in context—will immediately refute their presentation."[23] As for the "proof texts" used by Christians to argue for Jesus' messianic credentials, they are "based on circular reasoning, quoting verses out of context, and mistranslation."[24]

Kaplan, another Orthodox rabbi, was especially blunt. "What can a

Jew lose by embracing Christianity?" he asked. "The answer is: Everything." He added:

> The Jews had one major objection to the Christian Messiah, and that was the fact that he had been unsuccessful. Judaism had always taught that the Messiah would redeem Israel in a political sense, and Jesus had failed to accomplish this. Instead, he had been scourged and humiliated like a common rebel, and finally crucified along with two ordinary thieves. How could the career of Jesus be reconciled with the glorious picture of the Messiah as taught by the Prophets of Israel? The early Christians faced this dilemma, and, in justifying Jesus as the Messiah, radically altered the entire concept.[25]

Amy Jill Levine, a Jewish expert in Jesus and the New Testament at Vanderbilt Divinity School and author of *The Misunderstood Jew*, said there's no "messianic checklist" that establishes Jesus as the one who was foretold. "The Messiah is someone who establishes justice throughout the world, and I look out my window and I know that hasn't happened," she said. "The Messiah is someone who conquers death, conquers disease. And I know that hasn't happened. One might even say, for example, the death of the Messiah — his torture, his crucifixion — is predicted in the Old Testament. Well, in fact, it's not."[26]

Christians, of course, offer a radically different perspective. "Not all the prophecies in the Old Testament about the Messiah were fulfilled in Jesus' lifetime," said Edwin Yamauchi, now-retired professor of ancient history at Miami University of Ohio. "The Christians' answer is that those prophecies will be fulfilled when Christ comes again."[27]

Comes *again*? Jewish scholars point out that the terms "first coming" and "second coming" aren't even mentioned in the Old Testament. They contend that Christians invented the idea of Jesus coming again out of embarrassment that he failed to usher in the universal peace that the Messiah is predicted to bring. In fact, they argue, *anyone* could claim to be the Messiah — and when someone points out he hasn't brought peace to the world, he can merely use the excuse that this will be fulfilled at some unspecified future date. In short, they say, the second coming is nothing more than an escape clause for charlatans.

One thing's for sure: history and logic either support the conclusion that Jesus is the Messiah or they don't. How convincing is the affirmative case, and how deflating are the latest counterarguments raised by Jesus' detractors? Those are the issues that prompted me to fly to North Carolina and to seek out one of the world's leading authorities on the messianic prophecies. On a brisk morning, with the sun shining through fiery autumn leaves, I found his office in a nondescript white office building in a northern suburb of Charlotte.

INTERVIEW #5: Michael L. Brown, PhD

As a teenager growing up on Long Island, Michael Brown's insatiable appetite for illicit drugs earned him the nicknames "Iron Man" and "Drug Bear." By the age of fifteen, the aspiring rock and roll drummer was shooting heroin and had burglarized some homes and even a doctor's office for amusement—an incongruous lifestyle for the son of the senior lawyer of the New York Supreme Court.

He grew up in a Jewish family but was uninterested in spiritual matters. When he was bar mitzvahed at the age of thirteen, he was given a Hebrew passage to memorize—but nobody ever translated it for him, and he never bothered to ask anyone what the words meant. For him, it was a meaningless ritual.

In 1971 the two other members of his band began attending a local church in pursuit of two girls related to the pastor. Little by little, they began to be influenced by the gospel. Upset at the changes in their lives, Brown decided to visit the church in an effort to extricate them. One of the girls, aware of his reputation, wrote in her diary that night: "Anti-Christ comes to church."

Unexpectedly, in the months that followed, Brown discovered a new emotion: a gnawing sense of regret and conviction over his rebellious and drug-saturated behavior. He ended up in many discussions with Christians about spirituality. On November 12, 1971, when the pastor asked if anyone wanted to receive Jesus as their Savior, Brown walked the aisle—not because he really wanted to become a Christian, but so that he could give the congregation a thrill. After all, he was sure they regarded him as the worst of sinners.

Then something even more unexpected happened: as he repeated the words of the pastor in a prayer of repentance and faith, he found himself suddenly believing the message of Christ. "It was like a light went on," he said. Instantly, he believed Jesus had died for his sins and had risen from the dead. "I knew it was real," Brown said. "Now the challenge was: what was I going to do with it — because I wasn't ready to change my lifestyle." It wasn't until five weeks later that he permanently abandoned drugs and yielded his life to Jesus.

His father liked the subsequent reform of Brown's behavior, but he didn't like the Jesus part. He brought his son to talk to the local rabbi, who eventually took him to a community of ultra-Orthodox Jews in Brooklyn. None of them, however, was able to dislodge his belief, now confirmed by his own deep study, that Jesus is the Messiah of Israel.

But they did raise some serious questions, challenging him on his lack of a working knowledge of Hebrew. To better understand and test the messianic promises, Brown then pursued years of education that ultimately led to a master's degree as well as a doctorate in Near Eastern Languages and Literatures from New York University. His practice of tackling the most powerful arguments of critics has helped him develop into one of America's best-known defenders of Jesus the Messiah. Over the past thirty years, he has debated and dialogued with rabbis and leaders of the Jewish community on radio, television, college campuses, and even in synagogues.

Brown has taught at Trinity Evangelical Divinity School, Fuller Theological Seminary, Regent University, and in twenty-five countries. He has authored eighteen books, including the widely acclaimed, multi-volume series, *Answering Jewish Objections to Jesus*, which contains in-depth responses to the most common historical and theological issues regarding the messianic prophecies. His book *Our Hands Are Stained with Blood* examines anti-Semitism in church history.

He also has written a commentary on the book of Jeremiah for *The Expositor's Bible Commentary* and contributed to the *Oxford Dictionary of Jewish Religion, The Theological Dictionary of the Old Testament, The New International Dictionary of Old Testament Theology and Exegesis*, as well as several Semitic linguistic journals.

Warm and gregarious, with a satisfying mix of a pastor's heart and a scholar's mind, Brown greeted me with an enthusiastic handshake as he ushered me into his office at the FIRE School of Ministry, where he serves as president and professor of practical theology.[28] He was informally dressed, wearing a dark green shirt open at the collar. His wavy brown hair has almost totally surrendered to gray, while his graying mustache has now become nearly white.

He sat behind his desk, surrounded by bookshelves brimming with Jewish and Christian tomes. Over his shoulder, the shelf literally sagging under the weight, were the twenty volumes of the Babylonian Talmud, the 2.5-million-word foundational text for Jewish religious study, oversized and with its covers colored crimson.

Prior to the visit, I reviewed the most current objections to Jesus being the Messiah — an easy task since I had already overseen two debates on the topic. Frankly, I thought some of the arguments against Jesus' fulfillment of the prophecies were weak, their answers so obvious that they weren't worth bringing up, but I had to admit there were many others that raised significant and thorny issues. I wrote those down and then added the questions that had been troubling me personally.

I was anxious to see how Brown would try to answer them. But rather than cross-examining him right away, I decided to do what I had done in my earlier interview on the resurrection: I invited Brown to first set forth the affirmative case, promising to withhold substantive questions until he could establish why he believes Jesus is the Messiah.

"That sounds fair," he said, removing his glasses and putting them on his desk. He cleared his throat. After gathering his thoughts, he decided to start with some background.

"The Jews are God's chosen people," he said, "but it's important to understand that when God chose Abraham and his descendants, there was a divine purpose. It was not just to have a separated people who would be loyal to him: it was so that through Israel the entire world would be blessed and come to know the one true God. We need to keep that in mind as we proceed."

I nodded in acknowledgment. Then, with virtually no interruption, Brown began to unfold the evidence for the messiahship of Jesus, fluidly moving from point to point, quoting scripture and rabbinic commentaries with equal ease, and weaving together a tapestry of facts and clues and arguments and history and implications. The pace of his impromptu presentation quickly outstripped my ability to take notes; instead, I sat back, crossed my legs to get comfortable, and let my tape recorder soak it in.

The Case for Jesus the Messiah

"There are specific promises given to the tribe of Judah and to David, who was from the tribe of Judah and was the son of Jesse," Brown said. "Genesis 49:10 says, 'The scepter will not depart from Judah,' while Isaiah 11:1 says, 'A shoot will come up from the stump of Jesse; from his roots a Branch will bear fruit.' The term 'Branch' is commonly used to refer to the Messiah. It's said there would be a lasting kingship through David. The Lord declares in Jeremiah 23:5 that he will raise up from David's line 'a righteous Branch, a King who will reign wisely.'"

So far, nothing controversial.

"When we get to Isaiah, we see references to the servant of the Lord. A number of these verses are also recognized as referring to the Messiah in some ancient Jewish traditions. Isaiah 42 says he will not falter until he brings justice to the earth.[29] Isaiah 49 says the servant has the mission of regathering the tribes of Israel to bring them back to God. The servant feels as if he failed in his mission, but God says not only will he ultimately regather Israel, but he adds in Isaiah 49:6, 'I will also make you a light for the Gentiles, that my salvation may reach to the ends of the earth.'"

Then Brown brought up the most famous messianic passage of all — Isaiah 52:13 – 53:12. "These verses say the Messiah will be highly exalted but first will suffer terribly. He will actually be disfigured in his suffering," Brown explained. "And the narrative says the people of Israel didn't get it. They thought he was suffering for his own sins and wickedness; they didn't realize he was bearing *their* sins, suffering on *their* behalf, and by his wounds there was healing for them. Then it speaks of his death and his continued life after that.

"Now we narrow things even more. In 2 Chronicles 7, God says if Israel's sin reaches a certain level, he'll destroy the temple, exile the people, and leave them in a state of judgment.[30] Sure enough, this comes to pass. The prophet Daniel prays in Daniel 9 that God would have mercy. God gives him a revelation about the temple being rebuilt. Before this new temple is destroyed, Daniel is told, several things are going to take place, including the bringing of everlasting atonement — the final dealing with sin.[31]

"The prophet Haggai lives to see this second temple built, but it's nothing like the first. The first one, Solomon's temple, was not only a stunning physical structure far more imposing than the second temple, but it had the glory of God there. When sacrifices were offered, fire came down and consumed them. The second temple didn't have the presence of God or the divine fire.

"Yet Haggai said the glory of the second temple would be greater than the glory of the first temple. God would fill the second temple with his glory.[32] The Hebrew word for *glory* can sometimes refer to great wealth and abundance, but when God says he'll *fill* the temple with *glory*, that can only apply to his presence. Then the prophet Malachi, who lived later, says the Lord will come to his temple, purifying some of his people and bringing judgment on others.[33] He uses a Hebrew term that always refers to God himself: *the* Lord — *he* will come to that temple.

"Keep in mind the second temple was destroyed in AD 70. Atonement for sin had to be made and the divine visitation had to take place before the second temple was destroyed. There are even rabbinic traditions that put the Messiah's coming around two thousand years ago — right when Jesus came. In fact, Rashi, the foremost Jewish commentator on the Tanakh, put the date at more than 1,750 years ago, but that was based on the most famous chronological error in the rabbinic literature. When the error is corrected, we find ourselves in the middle of the first century, within one generation of the time of Jesus![34]

"So it's not a matter of maybe there's another one who's the Messiah. If it's not Yeshua, which is the Jewish name for Jesus, then throw out the Bible, because nobody except him accomplished what needed to be done prior to AD 70. What divine visitation *did* take place if not for Yeshua? When else *did* God visit the second temple in a personal way? Who else atoned for sin? How else *was* the glory of the second temple greater than the first? Either the Messiah came two thousand years ago or the prophets were wrong and we can discard the Bible. But they weren't wrong. Yeshua is the Messiah—or nobody is."

He paused for a moment to let the implications sink in. "Let's keep going," Brown continued. "The Talmud asks whether the Messiah will come 'with the clouds of heaven,' as written in Daniel 7:13, or 'lowly and riding on a donkey,' as in Zechariah 9:9.[35] The rabbis said if we're worthy, he'll come with the clouds of heaven, meaning swiftly and powerfully; if we're unworthy, he'll come meek and lowly. They believed it's 'either/or.' Actually, it's 'both/and.' They're both true—of the same person.

"Shortly before he died, Jesus rode on a donkey into Jerusalem, with the crowds hailing him as the Messiah. But then the people turned on him. Is it possible that he came 'lowly and riding upon a donkey' because we weren't worthy of his coming, and in the future, when we recognize him as the Messiah, he will return with the clouds of heaven, as he himself specifically foretold in his trial before the high priest?"

Brown moved ahead without waiting for an answer. "Now let's think about the roles of the Messiah," he continued. "In addition to being a king, he would be a priestly figure."

"How do you know?" I interrupted.

"Well, David is the prototype for the Messiah, and David performed certain priestly functions," Brown said. "Second Samuel 24:25 says, 'David built an altar to the LORD there and sacrificed burnt offerings and fellowship offerings.' That's what a priest does. According to 2 Samuel 8:18, David's sons were priests.

"Then look at Psalm 110:4. It says, 'The LORD has sworn and will not change his mind: "You are a priest forever, in the order of Melchizedek."' Here we have the Lord making an emphatic oath that the king in Jerusalem was to be a priest forever in the order of the ancient priest-king of that city. Either this prophecy directly refers to the Messiah or it refers to David. If it refers to David, and he's the prototype of the Messiah, it still means the Messiah will be priestly as well as royal.

"In Zechariah 3, we encounter Jeshua, who was the high priest. Incidentally, Jeshua is the short form of the name Joshua, which in English would be Jesus. Jeshua is said to be a sign and symbol of 'the Branch.' Remember, Jeremiah 23 and other passages tell us the Branch is the Messiah, because he's the branch that comes out from the tree, the root of Jesse. In Zechariah 6:11 – 13, Jeshua is sitting on a throne. They put a crown on his head. So think about this: in the most overt passage in the Bible where a human being is explicitly identified with a Messianic figure, it's a high priest sitting on a throne."

Brown paused for emphasis. "A *priestly* king!" he stressed. "Typically, priests don't sit on thrones and priests don't have crowns."

"Why is this important?" I asked.

"Because priests dealt with sin. Priests bore the iniquities of the people on their shoulders. They were intercessors. In fact, according to Numbers 35, the death of the high priest could serve as atonement for certain sins for which there were no other earthly atonement.

"Now consider Psalm 22. This isn't a prophecy; it's a prayer of a righteous sufferer who comes to the jaws of death and is miraculously delivered. Yet Jesus said that everything written up to his lifetime finds its full meaning and expression in him. He even applied Psalm 22 to himself on the cross.[36] And in Psalm 22, as a result of the righteous sufferer's deliverance from death, all the ends of the earth will worship God.[37] That's quite a significant deliverance from death!

"So let's put all of this together. God's intent was not to keep Israel as an isolated nation, but that through Israel the entire world will come to know the one true God. That has always been his heart. We see in the scriptures that this messianic figure will be both priestly *and* royal — he will deal with sin as well as rule and reign. He will first suffer before he is raised up and exalted; he will both come riding on a donkey meek and lowly, as well as come in clouds of glory.

"He will first be rejected by his people and will be a light to the nations. He will suffer terribly for our sins as a righteous substitute. The power of his deliverance from death will cause the ends of the earth to worship the one true God. We also see that redemption had to come and there had to be divine visitation before the second temple was destroyed in AD 70."

Brown reached his hands toward me as if soliciting a response. "Who might that be?" he asked. "Is there any possible candidate? It's not rocket science to say either the Bible is false — or it has to be Yeshua, also known as Jesus."

"It's Him or No One"

Brown wasn't finished. "Yeshua said he came to fulfill what had been written in the Law and the Prophets. He predicted the destruction of the second temple. No other significant Jewish leader did that," he continued. "Deuteronomy 18 says to pay attention to the prophet who's raised up in each generation.[38] Yeshua is the last great prophet who speaks to Israel. He brings this prophetic word: The temple is going to be destroyed, but the fulfillment of what's written in the scriptures points to him.

"In short, Yeshua fulfilled the essential prophecies that had a definite time frame and which had to be completed before the second temple was destroyed. This is not a matter of speculation; it's historical fact. And since he fulfilled the past prophecies—coming as our great high priest and making atonement for our sins—we can be sure that he will fulfill the future prophecies, reigning as the worldwide king and bringing peace to the earth.

"In fact, he already rules and reigns as a royal king over the lives of countless tens of millions of people from every nation under the sun. They give him their total allegiance and loyalty. His reign is already far greater and more influential than the reign of David himself. And that's only the beginning; he will reign over all when he returns.

"Think about this: for more than 1,900 years, traditional Jews have had no functioning temple. There has been no functioning priesthood with sacrifices. What happened? As you read through the Torah, or the first five books of the Bible, you find repeated references to sacrifices and offerings.[39] Isn't it significant that Isaiah 53 says the servant of the Lord will himself be a guilt offering?[40]

"Either God has left us completely bereft of the major atonement system, a functioning priesthood, and a functioning temple, or else everything that we're speaking of finds its fulfillment in the One who came when he had to come.

"We're not talking about things Yeshua could have arranged. How do you arrange being the most influential Jew who ever lived? How do you arrange bringing hundreds of millions of people into the worship of God? How do you arrange being rejected by your people and yet being accepted by the nations? How do you arrange being the only possible candidate who can fulfill the scriptures, prophesying the end of one system, and then bringing the reality of the new system?

"So I look at the broad strokes and then I begin to see how the New Testament authors saw that, even in the details, he is prefigured by the nation of Israel. For example, Israel in its infancy went into Egypt— Hosea 11:1 says when Israel was a child, God loved him and called his son out of Egypt. The Messiah as a child goes into Egypt and is called out of Egypt. As it happened to Israel, so it happens to him. David was betrayed by a close friend; the Messiah was betrayed by a close friend. As it happened to Moses, having to flee for his life from pharaoh, it happens to Messiah, who had to flee for his life from Herod.

"You begin to see these little details, which in themselves are not necessarily prophecies, but they prefigure him—they are types, shadows, and allusions. The rabbinic mind-set could extract from scripture things that we might not see. Actually, the New Testament is very conservative in its references to predictive scripture. It's not wild or outlandish. The broad strokes can only apply to one possible candidate, and then we get to put in all the finishing details into a beautiful picture.

"And here's something fascinating: there's a rabbinic tradition preserved in the Talmud that says on the Day of Atonement there were three different signs that the animal sacrifices the high priest offered had been accepted by God and atonement given to the nation.[41] In the years when the signs would come up negative, the people would be ashamed and mourn, because God had not accepted their sacrifice.

"Then it says that during the last forty years before the second temple was destroyed, all three signs were negative each and every time.[42] Think about that: Jesus probably was crucified in AD 30, and the temple was destroyed in AD 70. So from the time of his death to the time of the destruction of the temple—*a period of forty years*—God signaled that he no longer accepted the sacrifices and offerings of the Jewish people. Why?"

His answer was emphatic: *"Because final atonement had been made through Yeshua, just as he had prophesied."*

Brown let his words linger. Then, apparently sensing the need for elaboration, he said, "Please, let me explain how Yeshua fulfilled the Jewish sacrificial system."

My mind was racing to keep up with him. "Yes, go ahead," I said.

"If you go through the first five books of the Bible, called the Written Torah, you'll find several hundred references to animal sacrifices and offerings," Brown said. "The fundamental concept was life for life, as recognized in some of the rabbinic commentaries. Why was it so important? Obviously, God was seeking to get something across—that sin required a penalty of death, and that God would receive a substitution on behalf of the guilty person. When an innocent lamb was slain and the blood drained out, that was quite a vivid lesson.

"Remember, it was foretold the Messiah would be a priestly figure. What did the priest do? He went between the people and God. He went into the holiest place of all. By his stature, position, and calling, he did what nobody else could do. Yeshua, as the great high priest, prays for us and then literally carries our sins on his shoulders as Peter expresses —'He himself bore our sins in his body on the cross.'[43] He takes the guilt, the punishment, and the suffering that we all deserve and bears them himself.

"What sacrifice is great enough to cover the guilt of the entire world? Who's pure enough? Who's perfect enough? Only this one, the great Son of God, takes the sin and guilt of the entire world on his own shoulders and dies on behalf of our sins so we can now receive forgiveness, cleansing, and righteousness.

"Hebrews 9:22 says that without the shedding of blood, there's no forgiveness of sins. Yes, there are secondary means of atonement other than blood, but the foundation of it all is blood atonement. On the holiest day of the Jewish calendar, the Day of Atonement, when the temple was purged, the people were purged, and atonement would come to the entire nation—all of that centered around blood. Take away the blood, and there's no atonement.

"God gave blood atonement because life is in the blood: it's life for life. Leviticus deals with the topics of sacrifice and atonement, and whenever atonement is mentioned—all forty-nine times—it's always in conjunction with blood sacrifices. Leviticus 17:11 says, 'For the life of a creature is in the blood, and I have given it to you to make atonement for yourselves on the altar; it is the blood that makes atonement for one's life.' An ancient midrash, or Jewish commentary, on Leviticus 1:12 says that when a sacrifice is killed, 'I consider it as if you have offered your very selves.'[44] In Leviticus 1:4, God says specifically, 'You are to lay your hand on the head of the burnt offering, and it will be accepted on your behalf to make atonement for you.'

"It's not just a matter of cutting your finger and putting a little blood on the altar. No, the sacrifice had to die. That's the terribly ugly picture of the cost of sin—that it's so serious to God that it requires death. The shedding of blood is our repayment of sin, but instead of us shedding our blood, Yeshua shed it for us as our substitute. As we know from John 1:29, Yeshua was called 'the Lamb of God, who takes away the sin of the world.' "

Brown had been sitting on the edge of his chair, pleading his case every bit as compellingly as his attorney father used to. Now, his presentation complete, he eased back.

"So add everything up," he said. "All of these clues point to Yeshua and Yeshua alone. He fulfills the prophecies in the most incredible way. Since the Messiah had to come almost two thousand years ago, according to the testimony of the Jewish scriptures, then if Yeshua isn't the Messiah, there will never be a Messiah. It's too late for anyone else. It's him or no one. If Yeshua didn't come and do what had to be done in the first phase of things, when there was a definite deadline, then there's no hope that the second phase will ever come, when he will come in the clouds of glory to rule and reign."

He smiled. "We have the deposit," he said. "We have the down payment. We can be confident he will return to accomplish the remainder."

The *Shekinah* and the *Memra*

The room fell quiet except for the faint buzz of a distant lawn mower. For a few moments, I contemplated what Brown had said. From his sweep through the Old Testament, from Genesis to Malachi, he had marshaled powerful evidence in building a convincing case for Jesus — and only Jesus — having fulfilled the messianic prophecies. Standing alone, unchallenged by objections, his arguments seemed conclusive.

Still, my clipboard, which was brimming with questions, reminded me there was another side to the story. No verdict could be reached until Brown's case could be tested by opposing views. With his permission, I began to probe potential soft spots in his presentation.

"Let's be really honest," I began. "The prophecies don't foretell that the Messiah would be divine, do they?"

Brown leaned forward. "Actually, Lee, yes, they do," he replied.

I glanced down at my clipboard. "Not according to the late rabbi Aryeh Kaplan," I told him. " 'In no place do the Prophets say that he will be anything more than a remarkable leader and teacher,' he said. 'The Jewish Messiah is truly human in origin. He is born of ordinary human parents, and is of flesh and blood like all mortals.' "[45]

Moving to the edge of his chair again, Brown said, "Let's look at the facts. There are definitely verses that point toward his divine nature. Bear in mind, however, that the Jews were staunch monotheists, and it would have been totally misunderstood if the claim of the Messiah's divinity had been too explicit."

"So what's the evidence for his predicted divinity?" I asked.

"The Davidic king was described as being highly exalted and the one who will someday rule and reign. Several parallel descriptions are used of both God and this exalted king: people will praise God, and the people will praise the king; people will serve God, and the people will serve the king; people will bow down before God, and people will bow down before the king.

"Also, Psalm 110:1 says, 'The LORD says to my lord: "Sit at my right hand." ' That's a position of great exaltation. The figure in Daniel 7—the Son of Man—is highly exalted; he comes before the throne of God, is worshiped, is given sovereign power and authority, and his kingdom is eternal. Being worshiped, having sovereignty, being eternal —those sound a lot like divine characteristics to me. And of course, Jesus' favorite self-description was the Son of Man, and he applied Daniel 7 directly to himself.[46]

"Even more explicitly, Psalm 45:6 says of the Messiah-king, 'Your throne, O God, will last for ever and ever.' God is anointing this king, yet the king himself is called *Elohim*, a Hebrew name for God. That's very significant. We know that sometimes *Elohim* can be a reference to earthly judges and angels, but to call an individual *Elohim* in this context is really stretching things.

"Isaiah 52:13 says the servant will be 'raised' and 'lifted up.' In Isaiah, those words only occur in reference to the Lord. And even more directly, in Isaiah 9:6–7, the king is given various names, including 'Mighty God' and 'Everlasting Father.' So you have the royal king, or the messianic figure, being described as divine."

"Did the people of that day anticipate a divine Messiah?"

"It wasn't really until Yeshua came and they looked back at the Hebrew scriptures and said, 'Oh, *that* explains it!' In hindsight, it becomes much clearer."

"But the Hebrew scriptures say God is one and incorporeal," I protested.[47] "The Bible says nobody can ever see God.[48] So how could Jesus be God?"

"It's clear there's only one God, yet it seems that he's somehow complex in his unity," Brown explained. "On the one hand, he's ruling from his throne in heaven, and yet on the other hand he's present on the earth. There are other times when he himself is seen, even though the Bible says no one can see God, who's spirit. Let me give you a few examples. In Genesis 18, Yahweh and two angels appear to Abraham. Jacob saw God face to face.[49] Isaiah says, 'I saw the Lord.'[50] Exodus 24:9–10 says, 'Moses and Aaron, Nadab and Abihu, and the seventy elders of Israel went up and saw the God of Israel.'"

I jumped in. "Wasn't that just a *vision*?"

"No, because verse 11 says, 'God did not raise his hand against these leaders of the Israelites.' That doesn't sound like a vision to me," Brown said, a chuckle in his voice. "So who is it that all these people saw if they can't see God and yet they saw God? Could it have been the Son?"

Without waiting for a response, he said, "Yes, I believe it was. Then the New Testament begins to enlighten us—God is complex in his unity and this one God makes himself known as the Father, Son, and Spirit. The Father has never been seen; the Son is the one who reveals him and makes him known, and who now takes on flesh and blood. So in a sense God did not become a mere man, as the Hebrew scriptures emphatically say. But can he make himself known in flesh and blood? Can he, while remaining enthroned in heaven, come down among us?

"This explains how all these things can be said at the same time about God. Interestingly, the rabbis came up with different concepts about how God can be untouchable and invisible, yet touchable and known. One of the concepts was the *Shekinah*, which is the dwelling presence of God on earth. God said in Exodus 25:8, 'Have them make a sanctuary for me, and I will dwell among them.' One rabbi said to me, 'So Jesus was like a walking *Shekinah*—that's what you believe?' I said, '*Exactly.*'

"We also see references in the Hebrew scriptures to the Word of God. The Word is something that proceeds forth from him, yet *is* him. We see in Genesis that God created all things through his spoken word—in fact, Psalm 33:6 says: 'By the word of the LORD the heavens were made.' His Word is even worthy of praise: Psalm 56:4 says, 'In God, whose word I praise—in God I trust.' The Targums, which are Aramaic paraphrases of the Hebrew scriptures, use the expression *Memra*, which is 'Word.' For instance, instead of saying the Lord spoke to Moses, it says the Word of the Lord spoke to Moses.

"So now go to John 1 and merely substitute *Memra* for Word: 'In the beginning was the *Memra*, and the *Memra* was with God, and the *Memra* was God.' This is God drawing near. He was in the tabernacle; now he's in Yeshua, who combines deity and humanity. Though God remains invisible, though he remains God transcendent and not a man, yet he reveals himself fully in bodily form.

"If John had simply written, 'God became a human being,' it would have given the false impression that the Lord was no longer filling the universe or reigning in heaven, but that he had abandoned his throne to take up residence here, like one of the pagan deities. Instead, John tells us that it was the divine Word that became a human being, and through the Word, we can know God personally. As John said, 'No one has ever seen God; the only Son, who is in the bosom of the Father, he has made him known.'[51]

"Think about Genesis 18 again, where God appeared to Abraham. This clearly teaches that God can come to earth in human form for a period of time if he wants to. If he could do this for a few hours, in a temporary human form, could he do it for a few years, in permanent human form? Of course. This is called the incarnation—God coming down to earth in the person of his Son. When we recognize the Son as the exact representation of God, yet God himself, then we can explain how God remained the Lord in heaven while also appearing as the Lord on earth in Genesis 18.

"Seeing Jesus was seeing God. Jesus said in John 14:9, 'Anyone who has seen me has seen the Father.' He said, 'I and the Father are one.'[52] Notice that Jesus didn't call himself God; he called himself God's Son[53] — the one in whom the fullness of God dwells in bodily form.[54]

"This doesn't contradict anything in the Hebrew scriptures," he said in conclusion. "In fact, this explains many verses in the Hebrew Bible that are otherwise unintelligible."

Where Is World Peace?

Nevertheless, as I mentioned at the beginning of this chapter, one of the biggest objections brought up by critics is the fact that Jesus didn't fulfill what they consider to be the main messianic prophecies: bringing about a world of peace and unity, and ending evil, idolatry, falsehood, and hatred. "In light of that," I said after mentioning this to Brown, "how can you say that Jesus is the Messiah?"

"Again, there are things that had to happen in a certain time frame before the second temple was destroyed," Brown replied. "If those have not happened, then there can be no other potential candidate. Secondly, these critics have identified prophecies six through ten as messianic, but have left out prophecies one through five. I'm saying Yeshua will fulfill prophecies six through ten because he has already fulfilled one through five. He will both suffer and be exalted. He will be both priestly and royal. He will be both rejected and accepted. He will be a light to the nations before being received by the Jewish people. So looking at the larger picture points me back towards Yeshua.

"Also," he added, "it's not as if Yeshua did certain tactical things that had to happen and now has been absent for two thousand years. Instead, we see certain things unfolding just as expected, with his kingdom continuing to advance. Look at how many people came to worship the one true God in the twentieth century alone. This tells me the pace is accelerating. So the fulfillment of the first stage, as well as the ongo-

ing fulfillment of those things that had to be ongoing, tells me that the
final stage is clear.

"For instance, imagine that two people owe me a lot of money. One
gives me a partial repayment of a hundred thousand dollars and says,
'When I come back, I'll give you the rest.' The other person says that
someday he'll repay me, but he doesn't even give me a deposit. Who am
I more likely to believe? Especially when I get ongoing letters from the
first one reassuring me that the remaining money will indeed be fully
repaid soon."

"But the term *second coming* isn't found in the Hebrew scriptures,"
I pointed out.

"The word *trinity* isn't used anywhere in the entire Bible either,
but the evidence is there supporting it," he countered. "The prophecies
require certain events to happen — like atonement and the visit to the
temple — before other events can happen, like the Messiah bringing
peace to the earth. The first act precedes the second act and prepares
the way for it. First atonement for sin, then peace on the earth."

I tried another tack. "Couldn't the idea of a second coming be used
by any false Messiah who failed to fulfill all the prophecies?"

"Well, if Yeshua had done nothing to fulfill any of the prophecies
and said he was going to do everything in the future, then, yes, I'd
agree. But that's not the case," said Brown. "He did what needed to be
done before AD 70, so we can have confidence he'll do what needs to
be done in the future."

"Some say he fulfilled none of the *provable* prophecies," I said. "Anyone could die, anyone could claim to have been born in Bethlehem, as
Micah 5:2 foretold, and so forth."

"One simple response: the story of his deliverance from death,
according to Psalm 22, was supposed to have such an effect that people
around the entire world turned to God," Brown said. "That's pretty
provable. Rejected by your own people but being a light to the nations
— that's pretty provable. There's the ongoing accreditation by God of
who he is, through the extension of his kingdom around the world. It's
convincing enough to read the amazing accounts of Yeshua in the New
Testament. It's quite another to see how he continues, without break,
to have worldwide impact."

Repentance and Sacrifice

Critics also have attacked Christianity's claim that Jesus' atoning death is the culmination of the Old Testament practice of animal sacrifices. I pulled out a document from Jews for Judaism and read it to Brown:

> None of the biblical prophets taught that animal or blood sacrifices were indispensable in order for the forgiveness of our sins. As a matter of fact, the prophets constantly berated people who mistakenly thought that sacrifices, in and of themselves, bring about forgiveness.[55] The Bible clearly teaches that the only way of atoning for sins is through repentance—a process of transformation that includes acknowledging our wrongdoing and confessing it to G-d, feeling regret, making restitution if we harmed someone, resolving to improve our behavior, returning to G-d and praying for forgiveness."[56]

I slipped the paper back into my briefcase and looked at Brown. "If repentance is all that's needed," I said, "doesn't that negate the belief that Jesus was the fulfillment of the Jewish sacrificial system?"

"Let's make something clear," Brown began. "The new covenant writings—that is, the writings of the New Testament—consistently emphasize the importance of repentance as well. They don't teach that Jesus died and therefore you're automatically forgiven. Jesus said, 'Repent, for the kingdom of heaven has come near.'[57] He said, 'I have not come to call the righteous, but sinners to repentance.'[58] In Mark 6, he sends out the Twelve—and what do they preach? That people should repent.[59]

"I don't argue that. But repentance has never existed independently from the larger system of atonement that God made. Go back to Torah. Every time you find something barely resembling the concept of repentance, I'll find fifty to a hundred that talk about blood sacrifice. God was trying to get something across, which was the foundational nature of the blood sacrifice. That system was pointing toward the one who would come. God never really wanted the blood of bulls and goats. The prophets repudiated sacrifices that were offered with an empty heart; they never repudiated sacrifices themselves—"

I cut in. "But doesn't God say in Hosea 6:6, 'For I desire mercy, *not sacrifice*, and acknowledgment of God rather than burnt offerings'?"[60]

"Jesus quoted that *twice* in the New Testament. I agree with that!" he declared. "The problem was *not* the sacrifice; it was the empty heart. First Samuel 15 says God prefers obedience to sacrifice. What he wants is an obedient heart.[61] Yet because we all fall short, he established the sacrificial system to ultimately point people toward the Messiah."

Another objection popped into my mind. "When God forgave the sins of the Ninevites in the book of Jonah, no sacrifices were offered," I observed.

Brown's answer was direct. "God never called the Ninevites to offer sacrifices," he said. "This was Israel's role as a priestly nation, and that role finds its fulfillment in the work of the Messiah."

I picked up my Bible, which was next to me on his desk, and opened it. "Leviticus 5:11 says if someone can't afford the animal sacrifice, they can bring 'a tenth of an ephah'—that would be a couple of quarts—'of the finest flour for a sin offering.' So there you have it—blood sacrifice wasn't always required."

Brown shook his head. "God didn't build a theology on the atoning power of flour," he said. "Have Jews through the ages just offered flour? If you read the next verse, it says a handful of the flour should be put on the fire offerings on the altar. So the flour is put on existing offerings, which is how poorer people would participate in the atonement system. The idea of just offering flour without offering blood sacrifices—they never did it. You needed repentance and you needed the blood. That's the whole message of the new covenant to Jew and Gentile alike: turn in repentance toward God and put your trust in Jesus' atoning sacrifice. He's the 'Lamb of God who takes away the sins of the world.'"

Though Brown had answered my basic questions about the atonement system, one last issue was hanging. "Sacrificing animals seems like such a barbaric practice," I said. "These days the animal-rights folks would howl in protest."

"In the culture of the day it was perfectly normal to offer sacrifices as part of worship," came his response. "It was saying, 'I'm taking something valuable that I have and offering it up to God,' but ultimately

God was not interested in that. He was interested in something of massive eternal value, which is showing us how ugly sin is and how he was going to send a substitute. So for centuries and centuries—because it takes people a while to get the point—he kept giving the same lesson, until he finally sent the one who brought an end to the necessity of blood sacrifices."

The Fifth Evangelist

A significant part of Brown's case for Jesus being the Messiah hinges on the prophecies of Isaiah, who was so prolific in foreshadowing "the anointed one" that he has sometimes been called "the fifth evangelist," adding him alongside Gospel authors Matthew, Mark, Luke, and John.

"According to some counts, the New Testament has over four hundred allusions to [the Book of Isaiah], and parts of forty-seven chapters of Isaiah's sixty-six are either directly quoted or alluded to in the New Testament," Walter Kaiser said. "This means that Isaiah is second only to the book of Psalms as the favorite Old Testament book from which the early church drew its predictions of what happened to Christ."[62]

Of special interest is the description of the suffering servant in Isaiah 52:13 to 53:12, which has probably prompted more people to put their trust in Jesus as the Messiah than any other passage in scripture:[63]

> See, my servant will act wisely;
>   he will be raised and lifted up and highly exalted.
> Just as there were many who were appalled at him—
>   his appearance was so disfigured beyond that of any human
>   being
>   and his form marred beyond human likeness—
> so he will sprinkle many nations,
>   and kings will shut their mouths because of him.
> For what they were not told, they will see,
>   and what they have not heard, they will understand.
>
> Who has believed our message
>   and to whom has the arm of the LORD been revealed?
> He grew up before him like a tender shoot,
>   and like a root out of dry ground.

He had no beauty or majesty to attract us to him,
> nothing in his appearance that we should desire him.

He was despised and rejected by mankind,
> a man of sorrows, and familiar with pain.

Like one from whom people hide their faces
> he was despised, and we held him in low esteem.

Surely he took up our pain
> and bore our suffering,

yet we considered him punished by God,
> stricken by him, and afflicted.

But he was pierced for our transgressions,
> he was crushed for our iniquities;

the punishment that brought us peace was on him,
> and by his wounds we are healed.

We all, like sheep, have gone astray,
> each of us has turned to our own way;

and the LORD has laid on him
> the iniquity of us all.

He was oppressed and afflicted,
> yet he did not open his mouth;

he was led like a lamb to the slaughter,
> and as a sheep before its shearers is silent,
> so he did not open his mouth.

By oppression and judgment he was taken away.
> Yet who of his generation protested?

For he was cut off from the land of the living;
> for the transgression of my people he was punished.

He was assigned a grave with the wicked,
> and with the rich in his death,

though he had done no violence,
> nor was any deceit in his mouth.

Yet it was the LORD's will to crush him and cause him to suffer,
> and though the LORD makes his life an offering for sin,

he will see his offspring and prolong his days,
> and the will of the LORD will prosper in his hand.

After he has suffered,
  he will see the light of life and be satisfied;
by his knowledge my righteous servant will justify many,
  and he will bear their iniquities.
Therefore I will give him a portion among the great,
  and he will divide the spoils with the strong,
because he poured out his life unto death,
  and was numbered with the transgressors.
For he bore the sin of many,
  and made intercession for the transgressors.

"Isaiah 52:13 – 53:12 — how important is this passage?" I asked Brown.

"It's almost as if God said, 'I want to make it so absolutely clear Yeshua is the Messiah that it's undeniable,'" Brown declared. "I almost feel as if God would have to apologize to the human race and to the Jewish people for putting this passage into the scriptures when it so clearly points to Yeshua if he didn't really mean that."

With so much depending on these verses, I decided to raise some of the most frequent objections to its fulfillment in Jesus and see how Brown would respond.

Objections to Isaiah

Some commentators, I pointed out, say this description of the suffering servant applies to the people of Israel as a nation, not to an individual who is the Messiah. "Doesn't the passage actually deal with the return of the Jewish people from the Babylonian exile, which occurred more than five hundred years before Jesus was born?" I asked.

"That's the backdrop of many of the messianic prophecies," Brown said, quickly dismissing my comment about the exile.

"Early Jewish interpretations about Isaiah 53 are varied," Brown went on. "But nowhere in the classical, foundational, authoritative Jewish writings do we find the interpretation that this passage refers to the nation of Israel. References to the servant as a people actually end with Isaiah 48:20.

CHALLENGE #5: *"Jesus Was an Imposter Who Failed*   225
to Fulfill the Messianic Prophecies"

"Many traditional Jewish interpreters, from the Targum to today, had no problem seeing this passage as referring to the Messiah," he said. "They didn't have any difficulty interpreting it independently of the preceding context of the return from the Babylonian exile. By the sixteenth century, Rabbi Moshe Alshech said, 'Our rabbis with one voice accept and affirm the opinion that the prophet is speaking of the Messiah, and we shall ourselves also adhere to the same view.' So he was saying all his contemporaries agreed with the messianic reading —even though it must have been very tempting to deny this because by that time Christians had been claiming for centuries that this passage describes Yeshua."

"Why can't this passage refer to Israel as a whole?"

"Several reasons," he said. "The servant of the Lord is righteous and without guile and yet suffers terribly. If this is the nation of Israel, it's a complete violation of Torah. According to Torah, if the nation is righteous, then it will be blessed. If it's wicked, it'll be punished. The idea that the nation as a whole could be righteous and yet punished is completely unacceptable on a scriptural level."

"But in another chapter," I said, "the psalmist himself says Israel suffered at the hands of its enemies even though it was righteous."[64]

"Not so," he responded. "This is a prayer of the righteous remnant on behalf of the sinning nation. It's the small group of the godly—the righteous—who are interceding on behalf of the unrighteous, ungodly, suffering majority."

"Okay," I said, conceding the point. "I interrupted you—you said there were several reasons why this passage doesn't refer to the nation of Israel."

"Yes, the second reason is because the text says the servant will be highly exalted, even to where kings stand in awe. That's not true of Israel, but it is true of Yeshua, who's worshiped by kings and leaders around the world. Third, the passage offers the picture of a totally righteous, guileless servant of God. But nobody can point to a time when Israel, as a nation, had no deceit on its lips or was a righteous servant of God. And fourth, Isaiah says the servant's sufferings brought healing to the people. Now, has Israel suffered through the ages? Yes, but our sufferings did not bring healing to the nations that afflicted us."

"All right, this passage might refer to an individual—but it can't be Yeshua," I said.

"Why not?"

"Let me give you several reasons." I consulted the series of objections I had jotted on my clipboard. "First, the Isaiah passage says nobody was attracted to the servant of the Lord, but we know that Jesus attracted huge throngs to himself—thousands of people flocked to him at times."

"Actually, Isaiah 53 first refers to his origins, which were very lowly and inauspicious—'He grew up before him like a tender shoot, and like a root out of dry ground.' That's a consistent theme in the New Testament—'Can anything good come out of Nazareth? The carpenter's son? *Him?* How could this be?'[65]

"Isaiah says, 'He had no beauty or majesty to attract us to him,' and certainly there's nothing recorded about the appearance of Jesus that would contradict that. Besides, the crowds around Jesus were very fickle —they shouted, 'Crown him!' one day and "Crucify him!' the next. But the primary thrust of Isaiah 53 is his rejection, suffering, and death— at that time, he's utterly forsaken. Yeshua fulfills all of that very well."

"His death?" I said. "Critics claim that the passage doesn't specifically and unambiguously say the servant would die."

"There's an accumulation of words that are used," Brown said. "He's stricken by God, he's smitten, he's pierced, he's crushed, he's oppressed, he's afflicted, he's led like a lamb to the slaughter, he's taken away, he's cut off from the land of the living, he's assigned a grave, he poured out his life unto death, he's with the rich in his death—what are all those phrases referring to, if not the fact that he did truly die?"

"But what about the resurrection?" I pressed. "Show me where that word is used."

"It's not—but it's plainly implied," replied Brown. "How does someone die and yet 'prolong his days'? Clearly, the passage speaks of the servant's continued activities after his death. And there's only one explanation for that—resurrection!"

Who but Jesus?

Brown's answers seemed persuasive enough, but there were still other reasons why critics reject Isaiah 53's fulfillment in Jesus. For instance, while the Isaiah passage refers to the nonviolence of God's servant, the Gospels describe Jesus as using a whip to drive money-changers out of the temple.

"That sounds like a violent act that would get a person arrested today," I said. "Wouldn't that disqualify Jesus from being the Messiah?"

"When the Hebrew scriptures speak of violence, which in Hebrew is *hamas*, it's describing illegal aggression like murder, bloodshed, and robbery—none of which Yeshua ever committed," Brown said. "Jesus' nonviolence was so well known that Mahatma Gandhi and Martin Luther King Jr. modeled their nonviolent resistance after him. When Peter drew a sword and cut off the ear of one of the guards who came to arrest Jesus, he was rebuked by Jesus—who then healed the guard's ear."

While that was true, it seemed to me he was skirting the question. "Specifically, what about the temple cleansing?" I asked.

"As for the temple incident—or incidents, since there may have been two separate events—this was praiseworthy and motivated by zeal for God," Brown replied. "If he wanted to hurt someone, he would have used a sword, but instead he made a whip out of cords, which was apparently used for the animals. The money-changers only got a verbal rebuke for making the temple 'a den of robbers.'[66] There's no record of anyone being injured, and this incident wasn't even brought up at Jesus' trial, where nobody could accuse him of wrongdoing."

I raised yet another issue. "Isaiah 53 says the Lord's servant will not lift up his voice or cry out, yet Jesus cried out several times on the cross," I said.

"Again, let's look at the context," Brown said. "The passage says he did not open his mouth but was led away like a lamb to the slaughter. Interestingly, the New Testament specifically applies this text to Jesus.[67] All through his ordeal—his arrest, his trial, his flogging, his crucifixion—he doesn't try to defend himself, he doesn't protest, he doesn't fight: just like a lamb being led to the slaughter. He truly turns the other cheek, as he taught in the Sermon on the Mount.[68] Is he crying out when he says on the cross, 'Father, into your hands I commit my spirit'? Is he crying out when he says, 'Father, forgive them'? Or is that also being like a lamb? The point is, he never fought what was happening to him.'

I glanced down at my notes: only one significant objection remained. "Isaiah 53 says the servant of the Lord will have descendants—or 'see seed' in the Hebrew," I said. "Jesus never married or had children, so he can't be the Messiah, can he?"

Brown smiled at a memory. "A rabbi once told me in a debate that every single time the term 'see seed' exists in scripture, it specifically refers to physical progeny. The only hole in that argument is that this is the only time the idiom occurs!" Brown said with a laugh.

"The question is, can 'seed' be used metaphorically, in terms of spiritual offspring?" he asked. "Isaiah himself uses it that way in other chapters; for example, he calls Israel 'a seed of evildoers.'[69] If we follow a standard Hebrew lexicon, we see that 'seed of evildoers' would mean 'a community of evildoers' or 'evildoers to the core.'[70] In the context of Isaiah 53, 'seed' would mean the servant of the Lord would see godly, spiritual posterity, true disciples transformed by means of his labors on their behalf.

"Also, the Hebrew word for 'seed' can mean 'a future generation' without reference to specific descendants of one individual in particular. It's used this way in Psalm 22. In the context of Isaiah 53, this would mean the servant of the Lord would see future generations of his people serving the Lord. One more point," he added. "Isaiah 53 doesn't say he'll see *his* seed. That's important. So I think it's entirely appropriate to interpret this metaphorically."

"Overall, then, you feel like Isaiah 53 remains the passage with the most clarity—," I began, but Brown interrupted.

"With all due respect to those who come up with objections, they're really swatting at flies," he said. "Any time I can get someone to read this passage, I ask, 'Of whom does this speak?' If you can read it in Hebrew, all the better. You'd be amazed at the reaction. I remember one time showing it to a respectful Jewish man. He read it, got red in the face, and yelled out: *Jesus Christ!'* It was an expression of anger, but I thought, 'How ironic is that?'

"Because who but Jesus could it be describing?"[71]

Born of a Virgin?

One of the most controversial prophecies is found elsewhere in Isaiah. In his Gospel, Matthew points to Isaiah 7:14 as being fulfilled in Jesus: "Therefore the Lord himself will give you a sign: The virgin will conceive and give birth to a son, and will call him Immanuel," which means "God with us."[72]

But critics claim several flaws. First, they say the word Isaiah used to describe the mother, *'almah*, doesn't mean "virgin" —and if he had wanted to convey the idea of virginity, he would have used a better word: *betulah*. Second, they deny this is a messianic prophecy at all, but it referred to a sign that God gave King Ahaz of Judah some seven hundred years before Jesus' birth. Third, this prophecy can't refer to Jesus because he wasn't given the name Immanuel.

"Those are pretty tough issues," I said to Brown after summarizing the objections. "Did Matthew misinterpret this?"

"It's a tough passage," Brown conceded. "I've analyzed Isaiah in general and this passage in particular for thirty years."

"What's your conclusion?" I asked.

"That it's impossible to determine exactly what the prophecy meant to the original hearers when it was delivered."

I was a little relieved that it was as murky to others as it was to me. "What's the background of it?" I asked.

"The people of Judah were being threatened by the Israelites in the north, who were joined by the Arameans," Brown said. "Their intent was to seize Jerusalem and remove the reigning king, Ahaz, who was from the line of David. This was a frontal attack on the dynasty from which the Messiah would come.

"Unfortunately, Ahaz was a faithless ruler. The Lord sent the prophet Isaiah to reassure him that his enemies would be defeated if he would trust in God alone. He refused to stand firm in his faith. Isaiah told him to ask God for a sign to assure him, but Ahaz didn't. So God unilaterally provides him a sign: the *'almah* will give birth to a son and he will be called Immanuel. And incidentally, Ahaz was being addressed not simply as the king but as a representative of the house of David, and in two verses he was referred to in the plural, so Azah was not being addressed alone."

"How did Matthew see this promise?" I asked.

"I'm sure he didn't see it in isolation. I believe he read it in the broader context of Isaiah 7–11, one of the key prophetic sections that point toward Jesus as Messiah. In Isaiah 7, he is about to be born; in Isaiah 9, he is already born and declared 'mighty God,' the divine king; and in Isaiah 11 he is ruling and reigning in the supernatural power of the Spirit.

"As Matthew looked back at these prophecies, it would have been apparent that these chapters were linked together and that the promises of a worldwide, glorious reign of the promised Messiah were not yet realized. In chapter 8, Maher-Slalal-Hash-Baz is born. It seems that for Isaiah's contemporaries, this birth virtually took the place of the birth of Immanuel, leaving this important prophetic announcement without any record of fulfillment for more than seven hundred years."

Something didn't seem right to me. "If Immanuel's birth was supposed to be a sign for Ahaz," I said, "then it wouldn't make sense that it would refer to the birth of Jesus seven centuries later."

"That fails to account for a few things," said Brown. "First, this was a promise to the house of David as a whole, and promises to Davidic kings often had meaning beyond their own generations. Second, the birth of Maher-Slalal-Hash-Baz seems to take the place of the Immanuel prophecy in terms of the immediate historical context. Third, the prophecy is shrouded in obscurity, and so Matthew could legitimately examine it afresh and seek its deeper meaning."

"So you think Matthew's interpretation was legitimate?"

"Yes, I do," he said. "He sees the supernatural birth, this Immanuel figure, as part of a larger messianic complex of passages, and he applies this difficult part of scripture with genuine insight to Yeshua."

Immanuel: God with Us

"What about Isaiah's use of the Hebrew word *'almah?*" I asked. "Does
it mean 'virgin'?"

"To be precise, *'almah* really deals with youthfulness," Brown said.
"Four other times when the word is used elsewhere in the Old Testament, the New International Version doesn't translate it as 'virgin.'
However, the foremost Jewish commentator Rashi said, 'And some
interpret that this is the sign, that she was a young girl'—an *'almah*
—'and incapable of giving birth.' So he was acknowledging that some
Jewish experts interpreted the text to mean that God's sign to Ahaz had
to do with the highly unusual nature of the birth.[73] Here was a young
girl, an *'almah,* for whom giving birth would not be normal. The birth
itself was unusual or perhaps even supernatural.

"Also, it's significant that the Septuagint, the Greek translation
of the Jewish scriptures, translated *'almah* as *parthenos,* which is the
primary Greek word for 'virgin'—and this was a couple of hundred
years *before* Jesus was born. So it's not misquoted or misused. We know
sometimes Matthew used the Septuagint, so he's just quoting from the
Jewish translation of his day."

"What about the word *betulah,* which critics say Isaiah would have
used if he had truly meant virgin?"

"*Betulah* can refer to a virgin, but more often than not it simply
means a young woman or maiden. In fact, more than three out of
every five times the word occurs in the Old Testament, the most widely
used Jewish translation renders it 'maiden.' Joel 1:8 speaks of a *betulah*
mourning for the husband of her youth. An ancient Aramaic inscription speaks of a *betulah* who struggled in labor to give birth. So neither
'almah nor *betulah,* in and of themselves, would clearly and unequivo-
cally mean virgin. They're consistent with virginity, but there is no
single word in biblical Hebrew that always and only means virgin."

"What about the argument that Jesus was never called Immanuel?"
I asked.

"We know that Solomon was to be called Jedidiah, but he was never
referred to by that name in the Old Testament," Brown said.[74] "And let's
face it, Jesus is acknowledged as Immanuel—or 'God with us'—by

millions of people around the earth to this day. He's called Immanuel in hymns sung in churches around the world. Names were often symbolic. And in the deepest ultimate way, he *is* God with us.

"Again, I look at messianic prophecies and see some passages that are indisputable—they can be referring to no one but Jesus. Then you fill in the other details. This is an obscure prophecy in Isaiah 7:14. It's amazing the amount of diversity in the rabbinic commentaries about it. Matthew comes up with a tremendous insight to rightly apply it to Jesus. The miraculous nature of the sign ultimately becomes clear in light of its fulfillment in Jesus—who was actually born of a virgin—whatever the original expectations and understanding might have been."

"So it was not seen in its day as being a messianic prophecy?"

"I don't believe many prophecies were seen in their day as messianic in the sense of a future, yet to come, Messianic King," Brown said. "In other words, they were spoken with anticipation. In the ancient world, there was tremendous hope with each new king who came: the prophecies were going to be fulfilled. Then it failed to happen, but still the words were considered prophetic because the prophets were proven accurate in everything else. Now who's going to fulfill the prophecies? So they looked with anticipation toward the future. You could look at any unfulfilled promise given to a descendant of David that has universal implications as messianic. Any Davidic promise that transcends the generation and that remains unfulfilled is messianic."

I was looking for a way to wrap up this issue in my mind. "So is Isaiah 7:14 an explicit prophecy of the virgin birth seven hundred years in advance?" I asked.

"I don't read it like that," said Brown. "Is it a prophecy of a supernatural birth in the house of David of one called Immanuel, which was part of the larger complex of messianic prophecies that reach their fulfillment in the miraculous conception of Jesus? Absolutely."

The Righteous Sufferer

Psalm 22, the prayer of the righteous sufferer, has been cited by Christians for centuries as foreshadowing the crucifixion of Jesus. The description in the psalm, said one nineteenth-century Christian scholar, is even "more vivid" than the Gospels: it describes the piercing of the hands and feet, the stretching of the body until the "bones are out of joint," the intensity of the thirst, and the dividing of the victim's garments among his persecutors.[75]

The piercing of the hands and feet seems especially prescient, particularly since it was written hundreds of years before crucifixion was even implemented as a method of execution by the Romans.

Or was it?

Rabbi Tovia Singer has accused Christians of "deliberately mistranslating" this psalm to make it appear that it points toward Jesus on the cross. He said that while the King James Version renders the Hebrew as, "They pierced my hands and feet," this is actually "a not-too-ingenious Christian interpolation." The unadulterated Hebrew, he said, should be rendered, "Like a lion, they are at my hands and feet."[76]

"This is a serious allegation," I said to Brown. "Did Christians maliciously tamper with the text?"

Brown sat back. "It's fascinating that this verse isn't even quoted in the New Testament, even though other verses of Psalm 22 are," he replied.

"But do you consider this psalm to be messianic?" I asked.

"When he was on the cross, Jesus quoted the opening line from Psalm 22: 'My God, my God, why have you forsaken me?'" replied Brown. "By doing so, he was applying the psalm to himself. The psalm describes the righteous sufferer, publicly mocked and shamed, brought down to the jaws of death in the midst of terrible suffering and humiliation, and miraculously delivered by God, to the praise of his name. So it applies powerfully to Jesus, the ideal righteous sufferer."

"The psalm," I noted, "is written by David in the first person."

"Many events in David's life were repeated in the life of the Messiah, since David was in many ways the prototype of the Messiah," said Brown. "In fact, a famous rabbinic midrash, or commentary, that was written some twelve hundred years ago, makes the point that David was speaking of the Messiah's sufferings."[77]

Brown picked up a copy of his book from the desk and thumbed to a quote from Old Testament scholar James E. Smith, which he read to me:

No Old Testament person could have imagined that his personal deliverance from death could be the occasion for the world's conversion. Such a hope must be restricted to the future Redeemer. Under inspiration of the Holy Spirit, David in Psalm 22 saw his descendant resembling, but far surpassing, himself in suffering. Furthermore, the deliverance of this descendant would have meaning for all mankind.[78]

"What other person's terrible suffering and death was worthy of worldwide attention to the point that the nations actually turned to the God of Israel because of it?" Brown asked. "Applying this psalm to the Messiah is in keeping with the clear meaning of the text."

I brought Brown back to my question about the alleged mistranslation. "Did Christians doctor the Hebrew to make it say 'pierced my hands and feet' instead of 'like a lion, they are at my hands and feet'?"

"This is definitely not a Christian fabrication," he said firmly. "The oldest Jewish translation—the Septuagint—translated it as, 'they pierced.' The oldest Hebrew copy of the Psalms we possess, from the Dead Sea Scrolls, dating back to the century before Jesus, uses the Hebrew verb *ka'aru*, which comes from the root meaning 'to bore through'—not *ka'ari*, which means 'like a lion.' The same with about a dozen medieval Masoretic manuscripts, which are *the* authoritative texts on traditional Jewish thought. But let me tell you why this really doesn't matter."

"Why?" I asked.

"Because let's make the assumption that the correct translation is, 'like a lion at my hands and feet.' What is this lion doing with the victim's hands and feet—*licking them?*" His voice was thick with sarcasm.

"Rashi says it means 'as though they are crushed in a lion's mouth.' Another prominent Jewish commentator, Metsudat David, said, 'They crush my hands and my feet as the lion crushes the bones of the prey in its mouth.' So the imagery is clear: the metaphorical lions are tearing and ripping at the sufferer's hands and feet. This mauling and biting graphically portray great physical agony.

"Would this contradict the picture of a crucifixion? In no way. It's entirely consistent with what occurs in a crucifixion. So either translation could be said to foreshadow the suffering of the Messiah. But the bottom line is there's no Christian tampering with the text, just honest efforts to accurately translate the Hebrew, where only one character determines the difference between *ka'aru*, or 'pierced,' and *ka'ari*, or 'like a lion.'"

"God's Very Best"

The stunning picture of the righteous sufferer in Psalm 22, the haunting portrait of the suffering servant in Isaiah 53, the prophecies that had to be fulfilled before the second temple's demise, the bloody sacrificial system that presaged the lamb of God—all of it, down to the predicted details of the priestly king and his ancestry and his birthplace and his crucifixion and his ongoing worldwide influence, was too eerily accurate to be the product of happenstance or manipulation.

How else could I account for dozens of detailed predictions miraculously coming true in the life of only one individual In all of history? The facts forced me to conclude that the messianic prophecies are an incredible affirmation of the supernatural nature of the Bible and the identity of Jesus being the redeemer of Israel and the world. The most recent objections, propagated on the Internet and in "anti-missionary" literature, simply failed to overturn the powerful case for him having fulfilled the ancient predictions against all odds.

"I think it would be mathematically impossible for anyone else ever to fulfill all these parameters of prophecy in the Old Testament any better than Jesus did," said noted ancient history professor Paul Maier.[79]

Walter Kaiser, the prominent Old Testament expert and author of thirty books, including *The Messiah in the Old Testament*, said that "a straightforward understanding and application" of the Hebrew text "leads one straight to the Messiah and to Jesus of Nazareth."[80] Declared Norman Geisler: "All the evidence points to Jesus as the divinely appointed fulfillment of the Messianic prophecies. He was God's man, confirmed by God's signs."[81]

Since the facts inexorably lead to Jesus, one more topic begged to be addressed. I had to ask Brown: "Given the depth and breadth of the

prophecies—given the compelling portrayal of Jesus in Isaiah 53 alone
—why don't more Jewish people come to faith in him?"

Brown had heard the question many times before. "There are several answers," he began. "For the most part, many Jewish people simply don't examine the issue. Religious Jews are engaged in the biblical text, but they don't spend most of their time looking at the prophets; instead, they study the Talmud and rabbinic traditions. They're not looking in the right place to find Yeshua. But many Jews today are not even following God in a devoted way. There's a general lack of God-consciousness. Also, there's a price to pay if a Jewish person decides to follow Jesus: they could be ostracized from their family and community. And another reason, unfortunately, is the barrier put up by anti-Semitism in the past."

That remark stopped me cold. "Do you think Christians are generally oblivious to the history of anti-Semitism and Christianity?" I asked.

"Yes, often they are—for good reason: they haven't seen it, and it isn't in their hearts," he replied. "With almost no exception, the Christians I've met around the world have a special attachment to Jewish people and Israel. So the history of anti-Semitism is very much unknown for that positive reason—but there's also a bad reason."

"Which is ...?"

"Many Christians today, especially evangelicals, don't have a sense of history. They'll quote Martin Luther left and right, but they won't talk about the horrific things he wrote that Adolph Hitler adopted, like his 1543 tractate *Concerning the Jews and Their Lies*, where he recommended, among other things, that synagogues be burned, Jewish homes destroyed, and rabbis forbidden to teach under the threat of death.[82] They'll quote the powerful preaching of John Chrysostom a thousand years before Luther, but they won't mention his seven sermons against the Jews, where he said, 'I hate the Jews,' called them 'possessed by the devil,' and said the Jewish religion is 'a disease.'[83]

"Someone once said that those pages of history that Jews have memorized, Christians have torn out of their history books. There's no denying these things occurred, but they were a complete and horrible aberration that, unfortunately, have been used to keep many Jews away from Jesus."

My heart sank at the prospect of anyone being repelled from seeking out the real Jesus because of atrocities perpetrated by those who claimed to follow him but who, by their repugnant behavior and attitudes, betrayed his most fundamental teachings.

"What can be done about it?" I asked.

"There was a Scottish Presbyterian conference 150 years ago where they were asking the question, 'To reach out to the Jews, what's the most pressing need?'"

"What was the answer?"

"More tears," Brown said somberly. "And I still believe that remains a pressing issue—more tears. It's essential that, as followers of Jesus, we repudiate these aberrations of history and tell Jewish people, 'Allow us to show you who Yeshua really is and what he really teaches.'"

I recalled a comment made by a mutual acquaintance, Rabbi Shmuley Boteach, who once told me Christianity is "a beautiful religion for Christians," but it's just not for Jews. "Can Jesus be the Messiah for Christians but not for others?" I asked Brown.

"That would be a complete contradiction of all of Jesus' claims," he replied, shaking his head. "He's either the Messiah of everyone or the Messiah of no one. To say the New Testament is beautiful but Jesus is not the Jewish Messiah—well, it's filled with fabrications and fantasies then. Christians are deluded in believing he died for the sins of the world and rose from the dead. Either he did or he didn't.

"Thankfully, over the last century there's been a great recovery of Jews saying, 'I worship the God of Israel, I worship the Messiah of Israel in light of the new covenant, and Torah is written on my heart.' In fact, many Jews who were secular have become appreciative of their heritage and background because of faith in Jesus. That trite saying—'Jesus made me kosher'—actually has a lot of truth to it."

"And what about for you, personally?" I said. "Who's the real Jesus to you?"

Brown glanced off to the side, collecting his thoughts, and then looked back at me. He was no longer methodically building a case; now, in a tone that blended gratitude with conviction, the words flowed almost poetically. I couldn't think of a better way to cap our time together.

"Yeshua is the right continuation of my Jewish roots," Brown said. "He's the Messiah of Israel and the savior of the world. He's the one to whom I owe my life, and through him I've come to know God. He is the one who provided me complete forgiveness of sins, who loved me when I was a miserable, ungrateful, rebellious, proud wretch. He put a new heart and a new spirit within me; he has turned my life around and given it meaning. He's the fullness of God in bodily form. He's the very expression and image of the Father—in seeing him, I see and know God.

"And he's the only hope of the world. Outside of him, all we see is darkness. He's the hope of Israel. Israel will run out of options and finally in the end recognize that the one that it thought was the source of all its pain and suffering through the years actually is its only hope.

"He's the beginning and end, the all in all. I cannot imagine existence outside of him. I cannot imagine truth outside of him. I can't imagine purpose in life outside of him. So really he is the ultimate expression of God to the human race. That's why I'm spending my life talking to Jewish people—as compassionately and accurately as I can—about the reality of Jesus the Messiah.

"I just can't withhold God's very best from those he dearly loves."

For Further Investigation
More Resources on This Topic

Brown, Michael L. *Answering Jewish Objections to Jesus.* Vol. 1, *General and Historical Objections.* Grand Rapids, Mich.: Baker, 2000.

———. *Answering Jewish Objections to Jesus.* Vol. 2, *Theological Objections.* Grand Rapids, Mich.: Baker, 2000.

———. *Answering Jewish Objections to Jesus.* Vol. 3, *Messianic Prophecy Objections.* Grand Rapids, Mich.: Baker, 2003.

———. *Answering Jewish Objections to Jesus.* Vol. 4, *New Testament Objections.* Grand Rapids, Mich.: Baker, 2006.

Kaiser, Walter C., Jr. *The Messiah in the Old Testament.* Grand Rapids, Mich.: Zondervan, 1995.

Smith, James E. *What the Bible Teaches about the Promised Messiah.* Nashville: Nelson, 1993.

Wright, Christopher J. H. *Knowing Jesus through the Old Testament.* Downer's Grove, Ill.: InterVarsity, 1995.

"People Should Be Free to Pick and Choose What to Believe about Jesus"

Designer God: In a Mix-and-Match World, Why Not Create Your Own Religion?

Headline of cover story in *Utne Reader*[1]

Americans write their own Bible. They fashion their own God, then talk incessantly about him.

Hanna Rosin, *Washington Post*[2]

Wendi was forced to go to Sunday school as a youngster, but she never believed what she heard. Years later, after a miscarriage, she wanted to know what happened to the unborn baby's soul. "I explored Christianity, but I didn't get any answers that satisfied me," she said. So she took a class in metaphysics, where she learned about life after death, intuition, and other intriguing topics.

Now the motivational speaker and life coach has created her own belief system, patching together bits and pieces from Christianity, Buddhism, paganism, metaphysics, and a lot from the Tao-te Ching, which teaches that everything is made of energy. "I take what resonates with me from each religion," she said. Her criterion for picking and choosing elements is based on "what works."

Moral codes? "Just religion's excuse to judge other people." Ethical behavior? "I don't believe in right or wrong. It just is. If it feels like something that I should do, then I'll do it." The afterlife? "There isn't some man in the sky waiting to send you to hell every time you do something wrong. And there is no Santa Claus sitting, waiting to reward you for doing good things, either."

Tolerance is an overriding virtue. "I believe everybody's belief system is right for them," she said. "Mine is right for me, yours is right for you, my mom's is right for her, and so on. I don't believe in judging each other the way that I see happening in Christianity and other religions." Rather than trying to convert anyone to her beliefs, she helps others find their own personal god or goddess.[3]

For Ed and Joanne, years of Catholic education only made them more neurotic rather than teaching them how to cope. So like Wendi, they've cobbled together their own religion. They decided to keep Jesus, because he's "big on love," and then they mixed in elements from popular Zen and New Age authors. The concept of hell was quickly jettisoned. "That's just something they say to scare you," according to Ed. Said a *Washington Post* article on their self-fashioned spirituality:

> Now they commune with a new God, a gentle twin of the one they grew up with. He is wise but soft-spoken, cheers them up when they're sad, laughs at their quirks. He is, most essentially, validating, like the greatest of friends. And best of all, he had been there all along. "We discovered the God within," said Joanne. "That's why we need God. Because we are God. God gives me the ability to create my own godliness."[4]

For many seekers, the quest for spiritual answers doesn't take them down the path toward a high-tech suburban megachurch or the liturgy of a mainline denomination. They're not interested in what a black-robed clergyman tells them they should believe—after all, why should his opinions trump anyone else's?

"People have shifted religious authority away from creeds, traditions, and churches and assumed it themselves," said James R. Edwards of Whitworth College. "People are less inclined today to defer to established religious authorities, and more inclined to express their own religious preferences."[5]

Increasingly, people seeking religious input draw more from the Internet than from church history, more from their own intuition than formal study. They stress sincerity over doctrinal specifics. They feel untethered to their religious upbringing and are more than willing to interpret Jesus in a fresh light for a new generation. According to a 2005 survey by CBS, 38 percent of Americans say the search for spirituality — no matter where that takes them — is more important than sticking to the traditions of their church.[6]

"This tendency to mix elements of different traditions into new hybrid forms will continue in the new millennium, as seekers separated from their religious heritage search out new expressions of faith," Richard Cimino and Don Lattin wrote in their examination of American spirituality called *Shopping for Faith.* "Brand name religion is on the wane. The wide range of spiritual texts and self-help books comprise an endless menu of spiritual teachings that can be selected and combined to suit individual needs."[7]

Do-It-Yourself Spirituality

When you wed the American independent streak with a postmodern skepticism toward institutions, you set the stage for what theologians call "syncretism," which is the blending of elements from various faiths into a new form of spirituality. Like grazing at the buffet table at a sumptuous banquet, syncretists adopt doctrines that seem appropriate to them and leave behind others that they regard as offensive or outdated. Orthodoxy becomes "flexidoxy."

The CBS survey disclosed that 36 percent of Americans combine the teachings of more than one religion into their own faith.[8] Thus, Los Angeles Lakers basketball coach Phil Jackson calls himself "a Zen Christian," while a well-known actress once identified herself as a Christian who is "into goddess worship." One Presbyterian minister described how he was taken aback when a woman introduced herself to him by saying, "I'm a Presbyterian Buddhist."[9]

"It's an eclectic approach," said Lynn Garrett, who tracks religious trends in the book industry. "People borrow ideas from different traditions, then add them to whatever religion they're used to. But they don't want anything to do with organized religion."[10]

Indeed, the attitude of many Americans is that they like Jesus but not the church, which they see as exclusivistic, condemning, intolerant, and intent on strapping people into a straitjacket of rigid dogma. But the Jesus they like may look very different from the historical Jesus. If the traditional church imagines Jesus as a finely painted portrait, then syncretists often render him as abstract art—many times to the point where he's unrecognizable from the Jesus of ancient creeds.

For syncretists, that's okay. Many of them find their Jesus more satisfying than the judgmental Jesus they learned about in Sunday school. Besides, they assert, who's to say which Jesus is more "real" than the other? If history is all based on someone's interpretation, then nobody can be certain who Jesus was and what he taught anyway. In this age when "you have your truth and I have mine," the important issue becomes what "works" for each individual life.

"What seems to have happened is that the concept of a personal God or of a historical Jesus has been replaced by an *idea* of God or of Jesus," said Edwards. "And like any idea—that of freedom of speech, for example—ideas of God and Jesus can be interpreted differently."[11]

When looking through the kaleidoscope of syncretism, the image of Jesus is broken up into all sorts of new and exciting colors and shapes. Freed from belief in an absolute truth, syncretists graft elements of Native American religion, Eastern philosophies, Jewish mysticism, or pre-Christian paganism onto his identity. What emerges is a Jesus customized for their worldview—a designer Jesus.

Thomas Jefferson is a good example. A skeptic toward the supernatural, he used a razor blade to excise references in the Gospels about Jesus' miracles, deity, and resurrection, leaving behind only his moral teachings. This radically altered view of Jesus matched Jefferson's philosophy perfectly. "I'm a sect myself," he said—a church of one.

Today, Oprah Winfrey is the queen of syncretism. She grew up in Faith United Mississippi Baptist Church, where she garnered the nickname "Miss Jesus," and attended Chicago's progressive Trinity United Church of Christ for a while as an adult. But she has embraced and endorsed so many religious trends through the years that one journalist said, "It's almost impossible to answer this simple question: What does Oprah believe?"[12] Marcia Nelson, who wrote a book on Winfrey's spirituality, observed, "The gospel according to Oprah doesn't appear to require some kind of doctrinal commitment."[13]

Said journalist David Ian Miller:

America has a long history of do-it-yourself spirituality going back at least as far as Ralph Waldo Emerson and the Transcendentalists. And that desire to "roll your own religion" shows no sign of fading away. A September 2005 *Newsweek* poll found eight in ten Americans do not believe any one faith is the sole path to salvation. So it's no surprise that some are weaving together strands from a variety of faiths to create their own personal religions.[14]

All of this sounds appealing to many people. What could be wrong with Wendi's nonjudgmental approach and her willingness to grant everyone the freedom to personally fashion a faith to fit themselves? Why shouldn't Ed and Joanne be able to accept the love of Jesus while overlooking his teachings about hell? Why can't people follow what's in their heart without condemning others who believe differently? Certainly that would seem to be helpful in calming tensions between world religions.

In the end, isn't a person's sincerity more important than whether he or she adheres to every clause in a denominational statement of faith? As Winfrey asked, "Does God care about your heart or whether you called his Son Jesus?"[15]

My wife and I were chatting about these sorts of issues in my office one Saturday afternoon. The particularly apt title of a book, crowded among many others on my shelves, caught her eye: *True for You, but Not for Me*.

She pulled it out and perused it. "Maybe you ought to talk to the person who wrote this," she suggested as she closed the book and handed it to me.

I was familiar with the author, Paul Copan, chair of philosophy and ethics at Palm Beach Atlantic University. Now that Leslie had mentioned him, I recalled that he's among the leading experts in this area. "That's a good idea," I said — and within days I had made arrangements to fly to Florida and meet with him in his offices in West Palm Beach.

INTERVIEW #6: Paul Copan, PhD

Tall and slender, his light brown hair neatly parted on the side, Paul Copan looks considerably younger than his forty-four years. A father of five, with a low-key and self-effacing manner, Copan is engaging, easygoing, and erudite in conversation. He's equally at home speaking with college students or interacting with the intellectual elite in philosophy of religion, having edited books with contributions by conservative scholars Craig Evans, Ben Witherington III, and Alister McGrath; liberals John Dominic Crossan, Marcus Borg, and Roy Hoover; Jewish intellectuals Jacob Neusner and Herb Basser; and skeptic Gerd Lüdemann.

After graduating *cum laude* with a master's degree in philosophy of religion from Trinity International University (thesis topic: "The Impossibility of an Infinite Temporal Regress of Events"), Copan earned his doctorate in philosophy from Marquette University. He has taught at Trinity and Bethel seminaries, worked alongside well-known Christian apologist Ravi Zacharias, and is a member of half a dozen professional philosophy societies. He has authored scores of articles and reviews for philosophical journals and lectured at a number of notable institutions, including Harvard, Boston College, State University of New York, and Moscow State University.

Copan has written and edited nearly a dozen books. *True for You, but Not for Me* isn't the only one relevant to the topic I wanted to discuss with him. He has also authored *That's Just Your Interpretation, How Do You Know You're Not Wrong?* and *Loving Wisdom: Christian Philosophy of Religion.* He coedited *The Rationality of Theism, Who Was Jesus? A Jewish-Christian Discussion, Jesus' Resurrection: Fact or Figment, Philosophy: Christian Approaches in the New Millennium,* and *Science: Christian Approaches in the New Millennium.*

Though his five children consume much of his free time, Copan also has been involved with an all-volunteer organization that raises funds for micro-enterprise development loans in such countries as Nigeria, Peru, India, Mexico, Thailand, and Haiti.

We sat down at a round wooden table in the corner of his office, flanked by floor-to-ceiling shelves teeming with books. Random traffic noises from a downtown street, including the occasional moan of a delivery truck, leaked into the room. I started with a broad question to lay the foundation for our discussion. As I did so, I thought of Pontius Pilate's question two millennia ago: "What is truth?"[16]

It's All Relative

"We're living in a postmodern era in which concepts like 'truth' and 'morality' are more elastic than in the past," I said to Copan. "How do you define postmodernism?"

Immediately, I noticed something about Copan: he's an intense listener. He concentrates with laser-beam focus on whatever topic is being raised. After mulling over my question for a few moments, he offered a brief historical perspective on the issue.

"First, it's helpful to know what modernism involves," Copan said. "Modernism can be traced back to René Descartes, the seventeenth-century French philosopher who is famous for his pursuit of certainty. Even though he was a committed Roman Catholic, he displaced God as the starting point for knowledge, replacing him with the individual knower who can find certainty on his own.

"Descartes said that one thing he couldn't doubt was that he was thinking, so his starting point for knowledge became, 'I think, therefore, I am.' There was a sense in which you had to have a hundred-percent certainty or you can't know something," Copan continued. "Later, Georg Wilhelm Friedrich Hegel offered huge explanatory systems that attempted to put everything into neat packages.

"So postmodernism is a reaction to Descartes's quest for certainty and to the creation of systems like rationalism, romanticism, Marxism, Nazism, or scientism. These systems tend to oppress people who disagree with those in power—the Jews under Nazism and the capitalists under Marxism, for example. French philosopher Jean-François Lyotard said that, simplifying to the extreme, postmodernism is suspicion toward a metanarrative, which is a 'world story' that's taken to be true for all people in all cultures and which ends up oppressing people."

I was thinking through the implications as he was talking. "The idea, then, is that certainty leads to oppression?" I asked.

"When people are so certain that they've got the truth and believe their system explains everything, then people who disagree with them are on the outside. They end up in Auschwitz or the Soviet gulags," he said. "So instead of metanarratives, postmodernism emphasizes mini-narratives. In other words, each person has his or her own viewpoint or story."

"And each viewpoint is as valid as any other," I said, more of an observation than a question.

"That's the postmodern view, yes. Each person has his own narrative, and who's to say anyone is wrong? Postmodernism celebrates diversity. Postmoderns approach certainty and objectivity by pointing out that we're finite and limited. We're limited by our cultural and family background, our place in history, and our personal biases. We're not totally objective or neutral. There's a suspicion toward sweeping truth claims, which are seen as power-grabbing: whoever is in charge can say 'this is true' and then back it up by oppressing those who disagree."

"And suspicion of truth contributes to relativism," I commented.

"Right. To the relativist, no fact is true in all times and all places. *Objective relativism* says that the beliefs of a person are 'true' for him but not necessarily for anyone else. No truth is objectively true or false. This means that one person's 'truth,' which really amounts to his opinion, can directly conflict with another person's 'truth' and still be valid.

"*Religious relativism* says one religion can be true for one person or culture but not for another. No religion provides a metanarrative or 'big picture' for everyone. No religion is universally or exclusively true. You can have your kind of Jesus and I can have mine; it doesn't matter if our views contradict each other. *Moral relativism* says there's no universal right and wrong. Moral values are true — or 'genuine' — for some but not for others. Since there are different expressions of morality in the world, there's no reason to think that one viewpoint is any more true than any other."

I searched my mind for an example. "So adultery can be okay for some people but not for others?" I asked.

"In the view of the moral relativist, yes," he replied. "Something is wrong only if you *feel* it's wrong. Now, relativists may not *approve* of adultery and may even have strong reservations about it. But they'll say, 'Who am I to say someone else is wrong?'

"Then there's *historical relativism*, which says we can't know for sure what happened in the past, so we're merely left with differing opinions or interpretations of these events. As the saying goes, 'You've got your truth, I've got mine.' "

Even his cursory survey of relativism was enough to surface a host of obvious problems. "What are the greatest shortcomings of relativism?" I asked.

"Relativism falls apart logically when you examine it. As a worldview, it simply doesn't work," he said.

I was looking for specifics. "Tell me why," I said.

"For instance, the relativist believes that relativism is true not just for him but for *every* person. He believes that relativism applies to the nonrelativist ('true for *you*'), not just to himself ('true for me'). The relativist finds himself in a bind if we ask him, 'Is relativism *absolutely* true for everyone?' If he says yes, then he contradicts himself by holding to an absolute relativism, which would be an oxymoron. To be consistent, the relativist must say, 'Nothing is objectively true, including my own relativistic position, so you're free to accept my view or reject it.'

"There's no reason to take seriously the claim that every belief is as good as every other belief, since this belief itself would be no better than any other. If we do take it seriously, it becomes self-refuting, because it claims to be the one belief everyone should hold to. The claims of the relativist are like saying, 'I can't speak a word of English,' or, 'All generalizations are false.' His statements are self-contradictory. They self-destruct under examination."

Even so, I knew that there must be reasons why postmodernism has taken root. "Are there aspects of postmodernism that make sense to you?" I asked.

"Despite some of its own incoherencies, yes, there are some lessons we can learn from it," he said. "For example, we *do* have our limitations, biases, and perspectives. We should admit that. Also, the culturally or politically powerful—even the religious—many times *do* try to spin the truth to suit their own agenda. And metanarratives often *do* alienate and marginalize outsiders—although I should note that Christianity teaches the intrinsic value of every individual, including the disfranchised. Finally, the quest for absolute certainty in every area of life *is* impossible — but I have to add that it's also unnecessary."

"What do you mean by that last statement?"

"We can know many things — like the expansion of the universe or that various planets orbit the sun — even if we don't have a hundred-percent certainty. Between absolute, mathematical certainty and utter skepticism are degrees of knowledge — the highly plausible, the probable, and the reasonable, for instance. We rely on these standards every day. Certain beliefs are more plausible or likely than others. We can know *truly,* even if we don't know exhaustively or with absolute certainty."

The Truth about Truth

I went back to the infamous question posed by Pilate two thousand years ago. "What *is* truth?" I asked.

I was expecting a complex answer laden with philosophical jargon. Instead, Copan's definition was surprisingly straightforward: "I think people instinctively understand that truth is a belief, story, ideal, or statement that matches up with reality or corresponds to the way things really are."

When I asked him for an example, he said, "If I say the moon is made of cheese, that's false because there isn't a correspondence, or a match-up, with the way things really are. Or consider an event in history: Martin Luther wrote out his ninety-five theses in 1517. That's factually true, and to disagree with that would mean that you believe something that's false.

"Something is true — or corresponds to reality — even if people don't believe it. I often use the example of the earth being round even when people thought it was flat. Some people have said to me, 'Well, wasn't the earth flat for them at that time?' I say, 'No, the earth was *still* round. It wasn't as though people could fall over the edge of the earth and be swallowed by dragons back then. The earth was round, even if people didn't believe it.'"

"So truth is true even if people don't acknowledge it," I said, cementing his point in my mind.

"That's right. In fact, truth is true even if no one knows it, admits it, agrees with it, follows it, or even fully grasps it."

"Some people," I observed, "believe that whatever *works* for them is true."

"Yes, that's the pragmatic view," he said, nodding in acknowledgment. "The problem is that people can have beliefs that are 'useful,' maybe temporarily and for certain ends, but they may be completely false. And some things can be true—like the temperature at the North Pole—even though they don't help us in any way. So truth isn't merely what works.

"On the other hand, the pragmatist does have a point when he asks, 'Can my beliefs be lived out practically?' If not, then it's highly likely that the view isn't true. What is true *can* be lived out consistently—there doesn't have to be a mismatch between 'theory' and 'practice.'

"Another view of truth is called coherence," he continued. "This means that our beliefs must have internal consistency. In other words, our beliefs cohere in a kind of web or fit together like a puzzle. Now, coherence is important. If something is incoherent, it can't be true. But coherence, *by itself,* isn't enough to determine if something is true."

"Why not?"

"Look individually at Buddhism and Christianity," he said. "They both have an internal coherence, right?"

"That's right," I replied.

"Yet both of them can't be true," he said. "The Buddhist rejects the existence of God, while the Christian embraces the existence of God. So by itself, internal coherence isn't enough: we have to ask whether either of these views matches up with reality. Coherence is an important component of truth, but it doesn't constitute truth. It's not *all* that there is to truth.

"Ultimately, any theory of truth is going to correspond with reality. Something true is like a socket wrench that matches up to a bolt—there's a fit. And truth isn't merely propositional. Look at the person of Jesus. When he said he's the truth in John 14:6, there was a correspondence with reality. There was a match-up: He was faithfully and authentically representing to us who God is. He was the revelation of God, and he genuinely lived out what human beings are supposed to be before God."

I was reminded of a quote I had come across in my research. I searched through my notes until I found the words of New Testament scholar Andreas J. Köstenberger and read them to Copan:

> The very notion of truth has largely become a casualty of post-modern thought and discourse. Truth is no longer "the" truth, in Jesus' terms who claimed to be "the truth." Rather it is conceived of as "your" truth or "my" truth — that is, different yet equally legitimate ways of perceiving reality. Hence truth is simply one's preferred, culturally conditioned, socially constructed version of reality.[17]

Copan was listening carefully as I read. "I agree with his analysis," he said. "Ultimately, it comes down to a theological question: Can there be an authoritative viewpoint? To put it in Christian terms, is there the possibility of a special revelation in which God speaks authoritatively for all times and all cultures? Can God break onto the scene and offer a way to know truth with confidence?"

He allowed the question to hang in the air for a moment, then added: "Not only do I believe he *can*, but I believe he *has*."

The "Yuck Factor"

While intrigued with the direction our conversation was taking, there were other topics I wanted to be sure we covered. Shifting the emphasis of my questions, I told Copan about Wendi and read her quote: "I don't believe in right or wrong. It just is. If it feels like something that I should do, then I'll do it." Turning to Copan, I asked, "What's the role of feelings in terms of what's true or false, right or wrong?"

"Feelings can be tricky," Copan began. "A person may say, 'I need to be true to myself by following my feelings' — and then run off with his secretary. Such people use their feelings to rationalize immoral behavior. The problem, of course, is that feelings are only one aspect of who we are. The capacity to feel is a God-given gift — but so is the capacity to think, to act in a morally responsible way, to discipline ourselves, and, by God's grace, to shape our character into something better than it presently is. If we follow only our feelings, then we're being false to *all* of who we are and what we were designed to be."

"Still," I countered, "there *is* a role for feelings."

"Absolutely. Feelings and intuition have their place. For instance, there's the 'yuck factor.'"

"The what?"

"The 'yuck factor' is when we don't even have to think through certain issues. We have a strong visceral revulsion against, say, rape or child abuse. We don't hem and haw by saying, 'Oh, well, maybe rape is right in some contexts.' We know immediately, on a gut level, that rape is wrong. This is evidence that there are objective moral values that aren't the product of sociobiological evolution. They are valid and binding for everyone, not just for some cultures. And we should take intuitions about these moral values—the 'yuck factor'—seriously.

"In Romans 2, Paul says that even though Gentiles weren't given the law of Moses, their conscience bears witness, alternately accusing or else defending them, because the law has been placed in their hearts.[18] There is this moral law, and people with a well-functioning conscience can get a lot of things right.

"As one author put it, there are things we can't *not* know. We'd have to suppress our conscience not to know those things—and that's exactly what Romans 1 is talking about, that people may suppress the truth in unrighteousness.[19] They may even use 'reason' to avoid certain moral implications for their own lives, but they themselves recognize that there's a degree of self-deception going on for them to weasel out from those moral commitments."

"So we can use our feelings to justify virtually any behavior, even though deep down we often have a sense that we're doing something wrong," I said.

"Yes, that can certainly happen," he said. "We have to remember as well that our feelings can't change objective reality. Following our feelings wherever they go doesn't change who we are as human beings or how we were designed to function, and it doesn't make certain things true or right.

"For example, what happens when feelings conflict? If you have a Jew in Nazi Germany who has certain feelings and you've got Hitler who has feelings the other way, then the person with the greater power wins out. But that doesn't make his actions right."

A Mix-and-Match Jesus

I told Copan how the stories of Wendi, Ed, and Joanne were good examples of the way many people today feel comfortable in customizing their own religious beliefs. "It seems like a lot of people are trying to free themselves from the straitjacket of religious dogma and create their own Jesus by picking and choosing what they want from Christianity and other faiths," I said. "What's wrong with creating our own Jesus to suit our own needs?"

"We should clarify that Christianity isn't primarily about subscribing to a set of doctrines. Christianity is focused on the *person* of Christ. We're called into a relationship, not simply to believe a set of doctrines," he noted.

"The scriptures are basically a narrative of God's interaction with humankind. If we lose this notion of God's desire for relationship with human beings, we're in danger of losing the heart of the Christian faith. Doctrines, of course, will flow from that, but when the scriptures call us to *believe*, we're being called to put our trust in *someone*, not just agree with a bunch of doctrine. Demons could do that. We are to commit ourselves to Christ.

"I'd also like to know what people mean by 'dogma.' When a person rejects dogma, does this mean that he has no convictions about reality, about God, about salvation? I'd ask those who reject dogma or doctrine—what do you live by? Is there anything you think is worth dying for? If there's nothing worth dying for, is there anything worth living for? Often, people reject Christian dogma or doctrines because they disagree with them—and then they end up adopting their own set of dogmatic beliefs. So why choose one set of dogmas over another?

"But I want to bring it back to the personal," Copan continued. "The apostle Paul in 2 Corinthians 11:3 commends a pure and simple devotion to Christ. The Corinthians had lofty aspirations of a sophisticated faith, but that can result in pride and arrogance that diminishes devotion to Jesus. Paul was trying to get them back to the basics. Jesus put it very simply: '"Love the Lord your God with all your heart and with all your soul and with all your strength and with all your mind"; and, "Love your neighbors as yourself."'[20] Everything hangs on that. Yes, there will be dogma attached to those things—true doctrines that we ought to believe in light of God's existence and his relationship to human beings. But Jesus simplified it for us: Love God and love your neighbor."

"What about this tendency to pick and choose aspects of other faiths and incorporate them into Christianity?" I asked.

"Well, if we *do* love God, then we want to follow his teachings. If Jesus *is* God's unique revelation to us, then we want to follow what he said and did. So certain doctrines flow naturally from that: Jesus' divinity, his death for our salvation, his resurrection, his command that we live righteous lives, and so forth. We shouldn't be trying to create our own Jesus or our own set of doctrines, because then we are denying reality. Jesus reflects reality, so we need to align ourselves with him."

"If Jesus defines reality," I pressed, "then are you saying there's no truth in any other religion?"

"I believe there *are* some truths in other religions," he quickly replied. "As Scottish writer George MacDonald said, 'Truth is truth, whether from the lips of Jesus or Balaam.'[21] We need to affirm truth where we see it, but we need to remember there are entailments that come with certain beliefs. If you believe God exists, then you're going to have to reject certain aspects of, say, Buddhism—mainly, God's nonexistence. If you accept the existence of God, then large portions of Eastern philosophy are going to be wrong *at that point.* That doesn't mean they're a hundred percent wrong, but they're wrong when they conflict with a view that is correct. You can't say, 'Well, I believe in Jesus' resurrection, but I also believe in reincarnation.' If it's true that Jesus really did rise from the dead, then reincarnation is not true. Human beings have one earthly opportunity and then face judgment."

"So we ought to let Jesus speak for himself?" I asked.

"Yes. A lot of times, people will put words into his mouth. This kind of an approach to the Christian faith is both misguided and superficial

— *oh, yeah, sure, I'm a Christian, but I believe in reincarnation.* Well, you haven't really taken a serious look at the Christian worldview. It's like the person who says all religions are basically the same. Apart from their view of whether God exists, what the human problem is, what the solution to the human problem is, or the nature of the afterlife — yeah, sure, apart from those *massive* things, they're pretty much the same," he said, a chuckle in his voice.

"If God has broken into the world and spoken through Christ, then there are going to be certain beliefs that we're going to have to accept. It's not up to us to say, 'I like this, I don't like that.' C. S. Lewis said he'd gladly get rid of the doctrine of hell, but he concluded he can't, because there are certain things that flow from the claims of Christ and the teachings of the New Testament that precluded him from doing that. I think there needs to be that kind of honesty.

"We can say we find certain doctrines troubling — fine. But to try to pick and choose which doctrines we accept is denying the teachings of Jesus, who through his resurrection has demonstrated the reliability of his claims about being the Son of God and thus knowing what's true and what isn't.

"Look at it this way: we may have subjective preferences about what doctrines we like and don't like. But our subjective preferences can't change the objective reality that Jesus is God's unique revelation to humankind. If we want to sync up with reality, we need to sync up with him. We can't change reality just by refusing to believe certain doctrines that Jesus affirms. We may not like the doctrine of hell, but that can't change the objective reality of whether hell exists. We can't wish it out of existence. It either exists, as Jesus affirms, or it doesn't."[22]

I pondered his point for a minute as I tried to crystallize a response. "In a way," I said finally, "everything goes back to the resurrection."

"That's true," he replied. "If Jesus really was resurrected from the dead, then this vindicates his claims that he really is the unique Son of God. And if he's the unique Son of God, then we can rely on his teachings being true. And so when we add things or subtract things from his teaching, we're in error, because we'd be believing something that doesn't correspond with reality."

Which Jesus?

Copan's mention of reincarnation turned my thoughts to a related line of inquiry. "So often, people who want to create their own religion will include the idea of reincarnation," I said. "Why is that?"

"Some people in the West see reincarnation as another crack at life in order to get things right, sort of like the movie *Groundhog Day.* There's an attraction to saying we have many opportunities and not just one lifetime. Actually, the reality is quite different." He gestured toward me. "You've been to India, right?"

"I've spent some time there, yes," I said.

"I have too. And I'm sure you've noticed that reincarnation is a very oppressive burden in that Hindu culture, as it is in the Buddhist world," he said. "For example, if you're a low caste or no caste Hindu, then you're stuck at that low level because that's what you deserve from your previous life. And people shouldn't reach out to help you, because they might jeopardize their own karma by interfering with you living out the miserable existence that you deserve."

I knew he was right. What sounds on the surface like a magnanimous belief that gives people multiple opportunities to live a better life turns out to create a devastating situation for millions upon millions of people who are mired in hopeless poverty day to day.

Another belief that people frequently add to their customized faith is the idea that we're all divine. "What about this tendency to make ourselves God?" I asked. "Shirley MacLaine said, 'The tragedy of the human race was that we had forgotten that we were each Divine.'[23] Why do people tend to gravitate toward that conclusion?"

Copan smiled. "I would rewrite her statement by saying the tragedy of the human race is that we've forgotten we're God's creatures! *That's* the problem," he said, his tone lighthearted but emphatic at the same time. "Given a choice, we tend to select beliefs that elevate who we are, that diminish personal responsibility, that give us greater freedom to call 'good' what the scriptures call 'sin,' and that put ourselves in charge of our own destiny, rather than saying to God, as the psalmist did, 'My times are in your hands.'[24] We want to create our own guidelines that don't put any demands on us.

"We all know deep down that we're flawed and imperfect. What kind of god would that make us? We flatter ourselves when we try to put ourselves in the place of God rather than acknowledge that we are God's creation and that we need to give God his rightful place. We don't need to be more self-centered than we are; we need to be more God-centered. We can't find the real Jesus by thinking that we're his equal."

His comment about the "real Jesus" sparked a thought. "These days if someone says he believes in Jesus, you almost have to say, '*Which Jesus?*' " I observed.

"Unfortunately, that's true," he replied. "We're living in an age of biblical illiteracy, where a lot of people have cobbled together beliefs of Jesus. If we ask which Jesus a person believes in, we may be surprised to find that it's a Jesus who said and did things that no serious scholar believes the historical Jesus did. Or he may be a Gnostic Jesus, sort of an abstract teacher of amorphous sayings who's divorced from history. But I can't stress this enough: *What we believe about Jesus doesn't really affect who he is,*" he said, his voice emphasizing each word.

That statement seemed pivotal. "Please, elaborate on that," I urged.

"Our beliefs can't change reality," he said. "Whether we choose to believe it or not, Jesus is the unique Son of God. How do we know? Because he convincingly demonstrated the trustworthiness of his remarkable claims through his resurrection. He is who he is, regardless of what we think. So we have a choice: we can live in a fantasyland of our own making by believing whatever we want about him; or we can seek to *discover* who he really is—and then bring ourselves into alignment with the real Jesus and his teachings."

The Jesus of History

Copan's conclusions about Jesus, of course, depend on whether he has an accurate assessment of what occurred in ancient history. Postmoderns, however, contend that history is—above all else—interpretive, and thus we can't be absolutely sure what happened in the past. The implication is clear, I said to Copan: if we lack certainty about history, then one person's version of Jesus would be just as valid as anyone else's — or the church's.

Copan furrowed his brow as I made my point. "The Australian historian Keith Windschuttle says in his book *The Killing of History* that for 2,300 years we have taken history seriously and believed we can know certain things about the past," he began.[25] "Now, in our day, there's skepticism about whether we can come to any solid conclusions about history. The study of history is seen as nothing more than one set of interpretations that come to be replaced by another. We're left without any confidence about how to approach history."

"Precisely," I said.

Copan thought for a moment, then grinned. "It's interesting that when people say we have to be historical skeptics, they speak with great confidence about skepticism!" he said, amused by the irony. "They're making remarkably strong assertions about the uncertainty of the study of history. The question needs to be asked, 'Why should we take *their* interpretation of history instead of anybody else's?' It's amazing how many people will trash history as being purely interpretive — but they expect us to take their word for it!

"At the same time, we have to remember that when we're dealing with history, we're dealing with probabilities — what are the likely and reasonable conclusions that can be drawn? And that's okay. It doesn't mean that we can't be confident about certain historical events. We can know with great confidence, for example, that Hitler didn't overthrow the Roman Empire or that Stalin wasn't the first American president. We can know about the Reformation — Martin Luther posting his ninety-five theses in 1517, the church's sale of indulgences, Erasmus's influence on Luther in the translation of the New Testament, and so forth.

"The question comes at an interpretive level. Given the *facts* of history — which we can conclude from historical records, archaeology, and so forth — how do we put the historical picture together? Yes, there are going to be some differing interpretations, but it's not *all* a matter of interpretation. We can differentiate between more plausible interpretations and ones that are off-the-wall. Certainly you can't say one interpretation is as good as any other. Some explanations do a much better job of accounting for the historical facts—they're more comprehensive, they're less ad hoc, they're better supported. So I simply reject the idea that we have to embrace interpretive skepticism."

I brought the discussion back to Christ. "How much can we confidently know about Jesus?" I asked. "Is there enough historical data for us to have a sufficient understanding of who he is so we can reject interpretations that simply don't reflect reality?"

"We have excellent historical data concerning Jesus," was his quick response. "He is mentioned in extra-biblical writings, and we have lots of details in the New Testament, which withstands scrutiny very well. The transmission of the New Testament through time has been remarkable. And we have internal evidence of its reliability. The criterion of embarrassment offers strong support for the Gospels and Acts. In other words, we have sayings and acts by Jesus—including his ignorance about the time of his return, his cursing of the fig tree, and even his crucifixion itself—that would not have been included if the authors were fabricating the record.

"When we look at Acts, we see that Luke's account can be corroborated through archaeology in numerous ways. So we have to ask the question: 'If Luke is right about these details that *can* be verified, can't we trust him when it comes to events that *can't* be verified, such as miracles and the identity claims of Jesus?' Luke specifically states that he is taking objective evidence seriously by investigating the truth of what took place.[26] Plus, we know from the 'we' passages in Acts that Luke was a traveling companion of Paul's, so he was an eyewitness himself to some of the events that transpired.

"Then look at the transformation that takes place in the disciples and the very elevated view of Jesus in the earliest church. Paul cites early creeds and hymns that center on the death, resurrection, and deity of Jesus. Here is a monotheistic Jew, claiming to be following in the footsteps of his fathers before him, saying that, yes, there is one Lord as we've always affirmed, but then identifying Jesus with him in a remarkable way. As Larry Hurtado, professor of New Testament at the University of Edinburgh, wrote in his recent book *Lord Jesus Christ*, this high view of Jesus is rooted very early in the Jesusalem church."[27]

"Then it's not a later fabrication?" I asked.

"No, it's not—and the evidence Hurtado and other scholars have presented is very compelling. Plus, even before the four Gospels, we have the early epistles—1 and 2 Thessalonians, 1 Corinthians, and so forth—that have a very elevated view of Jesus within twenty years of his crucifixion. How did that emerge in a strictly monotheistic Jewish setting? The resurrection of Jesus does a much better job of explaining this than secular counterparts."

"But we can't have a hundred-percent confidence, can we?" I asked.

"Maybe not, but we have a very convincing picture that does a better job of explaining the facts than the competing theories. We can talk about the real Jesus of history as being a unique individual who claims to stand in the place of God, who does remarkable things, who claims that in him the Kingdom of God has come, who says that in him a new creation is dawning, and whose claims are vindicated by his resurrection and then corroborated by the lofty beliefs about him in the early church."

Copan's points were well taken, but there was still a problem. "Aren't many of Jesus' teachings open to differing interpretations?" I asked.

"The golden rule of interpretation is that you treat someone's teachings as you would want your own to be interpreted," he replied. "We can't read whatever we want into what Jesus said; we have to seek to accurately understand what he was communicating. This involves a certain amount of study to comprehend what he was saying. But picking and choosing verses out of context, spinning them to say what we want them to say—that's not responsible scholarship.

"The question is: Are we willing to take Jesus seriously—even if his teachings may not sit comfortably with us? They may challenge us, they may force us to overturn a lot of our cherished beliefs about ourselves, but are we willing to confront what he taught without distorting it?"

"Still, some people are very sincere in interpreting Jesus differently than the church traditionally has," I pointed out.

"I'll grant that they're sincere," Copan conceded. "As I said earlier, Paul talks about the importance of sincerity and simplicity in urging a pure devotion to Christ. Sincerity is important, but, Lee, we can't overlook this: *sincerity is not sufficient.*

"Weren't Hitler and Stalin sincerely committed to their beliefs? I'm sure they were. The idea that God would applaud their sincerity is absurd. Sometimes people can be very committed and seemingly sincere, but it's at the expense of suppressing their conscience. They've rejected and resisted the truth or suppressed their moral impulses."

"In other words, a person can be sincere but sincerely wrong."

"Exactly. Sincerity doesn't make a person right. Sincerity doesn't make something true. I could believe with all the sincerity in the world that the earth is flat, but that doesn't make it so. I can sincerely believe that I'm every bit as divine as Jesus, but that doesn't change the fact that I'm a creature, not the Creator."

The New Tolerance

Few things are as politically incorrect these days as saying that another person is wrong about his or her religious beliefs. Such a claim smacks of judgmentalism, which is to be studiously avoided at all costs. "Aren't you judging other people when you say they're wrong—and didn't Jesus say in Matthew 7:1, 'Do not judge, or you too will be judged'?" I said to Copan.

The mention of that verse brought a smile to his face. "That passage has replaced John 3:16 as the favorite verse that people like to quote," he said. "Unfortunately, though, many of them misinterpret what Jesus was saying. Jesus wasn't implying that we should never make judgments about people."

"How do you know?" I asked.

"Because in John 7:24, Jesus says, 'Stop judging by mere appearances, and make a right judgment.' So he's clarifying that it's all right —in fact, it's a good thing—to make *proper* judgments about people. What Jesus condemns is a critical and judgmental attitude or unholy sense of moral superiority.

"The Bible says in Galatians 6:1 that if a fellow Christian is caught in a sin, then those who are spiritual should seek to restore him or her 'in a spirit of gentleness. Look to yourself, lest you too be tempted.'[28] God wants us to examine ourselves first for the problems we so readily detect in other people. Only then should we seek to remove the speck in the other person's eye.[29] So judgmentalism is the ugly refusal to acknowledge that 'there but for the grace of God go I.' "

"So the key issue is our attitude?"

"Yes, that's right. We can hold our convictions firmly and yet treat people with dignity and respect even though they disagree with us. We can have a spirit of humility while at the same time explaining why we believe someone is wrong. Ephesians 4:15 talks about 'speaking the truth in love.' That should be our goal."

"It seems like *tolerance* has become the buzzword of the postmodern world," I remarked.

"Tolerance is a wonderful virtue — when it's properly defined. Its meaning, however, has become distorted in recent years."

"In what way?"

"Traditionally, to be tolerant meant putting up with what we find disagreeable or false. For example, some people will tolerate green beans when they're served them at a person's house. They'll eat them even though it's not their favorite food. In the same way, tolerance historically has meant that we put up with people even though we disagree with their viewpoint.

"These days, though, tolerance means that you accept the other person's views as being true or legitimate. If you claim that someone is wrong, you can get accused of being intolerant — even though, ironically, the person making the charge of intolerance isn't being accepting of *your* beliefs."

I thought of a Muslim acquaintance of mine who has come over to my house to grill steaks and discuss theology and history. We disagree on fundamental spiritual issues, but neither of us has drawn a knife on the other. We've found a way to be civil and respectful without pretending we agree on everything.

I shared that anecdote with Copan. "That's exactly what true tolerance is about," he said. "Dialogue shouldn't begin by assuming the equality of all truth claims, which is a ridiculous position. Instead, dialogue should begin with assuming the equality of all *persons*.

"Each of us is made in the image of God and therefore has dignity and value as an individual. You can say, 'I accept you as a person but that doesn't mean I embrace the beliefs that you hold.' You can have a discussion with your Muslim friend and thoroughly respect him even though you believe on rational grounds that he's mistaken.

"The very fact that both of your views can't be right is an impetus to engage in a meaningful dialogue. This becomes a chance for both sides to argue their positions. True tolerance grants people the right to dissent."

Arrogance and Exclusivity

Nevertheless, many people accuse Christians of being arrogant when they insist that their religious beliefs are right while others are wrong. Theologian John Hick says all the world's religions are 'different culturally conditioned responses to the ultimately Real.'[30] In other words, religion is the imperfect attempts by human beings to understand the Ultimate Reality.

"That would mean that while all world religions express themselves differently, they all should be respected and none should claim superiority," I said to Copan.

Copan was well-versed in Hick's philosophy. "Religious pluralists like Hick believe that all religions are capable of bringing salvation or liberation, and that this is evidenced by the moral fruits produced by those religions—people like Mahatma Gandhi and the Dalai Lama, for example," he explained. "But I think the pluralist is displaying the same arrogance that he accuses Christians of having when Christians claim Jesus is the only way to God."

That statement intrigued me. "In what way?" I asked.

"The pluralist is saying if you disagree with his viewpoint, then at that juncture you would be in error. He's saying that the Christian is wrong and that he's right. The pluralist believes that his view ought to be accepted and the Christian's view rejected. So he's being as 'arrogant' as he accuses Christians of being. The pluralist is just as much of an exclusivist as the Christian."

Copan waited for a moment while I digested his logical jujitsu. "Are you familiar with the parable of the blind men before the king of Benares, India, who are each touching an elephant?" he asked as he continued.

I told him I knew the tale about the one blind man who touches the elephant's tail and concludes it's a rope; another who touches the elephant's leg and thinks it's a pillar; a third who touches its side and thinks it's a wall; and the fourth who touches the trunk and thinks it's a snake. The parable is often used to explain how various world religions are reaching out to God but only seeing part of the picture.

"Well, where's the pluralist in all of this?" asked Copan. "Is he another blind man, touching his own part of the elephant — in which case, why should we believe him any more than anybody else? Or is he sitting back like the king and saying, 'They don't see the big picture like I do.' Now, there's nothing wrong with that — after all, Christians say Jesus broke into history and has given *us* the big picture. So how can it be arrogant for Christians to make that claim if the pluralist is basically claiming the same thing?

"Think about it: if Hick is right and the world religions are culturally conditioned attempts to reach out to the ultimate Reality, then what about Hick himself? Isn't his belief about the Real and the nature of religions culturally conditioned — and, if so, why should his viewpoint be preferred when he's just as culturally conditioned as everyone else?"

I couldn't help but interrupt. "Yet aren't we culturally conditioned to some degree?" I asked. "Isn't it true that if you were born in Saudi Arabia, you'd probably be a Muslim, or if you were born in India, you'd probably be a Hindu?"

"Statistically speaking, that could be true," he said. "And if the pluralist had grown up in medieval France or modern Somalia, he probably wouldn't be a pluralist. So the geography argument doesn't carry much weight. Besides, I could make the claim that if you lived in Nazi Germany, the chances are you would have been part of the Hitler Youth. Or if you lived in Stalin's Russia, you would have been a Communist. But does that mean Nazism or Communism is as good a political system as democracy?

"No — just because there has been a diversity of political systems through history doesn't prevent us from concluding that one political system is superior to its rivals. Presumably, there are good reasons for preferring one political system over another. There are good reasons for rejecting a system like Nazism or Communism in favor of democracies. So why can't it be the same with regard to religious beliefs?

"The point is: are there good reasons for believing one religious viewpoint over another? I conclude, based on the historical evidence for Jesus' resurrection, that he has been vindicated as the true Son of God. And if Jesus is who he says he is, then Hick would acknowledge that pluralism is done for. Pluralism cannot survive if Jesus Christ is the unique way to God. So the pluralist has to try to explain away the evidence for the incarnation and the resurrection. The pluralist has to reject the Trinity and salvation only coming through Jesus. He simply cannot allow the Christian faith to be what it claims to be.

"Now, isn't *that* being exclusive — *and* 'arrogant'?"

Jesus and the Marginalized

Even so, I still saw problems. "When one religion, like Christianity, claims a unique path to salvation, doesn't that inevitably lead to marginalizing and persecuting people who believe otherwise?" I asked. "Is common ground for discussion even possible when one group claims a monopoly on truth?"

"Again, it's important to affirm that all truth is God's truth. It's not as though Christians have a monopoly on truth and that if you don't believe the Bible, then you're a hundred percent in the dark," Copan said. "God has made himself generally known to people, and there are things we can hold in common, like reason, experience, and moral understanding. We can cooperate with one another on certain important moral and social issues, even if we don't share the same theological outlook.

"But let's be clear about something: Jesus is not seeking to marginalize anyone. We read 2 Peter 3:9 that God isn't willing that *any* should perish, but that *all* would come to repentance. It's not God who marginalizes people; actually, it's people who marginalize God. What prevents universal salvation is human freedom — a rejection of God's salvation. It's human beings who push God away and who want to keep him at arm's length. God makes his salvation available to all people, but not all choose to embrace it.

"Furthermore," he said, "the question of oppression is a separate issue from that of truth. Does truth necessarily oppress? Truth-claimants can, but it doesn't have to. Religious people can oppress, but so can nonreligious people—look at Marxism and Stalinism. But is oppression consistent with what Jesus taught—the Jesus who sat down with the hated tax-collectors, prostitutes, and the forgotten of society? Jesus actually came to the marginalized. He taught his followers to love all people. Christians may not always fully live out those principles, but this is the ideal Jesus tells us to strive for."

"But can we, as a world, avoid the violence that can come when a religion, like Christianity, says it's the only way to God?" I pressed.

"When we talk about religion and the potential for violence, it's instructive to look at the origins of Christianity versus Islam," Copan said. "It's quite a contrast. For the first several centuries, the Christian faith was spread through people being radical in their love for Christ and others. The church didn't grow as a result of a military campaign, as you see taking place within Islam, which grew by the sword. So when you ask whether religion oppresses—well, it depends on which religion we're talking about. With Christianity, unfortunately, there are periods of oppression that did come later. But we need to ask whether this was the sort of thing that Jesus espoused, or whether these were people giving Jesus a bad name.

"Truth doesn't necessarily marginalize people. You can still respect someone who disagrees with you. Sometimes religion gets the blame, but we just saw in the twentieth century how secular systems—like Communism, for example—oppressed and murdered millions and millions of people. So it's not necessarily religion that does the oppressing; it can be any viewpoint that takes an intolerant stance, does not allow for any sort of disagreement, and has political and military power to enforce the official position.

"As for Christianity, Paul says in Romans 12:18, 'If it is possible, as far as it depends on you, live at peace with everyone.' He rules out revenge and says we should overcome evil with good, just as Jesus taught.[31] And Acts portrays Christians as honorable, respectable citizens, who aren't creating chaos and turmoil, but on the contrary are the ones who take the law seriously."

"I think what upsets some people is that there are certain Christians who sound morally superior when they talk about their faith," I observed.

"Yes, unfortunately that happens. But as Martin Luther said, when Christians are evangelizing, they're like one beggar simply telling another beggar where to find bread. It's not as though we are sharing the Christian faith from a position of moral superiority—like saying, 'I'm better than you because I'm a Christian and you're not.'

"Let me give you an example. My wife and I like a restaurant called the Macaroni Grill. When we tell people about it, we're not saying, 'I'm better than you because I know about the Macaroni Grill and you don't.' No—we're merely happy to pass on the news about the place. And that's how it should be with the Christian faith. Our attitude shouldn't be, 'I'm better than you,' but, 'I found something really good; I urge you to check it out.'"

Whatever Became of Sin?

One thing I've noticed among people who customize their own religion is that one of the first doctrines to go is sin. We may see ourselves as making mistakes, committing errors, or having a lapse of judgment, but few people envision themselves as sinners. Said journalist Bryan Appleyard: "Sin doesn't really exist as a serious idea in modern life."[32]

In fact, we live in a blame-shifting culture, where we tend to evade responsibility for our actions and point the finger at everyone else —especially society or our early childhood trauma—for our behavior. As one scholar noted, therapists "make it a point of professional honor never to express moral judgments, so the word 'fault'—let alone the word 'sin'—will never pass their lips."[33] British theological consultant Alan Mann said the phrase, "It's not your fault," has become a major theme in the way we tell the contemporary story of human responsibility.[34]

I raised the issue with Copan. "If there is no such thing as sin anymore," I said, "then people wouldn't need a savior like the Jesus of the Bible, would they?"

"One of the problems of relativism is that it denies there's any moral standard to shoot for," he replied. "Consequently, there's no failure in meeting that standard—so then why, as you've asked, would you need a savior? Why do you need to be rescued? Why do you need redemption?

"But despite a lot of our therapeutic attempts to deal with human nature, the problem of evil in the human heart is something that keeps making realists of us. G. K. Chesterton talked about sin as being a fact as practical as potatoes. He said the doctrine of original sin is the only Christian doctrine that can be empirically verified—just look at the evening news on any given day. The Christian faith talks about human sinfulness and rebellion against God, which we readily see demonstrated throughout the world.

"If you take the therapeutic approach, then you're going to treat the killings at Columbine or the 9/11 terror attacks as being perpetrated by those who are aberrations. The killers failed to reach their full potential, which is why they were prompted to commit these atrocities. Some Eastern philosophies might say the problem is ignorance."

Copan shook his head. "Well, those are such hollow explanations for the depths of evil that exists around us," he said. "To simply gloss over these evil acts by using psychological categories is utterly inadequate to account for them. A better explanation is sin, which is being preoccupied with ourselves and doing things the way we want rather than as God wants, which produces destructive results.

"Until we bring *sin* back into our vocabulary, we're not going to take the depths of evil or our moral responsibilities—or God—seriously. We don't simply need more therapy to resolve our issues in this fallen world. We need to acknowledge our own guilt and humble ourselves in asking for forgiveness. Otherwise, the therapeutic mind-set relieves us from making any sort of moral judgments about ourselves or others. It relieves us of taking responsibility for our actions.

"There is a moral gap—an ideal we have fallen short of—and we need outside assistance to bridge it. We don't merely need therapy; we need someone to break into our human situation who can bring forgiveness, who can bring healing, and who can assist us in living the lives we ought to but can't on our own. So we need to recover this idea of sin in order to make better sense out of the evil we see in the world, rather than just papering it over."

To make sure we were both on the same page with our terminology, I asked, "What's the biblical definition of sin?"

"The Westminster Confession talks about sin being the lack of conformity to, or any kind of transgression of, the law of God. Basically, it's a violation of the character of God. It's something that falls short of what God desires for us. I guess if you want to put it in contemporary jargon, sin is doing what you want. Sin is having attitudes that are self-absorbed and self-centered, rather than being God-centered."

"It certainly is a word that has dropped out of our culture."

"It has. The title of psychiatrist Karl Menninger's popular book thirty years ago asked *Whatever Became of Sin?*[35] The doctrine of original sin has a lot of explanatory power, but the fact that we are born with a self centered tendency is not the whole story. There's also the story of redemption — that Christ has come to bring relief and resolution to a problem that, when left to ourselves, we simply aren't able to address."

Cosmic Child Abuse?

That brought me to my next topic. "Christians say Jesus died on the cross to pay for their sins, but is this concept of the substitutionary atonement outmoded?" I asked. "Episcopal Bishop John Shelby Spong said, 'A human father who would nail his son to a cross for any purpose would be arrested for child abuse.'"[36]

"We have to be careful about this notion being outmoded," came Copan's reply. "C. S. Lewis rightly warns us against chronological snobbery — saying, 'Oh, they used to do things that way, but we know better now because we're more enlightened.' Sometimes there is a mind-set that if no one believes something anymore, surely it has got to be false. G. K. Chesterton said if you take that view, you may as well say that on certain days of the week something is true and on others it's not. The question should be: Is there anything to this notion of substitutionary atonement?"

"Well, *is* there?" I asked. "Why can't God just say he forgives the sins of the world?"

Copan's answer came swiftly. "Why can't judges just forgive criminals? Why can't they let rapists and thieves back on the street and just say, 'It's okay, I forgive you'? For God to do something like this would be an insult to his holiness. It would look like he was simply endorsing rebellion against himself and his character. He is a righteous judge, and therefore he must find us guilty of sin because the truth of the matter is that we *are* guilty. We have fallen short of how God wants us to live. We violate even our own moral standards, so certainly we violate God's higher standard. To pretend otherwise would be a lie—and God is not a liar.

"Also, if God simply forgives, then he hasn't taken human responsibility with much seriousness at all. To simply let people go does not hold them accountable to the standards that people know they've transgressed. And he would be denying the gravity of sin, which we take far too lightly but which God takes very, very seriously."

That last remark made me think of a comment in a book I had been reading on the plane to Florida for the interview. As James R. Edwards, a professor of biblical languages and literature as well as a Presbyterian minister, said in *Is Jesus the Only Savior?*:

The doctrine of atonement obviously hangs on the doctrine of sin. A physician who removes a leg because of a splinter is a monster. A physician who removes a leg because of cancer or gangrene, on the other hand, is a hero who saves his or her patient's life. It all depends on the nature and seriousness of the problem. Spong and others see sin as a splinter; the New Testament sees it as a cancer that is fatal if left untreated. And that accounts for the sacrifice of Jesus Christ on a cross of cruelty and shame. The cross is indeed an outrage—an outrage of grace. If this is the kind of world in which we live—and I believe it is—then the death of God's Son for the sins of the world is the *only* way the world can be reunited with its Maker and Redeemer.[37]

Nevertheless, I continued to press the issue about why God simply couldn't magnanimously forgive people without having to sacrifice his Son. "What about the story in Matthew 18 about the king who forgave an enormous debt that was owed to him by his servant?" I asked Copan. "He seemed capable of forgiveness without sacrificing anyone on a cross."[38]

Copan's eyebrows went up. "Ah, but notice what happens in that parable: the king doesn't just forgive; he also absorbs the debt," he said. "The king basically says he's going to bear the burden of the loss even though the servant owes the money. Similarly, Jesus pays the cost of our sin on the cross. It's sort of like a child who breaks a neighbor's window. He may be too young to pay the price himself, so his parents pay it for him. Or when a small corporation is bought out by a larger one, the new corporation has to assume its debts.

"There's a cost to sin: Romans 6:23 says it's death, or eternal separation from God.[39] That's the penalty we owe. That's the cost we incur when our sins separate us from God. But Jesus willingly paid the price in our place, as our substitute — and offers forgiveness as a free gift. There's nothing illegitimate about that kind of representation. If we aren't able to handle our situation, what's wrong with someone who's willing to assume our indebtedness?

"From one perspective, Jesus' death was the very low point of God's career — he is crucified as if he were a criminal, exposed naked to the world, cursed on this tree, and tortured though he was innocent. But despite this ultimate degradation, John talks about the Son of God being 'lifted up,'[40] which is a double entendre. Yes, Jesus was physically lifted up on the cross, but this is also the point of God's exaltation. The crucifixion turns out to be a high point of God's career. The point is, Jesus was willing to go this low for our salvation — to be humiliated, to be degraded, to be insulted, that through this selfless act he was able to rescue us, bring an end to the powers of darkness, and bring about the restoration of a fallen world into a new creation.

"God isn't guilty of cosmic child abuse. It's not as though the Father consigns the Son to this humiliating death on the cross; it's something Jesus does voluntarily. Jesus says in John 10 that he lays down his life of his own accord.[41] It's important to see the Trinity being involved in this whole process. As 2 Corinthians 5 says, God was in Christ, reconciling the world to himself.[42] God the Father and God the Spirit suffer along with the Son as he hangs on the cross. The Father isn't pitted against his Son; this is something the Son willingly takes upon himself in order to pay the debt that humankind could not pay on its own."

"Some people say this seems utterly drastic," I observed.

"Well, yeah, if this were to happen to you or me, we would be terribly embittered and completely overwhelmed. But Christ bears the punishment perfectly. As British theologian John Stott said, 'For the essence of sin is man substituting himself for God, while the essence of salvation is God substituting himself for man.' "[43]

"The atonement, then, is not illogical or unfair," I suggested.

"That's right," Copan agreed. "Remember, the scriptures have a number of different pictures or metaphors for what was accomplished on the cross. But the substitutionary aspect of the atonement is deeply significant in that Christ our representative accomplishes for us what we can't do for ourselves.[44]

"So what should our response be? *Gratitude*—the Christian faith is a religion of gratitude. Why would we be reluctant to humble ourselves and receive the free gift of forgiveness that Christ purchased through his death—and also receive the gift-giver himself as the leader of our life?"

Solo Spirituality

Copan's description of Jesus' sacrifice was moving. Yet this love and grace isn't always the message that people hear from Christians. Often, they get a far different sermon. Along those lines, I quoted to Copan the words of emergent church leader Dan Kimball: "Today, Christians are known as scary, angry, judgmental, right-wing finger-pointers with political agendas."[45]

I asked Copan, "In light of that, isn't it understandable that people wouldn't want to hear about *their* Jesus?"

"Absolutely," Copan said. "Jesus said in John 13:35, 'By this everyone will know that you are my disciples, if you love one another.' Well, frankly, we can look around and see a lot of people who are not acting like Jesus' disciples. Instead of being able to say, 'Yes, look at us Christians and how we're living exemplary lives,' many times we have to say, 'Sorry, look at Jesus, not at us.' At the same time, though, some people can use this as an excuse not to take Jesus himself seriously."

I noted to Copan that the title of Kimball's book sums up the attitude of many people today: *They Like Jesus, but Not the Church*. As the rock star Bono said: "I'm not often comfortable in church. It feels pious and so unlike the Christ that I read about in the Scriptures."[46]

"Consequently," I said, "spirituality is very individualistic for a lot of people. They say they can worship God better while walking alone in the woods than in church. Can a Christian be divorced from Christian community?"

"I'm not sure Bono's concern about the church is a totally new phenomenon," Copan replied. "Even in the early Christian communities, you would probably have felt some discomfort."

"In what way?"

"If you were to visit the church in first-century Corinth, for example, you'd find division, spiritual arrogance, putting up with immorality in their midst, and a class-conscious mind-set. The apostle Paul wrote them to point out all these problems—but does he give up on them? No, Paul was writing to say, 'Get back on track.' He deals with them as a loving father would.

"Frankly, you can't live out the Christian life—with all of its commands about dealing with 'one another'—without being part of the church. As the author of Hebrews says, we need to stimulate one another to love and good works. He says we shouldn't abandon the gathering together as believers.[47] The church isn't perfect, but then neither are we as individuals."

"So solo spirituality is not something you'd recommend?" I asked.

"No, certainly not. Despite all of our failures, we cannot live the Christian life apart from one another. In fact, the fruit of the Holy Spirit—love, joy, peace, patience, kindness, goodness, faithfulness, gentleness, and self-control—requires community living.[48] These are community virtues that need to be cultivated in a way that can't be accomplished in isolation."

The Radical Jesus

The postmodern mind-set that has set the stage for so much syncretism has come under fierce attack in recent years. Critics have not only pointed out its philosophical inconsistencies, but also have deplored its effect on morality and ethics. One of its most vocal opponents has been Christian philosopher J. P. Moreland, who called postmodernism "an immoral and cowardly viewpoint that people who love truth and knowledge ... should do everything they can do to heal."[49]

I read Moreland's critique to Copan. "'Immoral and cowardly'— those are strong words," I said. "Is he being too harsh?"

Copan thought deeply before answering. "I love J. P., because he speaks forthrightly," he said, himself sounding a bit diplomatic. "Postmodernism is a nuanced movement, and I don't think either of us would want to paint it with a broad brushstroke. And as I said earlier, I do think postmodernism can remind us of some important things."

But Copan didn't stop there. "On the other hand, I can understand J. P.'s reaction. When a worldview declines to make moral judgments, when it sees all beliefs as being contextual, when it says we can't talk about absolute truth or what is right, when it claims we cannot know things for sure, well, that can be a dangerous—yes, cowardly—philosophy," he said.

"And, of course, the claim that we can't know is itself a claim to knowledge! There are some things we definitely *can* know—in fact, it's incredibly important that we *do* know them. God has revealed himself in the person of Jesus Christ so that we can *know* the Father through the Son. We can *know* of his love, because Jesus laid down his life for us. First John says we can have *confidence* about certain matters: 'I write these things to you who believe in the name of the Son of God so that you may *know* that you have eternal life.'[50] Galatians and Romans say we can have confidence that we're the adopted sons and daughters of God if we receive forgiveness through Christ—and this confidence goes against the spirit of postmodernism.

"So can we learn some lessons from postmodernism? Yes—we have a certain historical context, we don't always see things clearly, and so forth. But even though we may not know everything, we *can* know *some* things—indeed, some very important and life-changing things. We can know enough to encounter and experience the real Jesus."

"Then who is he?" I asked. "If the authentic Jesus can't be found in the cobbled-together beliefs of syncretism, then who is he, really?"

"We cannot separate the Jesus of history from what some people call the Christ of faith. They are one and the same," Copan answered. "We need to put Jesus back into his first-century context. If we disconnect him from history or come up with some sort of New Age Jesus who is detached from the cross or the resurrection, we've lost his real identity. The same goes with anti-Semitism in the name of a Jesus whose first-century Jewishness has been ignored or suppressed. How are we going to sort out the real Jesus from the fake, unless we have Jesus anchored in the historical Gospels?"

As he spoke, my mind flashed to the countless people who have disconnected Jesus from reality and then manufactured their own version of him—a Jesus who teaches them what they want to hear rather than what they desperately need to know. This Jesus is anemic—powerless and pale, because he exists only in their imaginations. All the while, the authentic Jesus—with his love and strength, his miraculous power and saving grace—stands patiently by.

I began to feel a sense of sadness. "Isn't it a shame," I said to Copan, "that so many people are creating a Jesus who matches their preconceptions about what they think he should be like, but in the process they're missing the real Jesus?"

Copan nodded in agreement. "Ironically, they're often talking about a 'radical new Jesus' they've discovered. *Radical?*" he repeated, incredulous. "No, these are silly or watered-down portrayals of Jesus. He's more than a good buddy, more than a social revolutionary, more than a Gnostic teacher. The real Jesus is the Jesus of orthodox Christianity: *He's no less than God incarnate.* God breaks into the world scene with Jesus. He conquers sin, Satan, and death through Jesus. He's bringing history to a climax through Jesus. *This* is what humankind has been waiting for.

"If you want a spectacular Jesus, or a hero for the ages, or a Jesus who shatters all expectations and pours out love beyond comprehension —*there* he is," he declared, thumping the table with his hand.

"How in the world can you get more radical than that?"

For Further Investigation
More Resources on This Topic

Beckwith, Francis J., and Gregory Koukl. *Relativism: Feet Firmly Planted in Mid-Air.* Grand Rapids, Mich.: Baker, 1998.

Carson, D. A., gen. ed. *Telling the Truth.* Grand Rapids, Mich.: Zondervan, 2000.

Copan, Paul. *How Do You Know You're Not Wrong?* Grand Rapids, Mich.: Baker, 2005.

————. *Loving Wisdom: Christian Philosophy of Religion.* St. Louis: Chalice, 2007.

————. *That's Just Your Interpretation.* Grand Rapids, Mich.: Baker, 2005.

————. *True for You, but Not for Me.* Minneapolis: Bethany, 1998.

Edwards, James R. *Is Jesus the Only Savior?* Grand Rapids, Mich.: Eerdmans, 2005.

Kimball, Dan. *They Like Jesus, but Not the Church.* Grand Rapids, Mich.: Zondervan, 2007.

Köstenberger, Andreas, gen. ed. *Whatever Happened to Truth?* Wheaton: Crossway, 2005.

Discovering
the Real Jesus

*I ask myself a question a lot of people have asked: Who is this
[Jesus]? Was he who he said he was, or was he just a religious
nut?... That's the question.*

Bono[1]

*It doesn't matter what I believe. It only matters what I can
prove.*

Tom Cruise's character in *A Few Good Men*

She was brought up Catholic, but by the age of eighteen she had left
the church and abandoned her belief in God. Two years later, she
married a fervent atheist. Soon she became not just a published novelist, but one of the best-read authors in America, penning a succession
of stories about vampires and witches—unaware at the time that her
books "reflected my quest for meaning in a world without God."

Anne Rice, author of *Interview with a Vampire* and the Mayfair
Witches series, spent thirty years as an atheist. Then she began studying
the Bible during her frequent periods of depression. Her faith rekindled,
she decided in 2002 to "give myself utterly to the task of trying to
understand Jesus himself and how Christianity emerged." She conse-
crated her subsequent book on Jesus—and herself—to him. And that's
when she discovered something very curious.

An inveterate researcher, Rice prides herself on the accuracy of the
historical world she creates for her novels. To prepare for writing about
Jesus, she spent more than two years delving deeply into first-century
Palestine, which included reading books on the New Testament era
written by skeptical and liberal historians.

"I expected to discover that their arguments would be frighteningly strong, and that Christianity was, at heart, a kind of fraud," she wrote. Surprisingly, the opposite occurred:

> What gradually came clear to me was that many of the skeptical arguments—arguments that insisted most of the Gospels were suspect, for instance, or written too late to be eyewitness accounts—lacked coherence.... Arguments about Jesus himself were full of conjecture. Some books were no more than assumptions piled upon assumptions. Absurd conclusions were reached on the basis of little or no data at all.

In short, she found the nondivine and impotent Jesus of liberal circles to be based on "some of the worst and most biased scholarship I've ever read." She was stunned that "there are New Testament scholars who detest and despise" the Jesus whom they spend their entire lives studying. "Some pitied him as a hopeless failure," she said. "Others sneered at him, and some felt an outright contempt. This came between the lines of the books."

In the end, she became "disillusioned with the skeptics and with the flimsy evidence for their conclusions." Instead, she discovered that the research and arguments from a wide range of other highly credentialed scholars—Richard Bauckham, Craig Blomberg, N. T. Wright, Luke Timothy Johnson, D. A. Carson, Larry Hurtado, and others—were more than enough to establish the early dating and first-person witness of the Gospels.[2]

If I were to sum up the lesson from her experience—which is quite similar to my own—I'd put it like this: *"The emperors of radical scholarship have no clothes!"*

For years, skeptical and left-wing historians have bedazzled the public with flashy new theories about Jesus—he's really a Gnostic imparter of secret wisdom; he's actually a reworking of the ancient myths about Mithras; he's a messianic pretender who fails the test of the ancient prophecies; he's buried in Galilee outside the city of Tsfat; or he's whatever anyone wants him to be in today's cacophony of postmodernism.

Didn't you know that the Christian idea of baptism comes from the sinking of the coffin of the pagan god Osiris in the Nile River? Or that Jesus held initiation rites with young men in the middle of the night?

Or that the first century was a cauldron of radically different views about Jesus, but the real story—which is that Jesus wants us to know we're all divine—was suppressed by the power-hungry church? Or that scribes have irretrievably contaminated the text of the New Testament? Or that Jesus wrote a secret letter to the Jewish authorities clarifying that he never claimed to be God's Son? Or that Jesus didn't utter most of what's recorded in the Gospels?

"These skeptical scholars," said Rice, "seemed so very sure of themselves."[3]

Very sure—but as it turns out, surely wrong. The truth is that skepticism does not equal scholarship.[4] Finally, other scholars are beginning to speak up to expose the leaps of logic, special pleading, biased interpretations, and tissue-thin evidence that underlies these outrageous claims about Jesus.

Righteous Indignation

Not long ago, Craig A. Evans had enough. With the same righteous indignation that prompted Ronald Nash to debunk the theory that Christianity stole its beliefs from the pagan mystery religions, Evans set out to demonstrate the sloppy scholarship that has confused the public about the real Jesus in recent years.

Coming from someone of Evans's impressive caliber, this was highly significant. Few Jesus scholars are as universally respected by both liberals and conservatives as Evans, the distinguished professor of New Testament and director of the graduate program at Acadia Divinity College in Canada and the first expert I interviewed in my quest for the real Jesus.

Evans looked at the current controversies swirling around Jesus—was he a mystic or Gnostic; did he fake his death; has his grave been found; did he deny his divinity; are the four Gospels unreliable; are there better sources about his life than the New Testament; is there a grand conspiracy to suppress the truth; did Jesus ever really exist at all?—and shook his head in disbelief.

"When I first began academic study of Jesus and the Gospels some thirty years ago, I could never have guessed that I or anyone else would find it necessary to write a book addressing such questions," he said. "Surely no one in all seriousness would advance such theories. Surely no credible publishers would print them. Yet, all of that has happened."[5]

Evans knows the sweep of historical evidence. He's well aware of what conclusions it reasonably supports and what it can't. And he was aghast at what he was reading in popular books about Jesus.

"We live in a strange time that indulges, even encourages, some of the strangest thinking," he wrote in the introduction to his well-titled book *Fabricating Jesus: How Modern Scholars Distort the Gospels.* "What I find particularly troubling is that a lot of the nonsense comes from scholars. We expect tabloid pseudo-scholarship from the quacks, but not from scholars who teach at respectable institutions of higher learning."[6]

Nevertheless, what he found were "daring theories that run beyond the evidence," distortions or neglect of the four Gospels, misguided suspicions, unduly strict critical methods, questionable texts from later centuries, anachronisms, exaggerated claims, and "hokum history"— all resulting in "the fabrication of an array of pseudo-Jesuses."[7]

In sum, he said, "Just about every error imaginable has been made. A few writers have made almost all of them."[8]

Evans is hardly alone in his assessment. Numerous other New Testament luminaries also have started to publicly condemn the way the public is being duped by ill-supported assertions concerning Jesus.

James H. Charlesworth, the highly regarded professor of New Testament Language and Literature at Princeton Theological Seminary and an expert on Jesus and the Dead Sea Scrolls, decried "the misinformed nonsense that has confused the reading public over the past few years."

James D. G. Dunn, professor emeritus at the University of Durham in England, agreed. "The quest of the historical Jesus has been seriously misled by much poor scholarship and distorted almost beyond recognition by recent pseudo-scholarship," he said.

Equally adamant was John P. Meier, professor at the University of Notre Dame, who wrote *A Marginal Jew*, the widely acclaimed multi-volume work on the historical Jesus. "For decades now," he said, "the unsuspecting public has been subjected to dubious academic claims about the historical Jesus that hardly rise above the level of sensation-alistic novels."

Gerald O'Collins, professor emeritus of the Gregorian University in Rome, warned of the "sensationalist claims about Jesus that quickly turn out to be based on mere wishful thinking." Gerd Theissen, professor at the University of Heidelberg, bemoaned "sensational modern approaches in Jesus research that do not live up to the standards of academic research."[9]

"Readers should beware of shocking new claims about Jesus or his earliest followers based on flimsy evidence," said New Testament professor Ben Witherington III in his 2006 book *What Have They Done with Jesus?*[10] Unfortunately, he added, Americans have been "prone to listen to sensational claims ... even when there is little or no hard evidence to support such conjectures."[11]

Meanwhile, scholars have been breaking new ground in academic research that flatly contradicts many of the recent radical assertions about Jesus, including the claims that his divinity was the product of legendary development and that the four Gospels lack eyewitness support.

Larry W. Hurtado, professor of New Testament Language, Literature, and Theology at the University of Edinburgh in Scotland, demonstrated in a 746-page volume that the exaltation of Jesus wasn't a later development. Rather, he said, "an exalted significance of Jesus appears astonishingly early in Christian circles."[12] He pointed out that early Christians defined and portrayed Jesus as God's "Son," "Christ/ Messiah," "Word," and "Image."[13]

"Well within the first couple of decades of the Christian movement [or AD 30–50] Jesus was treated as a recipient of religious devotion and was associated with God in striking ways," Hurtado concluded.[14]

Where would the monotheistic Jews of the early church come up with the idea of Jesus' divinity after his death if he had not made the claim himself during his ministry and then backed it up with his resurrection?

In a 2006 scholarly book that N. T. Wright called "a remarkable piece of detective work," Richard Bauckham, professor of New Testament studies at the University of St. Andrews in Scotland, meticulously documents how the four Gospels are closely based on the eyewitness testimony of those who personally knew Jesus.[15] That might not sound controversial to many people, but it dramatically deflates revisionist theories that say the Gospels are unreliable and disconnected from first-hand accounts.

In short, the four Gospels—once denigrated and mocked by skeptics—are making a powerful comeback. "When put to the test," summarized Evans, "the original documents hold up quite well."[16]

Answering the Challenges

After traveling a total of 24,000 miles on my mission to investigate six of the most current and controversial objections to the traditional view of Jesus, I went alone to my office, sat down in a comfortable chair, and flipped through reams of notes, transcripts, and articles.

In the end, none of these seemingly daunting challenges turned out to be close calls. One by one, they were systematically dismantled by scholars who backed up their positions not with verbal sleights of hand or speculation, but with facts, logic, and evidence:

- *Are scholars discovering a radically different Jesus in ancient documents just as credible as the four Gospels?* No, the alternative texts that are touted in liberal circles are too late to be historically credible—for instance, the Gospel of Thomas was written after AD 175 and probably closer to 200. According to eminent New Testament scholar I. Howard Marshall of the University of Aberdeen in Scotland, the Thomas gospel has "no significant new light to shed on the historical Jesus."[17] The Secret Gospel of Mark, with its homoerotic undercurrents, turned out to be an embarrassing hoax that fooled many liberal scholars too eager to buy into bizarre theories about Jesus, while no serious historians give credence to the so-called Jesus Papers. The Gnostic depiction of Jesus as a revealer of hidden knowledge—including the teaching that we all possess the divine light that he embodied—lacks any connection to the historical Jesus.

- *Is the Bible's portrait of Jesus unreliable because of mistakes or deliberate changes by scribes through the centuries?* No, there are no new disclosures that have cast any doubt on the essential reliability of the New Testament. Only about one percent of the manuscript variants affect the meaning of the text to any degree, and not a single cardinal doctrine is at stake. Actually, the unrivaled wealth of New Testament manuscripts greatly enhances the credibility of the Bible's portrayal of Jesus.

• *Have new explanations refuted Jesus' resurrection?* No, the truth is that a persuasive case for Jesus rising from the dead can be made by using five facts that are well-evidenced and which the vast majority of today's scholars on the subject—including skeptical ones—accept as true: Jesus death by crucifixion; his disciples' belief that he rose and appeared to them; the conversion of the church persecutor Paul; the conversion of the skeptic James, who was Jesus' half-brother; and Jesus' empty tomb. All the attempts by skeptics and Muslims to put Jesus back into his tomb utterly fail when subjected to serious analysis, while the overblown and ill-supported claims of the Jesus Tomb documentary and book have been decimated by knowledgeable scholars.

• *Were Christian beliefs about Jesus stolen from pagan religions?* No, they clearly were not. Allegations that the virgin birth, the resurrection, communion, and baptism came from earlier mythology simply evaporated when the shoddy scholarship of "copycat" theorists was exposed. There are simply no examples of dying and rising gods that preceded Christianity and which have meaningful parallels to Jesus' resurrection. In short, this is a theory that careful scholars discredited decades ago.

• *Was Jesus an imposter who failed to fulfill the messianic prophecies?* On the contrary, a compelling case can be made that Jesus—and Jesus alone—matches the "fingerprint" of the Messiah. Only Jesus managed to fulfill the prophecies that needed to come to fruition prior to the fall of the Jewish temple in AD 70. Consequently, if Jesus isn't the predicted Messiah, then there will never be one. What's more, Jesus' fulfillment of these prophecies against all odds makes it rational to conclude that he will fulfill the final ones when the time is right.

- *Should people be free to pick and choose what they want to believe about Jesus?* Obviously, we have the freedom to believe anything we want. But just because the U.S. Constitution provides equal protection for all religions doesn't mean that all beliefs are equally true. Whatever we believe about Jesus cannot change the reality of who he clearly established himself to be: the unique Son of God. So why cobble together our own make-believe Jesus to try to fulfill our personal prejudices when we can meet and experience the actual Jesus of history and faith?

Following the Unique Jesus

Not only had the six challenges been answered, but my journey also had yielded a fresh and powerful affirmative case for the overall reliability of the four Gospels, Jesus' fulfillment of the messianic predictions, and his resurrection. For me, it was further confirmation that the traditional view of Christ is amply supported by a firm foundation of historical facts.

Yet if that case is so convincing, then why do so many critics rely on flimsy evidence and feeble arguments in order to build a much weaker case for a fabricated Jesus? For instance, why would they ignore or denigrate the first-century, eyewitness-based Gospels of the New Testament and instead manufacture a different Jesus out of second century—or later—documents that lack historical credibility?

It's not always easy to discern people's motives. Still, I can't help but notice a common thread that runs through the efforts to discover another Jesus: many of them, in their own way, attempt to put humankind on the same level as him.

Some critics try to accomplish this by reducing Jesus. They reject his uniqueness, his miracles, and his divinity, transforming him into just another human being. This is the tactic employed by the Jesus Seminar, advocates of the "copycat" theory, and the skeptics who deny the resurrection. It's the message behind the Jesus Papers: Jesus never claimed to be God but only embodied God's Spirit in a way that anyone can.

Others take a different approach: rather than tearing Jesus down, they elevate themselves. In other words, they're fine with affirming the divinity of Jesus—as long as they too are indwelled by the same spark of the divine. This seems to be the strategy of many New Agers and Gnostics, as well as the people who set out to create their own do-it-yourself religion, only to "discover"—as Ed and Joanne did—that they're gods themselves.

Whether reducing Jesus or elevating ourselves, the result is the same: Jesus becomes our equal. As such, he doesn't deserve our allegiance or our worship. He cannot judge us or hold us accountable. His teachings become mere suggestions that can be followed or disregarded according to our whims. He isn't our savior; at most, he's a friendly guide.

On the other hand, the one Jesus that skeptics refuse to tolerate is a uniquely divine, miraculous, prophecy-fulfilling, and resurrected Jesus —even if the historical evidence points persuasively in that direction. After all, that would put them in the place of being beholden to him. Their personal sovereignty and moral independence would be at risk. The problem is: *that's* the real Jesus.

We are not his equals. We don't occupy the same stratum or possess the same status. He is God, and we're not. For many people, that's the crux of their predicament: if Jesus is God incarnate, then he could demand too much. And in fact, he does demand everything. Said C. S. Lewis:

> The Christian way is different: harder, and easier. Christ says, "Give me All. I don't want so much of your time and so much of your money and so much of your work: I want You. I have not come to torment your natural self, but to kill it. No half-measures are any good.... Hand over the whole natural self, all the desires which you think innocent as well as the ones you think wicked —the whole outfit. I will give you a new self instead. In fact, I will give you Myself: my own will shall become yours."[18]

That kind of surrender sounds scary for many people. But if Jesus really is God—if he really did sacrifice himself so that we could be forgiven and set free to experience his love forever—then why should we hesitate to give all of ourselves to him? Who could be more trustworthy than someone who lays down his life so that others might live?

This is what Jesus has done. The church has been telling this same story for two millennia. As I sat in my office, I found Evans's words echoing in my mind: "I come down on the side of the church," he declared. "Doggone it, bless their bones, I think they figured it out. They avoided errors and pitfalls to the left and to the right. *I think the church got it right.*"

As imperfect as she is, the church has preserved for us the four Gospels that constitute the most reliable reports about Jesus. The church has formulated the ancient creeds that efficiently sum up the implications of his life and ministry: Jesus is fully God and fully man, who offers forgiveness, hope, and eternal life as a free gift to all who want to receive it.[19]

As the church has affirmed from the beginning, he is utterly one of a kind. "Jesus was entirely different and new and stunning," said author Don Everts.

> There was just something so clear and beautiful and true and unique and powerful about Jesus that old rabbis would marvel at his teaching, young children would run and sit in his lap, ashamed prostitutes would find themselves weeping at his feet, whole villages would gather to hear him speak, experts in the law would find themselves speechless, and people from the poor to the rugged working class to the unbelievably wealthy would leave everything … to follow him.[20]

This is the *real* Jesus, who all along has been alive and well as he dwells in the lives of his people—the community whose door is always open.

A Summary of Evidence
from *The Case for Christ*

Here is a summary of the historical evidence for Jesus Christ from thirteen experts who were interviewed for my book *The Case for Christ*:

• Can the Biographies of Jesus Be Trusted?

I once thought that the Gospels were merely religious propaganda, hopelessly tainted by overactive imaginations and evangelistic zeal. But Craig Blomberg of Denver Seminary, one of the country's foremost authorities on the biographies of Jesus, built a convincing case that they reflect eyewitness testimony and bear the unmistakable earmarks of accuracy So early are these accounts of Jesus' life that they cannot be explained away as legendary inventions. "Within the first two years after his death," Blomberg said, "significant numbers of Jesus' followers seem to have formulated a doctrine of the atonement, were convinced that he had been raised from the dead in bodily form, associated Jesus with God, and believed they found support for all these convictions in the Old Testament." A study indicates that there was nowhere enough time for legend to have developed and wiped out a solid core of historical truth.

• Do Jesus' Biographies Stand Up to Scrutiny?

Blomberg argued persuasively that the gospel writers intended to preserve reliable history, were able to do so, were honest and willing to include difficult-to-explain material, and didn't allow bias to unduly color their reporting. The harmony among the Gospels on essential facts, coupled with divergence on some incidental details, lends historical credibility to the accounts. What's more, the early church could not have taken root and flourished right there in Jerusalem if it had been teaching facts about Jesus that his own contemporaries could have exposed as exaggerated or false. In short, the Gospels were able to pass all eight evidential tests, demonstrating their basic trustworthiness as historical records.

• Were Jesus' Biographies Reliably Preserved for Us?

World-class scholar Bruce Metzger, professor emeritus at Princeton Theological Seminary, said that compared to other ancient documents, there is an unprecedented number of New Testament manuscripts and that they can be dated extremely close to the original writings. The modern New Testament is about 99 percent free of meaningful textual discrepancies, with no major Christian doctrine in doubt. The criteria used by the early church to determine which books should be considered authoritative have ensured that we possess the best records about Jesus.

• Is There Credible Evidence for Jesus outside His Biographies?

"We have better historical documentation for Jesus than for the founder of any other ancient religion," said Edwin Yamauchi of Miami University, a leading expert on ancient history. Sources from outside the Bible corroborate that many people believed Jesus performed healings and was the Messiah, that he was crucified, and that despite this shameful death, his followers, who believed he was still alive, worshiped him as God. One expert documented thirty-nine ancient sources that corroborate more than one hundred facts concerning Jesus' life, teachings, crucifixion, and resurrection. Seven secular sources and several early Christian creeds concern the deity of Jesus, a doctrine "definitely present in the earliest church," according to Dr. Gary Habermas, the scholar who wrote *The Historical Jesus*.

• Does Archaeology Confirm or Contradict Jesus' Biographies?

John McRay, a professor of archaeology for more than fifteen years and author of *Archaeology and the New Testament*, said there's no question that archaeological findings have enhanced the New Testament's credibility. No discovery has ever disproved a biblical reference. Further, archaeology has established that Luke, who wrote about one-quarter of the New Testament, was an especially careful historian. Concluded one expert: "If Luke was so painstakingly accurate in his historical reporting [of minor details], on what logical basis may we assume he was credulous or inaccurate in his reporting of matters that were far more important, not only to him but to others as well?" Like, for instance, the resurrection of Jesus—the event that authenticated his claim to being the unique Son of God.

• Is the Jesus of History the Same as the Jesus of Faith?

Gregory Boyd, a Yale- and Princeton-educated scholar who wrote the award-winning *Cynic Sage or Son of God*, offered a devastating critique of the Jesus Seminar, a group that questions whether Jesus said or did most of what's attributed to him. He identified the Seminar as "an extremely small number of radical-fringe scholars who are on the far, far left wing of New Testament thinking." The Seminar ruled out the possibility of miracles at the outset, employed questionable criteria, and some participants have touted myth-riddled documents of extremely dubious quality. Further, the idea that stories about Jesus emerged from mythology fails to withstand scrutiny. Said Boyd: "The evidence for Jesus being who the disciples said he was ... is just light years beyond my reasons for thinking that the left-wing scholarship of the Jesus Seminar is correct." In sum, the Jesus of faith is the same as the Jesus of history.

• Was Jesus Really Convinced He Was the Son of God?

By going back to the very earliest traditions, which were unquestionably safe from legendary development, Ben Witherington III, author of *The Christology of Jesus*, was able to show that Jesus had a supreme and transcendent self-understanding. Based on the evidence, Witherington said: "Did Jesus believe he was the Son of God, the anointed one of God? The answer is yes. Did he see himself as the Son of Man? The answer is yes. Did he see himself as the final Messiah? Yes, that's the way he viewed himself. Did he believe that anybody less than God could save the world? No, I don't believe he did." Scholars said that Jesus' repeated reference to himself as the Son of Man was not merely a claim of humanity, but a reference to Daniel 7:13–14, in which the Son of Man is seen as having universal authority and everlasting dominion and who receives the worship of all nations. Said one scholar: "Thus, the claim to be the Son of Man would be in effect a claim to divinity."

• Was Jesus Crazy When He Claimed to Be the Son of God?

Gary Collins, a professor of psychology for twenty years and author of forty-five books on psychology-related topics, said Jesus exhibited no inappropriate emotions, was in contact with reality, was brilliant and had amazing insights into human nature, and enjoyed deep and abiding relationships. "I just don't see signs that Jesus was suffering from any known mental illness," he concluded. In addition, Jesus backed up his claim to being God through miraculous feats of healing, astounding demonstrations of power over nature, unrivaled teaching, divine understanding of people, and with his own resurrection, which was the ultimate evidence of his deity.

• Did Jesus Fulfill the Attributes of God?

While the incarnation—God becoming man, the infinite becoming finite—stretches our imaginations, prominent theologian D. A. Carson pointed out that there's lots of evidence that Jesus exhibited the characteristics of deity. Based on Philippians 2, many theologians believe Jesus voluntarily emptied himself of the independent use of his divine attributes as he pursued his mission of human redemption. Even so, the New Testament specifically confirms that Jesus ultimately possessed every qualification of deity, including omniscience, omnipresence, omnipotence, eternality, and immutability.

• Did Jesus—and Jesus Alone—Match the Identity of the Messiah?

Hundreds of years before Jesus was born, prophets foretold the coming of the Messiah, or the Anointed One, who would redeem God's people. In effect, dozens of these Old Testament prophecies created a fingerprint that only the true Messiah could fit. This gave Israel a way to rule out imposters and validate the credentials of the authentic Messiah. Against astronomical odds—by one estimate, one chance in a trillion, trillion, trillion, trillion, trillion, trillion, trillion, trillion, trillion, trillion, trillion, trillion, trillion—Jesus, and only Jesus throughout history, matched this prophetic fingerprint. This confirms Jesus' identity to an incredible degree of certainty. The expert I interviewed on this topic, Louis Lapides, is an example of someone raised in a conservative Jewish home and who came to believe Jesus is the Messiah after a systematic study of the prophecies. Today, he's a pastor of a church in California and former president of a national network of fifteen messianic congregations.

• Was Jesus' Death a Sham and His Resurrection a Hoax?

By analyzing the medical and historical data, Dr. Alexander Metherell, a physician who also holds a doctorate in engineering, concluded Jesus could not have survived the gruesome rigors of crucifixion, much less the gaping wound that pierced his lung and heart. In fact, even before the crucifixion he was in serious to critical condition and suffering from hypovolemic shock as the result of a horrific flogging. The idea that he swooned on the cross and pretended to be dead lacks any evidential basis. Roman executioners were grimly efficient, knowing that they themselves would face death if any of their victims were to come down from the cross alive. Even if Jesus had somehow lived through the torture, his ghastly condition could never have inspired a worldwide movement based on the premise that he had gloriously triumphed over the grave.

• Was Jesus' Body Really Absent from His Tomb?

William Lane Craig, who has earned two doctorates and written several books on the Resurrection, presented striking evidence that the enduring symbol of Easter—the vacant tomb of Jesus—was a historical reality. The empty grave is reported or implied in extremely early sources—Mark's Gospel and a creed in 1 Corinthians 15—which date so close to the event that they could not possibly have been products of legend. The fact that the Gospels report that women discovered the empty tomb bolsters the story's authenticity, because women's testimony lacked credibility in the first century and thus there would have been no motive to report they found the empty tomb if it weren't true. The site of Jesus' tomb was known to Christians, Jews, and Romans, so it could have been checked by skeptics. In fact, nobody—not even the Roman authorities or Jewish leaders—ever claimed that the tomb still contained Jesus' body. Instead, they were forced to invent the absurd story that the disciples, despite having no motive or opportunity, had stolen the body—a theory that not even the most skeptical critic believes today.

• Was Jesus Seen Alive after His Death on the Cross?

The evidence for the post-resurrection appearances of Jesus didn't develop gradually over the years as mythology distorted memories of his life. Rather, said renowned resurrection expert Gary Habermas, his resurrection was "the central proclamation of the early church from the very beginning." The ancient creed from 1 Corinthians 15 mentions specific individuals who encountered the risen Christ, and Paul, in effect, challenged first-century doubters to talk with these individuals personally to determine the truth of the matter for themselves. The book of Acts is littered with extremely early affirmations of Jesus' resurrection, while the Gospels describe numerous encounters in detail. Concluded British theologian Michael Green: "The appearances of Jesus are as well authenticated as anything in antiquity.... There can be no rational doubt that they occurred."

• Are There Any Supporting Facts That Point
toward the Resurrection?

Professor J. P. Moreland presented circumstantial evidence that provided strong documentation for the resurrection. First, the disciples were in a unique position to know whether the resurrection happened, and they went to their deaths proclaiming it was true. Nobody knowingly and willingly dies for a lie. Second, apart from the resurrection, there's no good reason why such skeptics as Paul and James would have been converted and would have died for their faith. Third, within weeks of the crucifixion, thousands of Jews became convinced Jesus was the Son of God and began following him, abandoning key social practices that had critical sociological and religious importance for centuries. They believed they risked damnation if they were wrong. Fourth, the early sacraments of communion and baptism affirmed Jesus' resurrection and deity. And fifth, the miraculous emergence of the church in the face of brutal Roman persecution "rips a great hole in history, a hole the size and shape of Resurrection," as C. F. D. Moule put it.

Taken together, I concluded that this expert testimony constitutes compelling evidence that Jesus Christ was who he claimed to be—and one and only Son of God. For details that support this summary, as well as other evidence, please refer to *The Case for Christ*.

Helpful Websites
to Investigate the Real Jesus

LeeStrobel.com
... a video-intensive site that explores what Christians believe about Jesus—and why. Also available is a free e-newsletter, "Investigating Faith."

JesusCentral.com
... a place to learn and dialogue about what Jesus said.

Tektonics.org
... a feisty site that answers critics of historic Christianity.

Christian-Thinktank.com
... a vast resource of answers to current objections to Christianity.

ReasonableFaith.org
... scholar William Lane Craig defends historic Christianity.

MarkDRoberts.com
... a wealth of material from this Harvard-educated scholar.

Willowcreek.com
... includes a guide to finding local churches that can help in your spiritual journey.

Metamorpha.com
... where the focus is on how to become more like Jesus.

Notes

INTRODUCTION: Searching for the Real Jesus

1. Andrew Greeley, "There's No Solving Mystery of Christ," *Chicago Sun-Times* (Jan. 16, 2004).

2. Lyric from "The Real Jesus," from the album *Wide-Eyed and Mystified* by downhere (Word Entertainment, 2006).

3. Doyle P. Johnson, "Dilemmas of Charismatic Leadership: The Case of the People's Temple," *Sociological Analysis* 40 (1979), 320.

4. See Sally Quinn and Jon Meacham, "Who Was Jesus?" available at newsweek .washingtonpost.com/onfaith/2006/12/who_was_jesus/comments.html #76008 (Dec. 26, 2006). The bulleted points are condensed from the submissions, but they preserve the author's original language as much as possible.

5. Chris Suellentrop, "Jesus Christ: Choose Your Own Savior," available at www.slate.com/id/2150645 (Oct. 4, 2006).

6. Paul Copan, *True for You, but Not for Me* (Minneapolis: Bethany, 1998), 94.

7. Charlotte Allen, *The Human Christ* (Oxford: Lion, 1998), 5.

8. For a summary of the evidence I found convincing, see appendix A.

9. Gregory A. Boyd, *Jesus under Siege* (Wheaton, Ill.: Victor, 1995), 14.

10. See Neil Gross and Solon Simmons, "How Religious Are America's College and University Professors?" available at www.wjh.harvard.edu/soc/faculty/gross/religions.pdf (Oct. 22, 2006).

11. See N. T. Wright, *Judas and the Gospel of Jesus* (Grand Rapids, Mich.: Baker, 2006), 31–34.

12. Ibid., 33.

13. Jay Tolson, "In Search of the Real Jesus: The Gospel Truth," *U.S. News and World Report* (Dec. 18, 2006).

14. Ibid.

15. Ibid.

16. Richard Cimino and Don Lattin, *Shopping for Faith* (San Francisco: Jossey-Bass, 1998), 19.

17. Ibid., 19–20.

18. Tolson, "In Search of the Real Jesus."

19. See Marvin Meyer and James M. Robinson, *The Nag Hammadi Scriptures* (San Francisco: HarperSanFrancisco, 2007).

20. Bart D. Ehrman, *Misquoting Jesus* (San Francisco: HarperSanFrancisco, 2005), 208.

21. The percentage who saw or heard about the Jesus Tomb documentary is based on a survey of 1,204 randomly selected American adults by Zogby International taken March 22–26, 2007. See www.churchexecutive.com/Page.cfm/PageID/8875 (April 18, 2007).

22. For example, see Dan Brown, *The Da Vinci Code* (New York: Doubleday, 2003), 232.

23. Jesus said in John 8:24: "If you do not believe that I am [the one I claim to be], you will indeed die in your sins."

CHALLENGE #1: "Scholars Are Uncovering a Radically Different Jesus in Ancient Documents Just as Credible as the Four Gospels"

1. Stevan L. Davies, *The Gospel of Thomas and Christian Wisdom* (New York: Seabury, 1983), 1. The year 1945 was when a cache of ancient nonbiblical texts, including the Gospel of Thomas, was discovered in Egypt.

2. Sullivan made the comment during *The Chris Matthews Show* on MSNBC, May 7, 2006, in a debate over *The Da Vinci Code*.

3. The reporters who broke the story, which won first place for investigative reporting among Illinois newspapers from United Press International in 1986, were Anne Burris, Thomas J. Lee, Pete Nenni, Chris Szechenyi, and Kathy Schaeffer.

4. See Robert J. Miller, ed., *The Complete Gospels*, rev. and exp. ed. (Santa Rosa, Calif.: Polebridge, 1994).

5. Ibid., back cover.

6. Ibid., 3.

7. Philip Jenkins, *Hidden Gospels* (Oxford: Oxford University Press, 2001), 7.

8. Miller, *Complete Gospels*, 360.

9. Ibid., 357.

10. Ibid., 357, 358.

11. Ibid., 401.

12. See Scott G. Brown, *Mark's Other Gospel: Rethinking Morton Smith's Controversial Discovery* (Ontario: Wilfrid Laurier University Press, 2005).

13. Morton Smith, *The Secret Gospel* (Middletown, Calif.: Dawn Horse, 2005), 107.

14. Ibid., 15–16.

15. Michael Baigent, *The Jesus Papers* (San Francisco: HarperSanFrancisco, 2006), 270.

16. See Robert W. Funk et al., *The Five Gospels* (San Francisco: HarperSanFrancisco, 1997).

17. Miller, *Complete Gospels*, 6.

18. Willis Barnstone and Marvin Meyer, *The Gnostic Bible* (Boston: New Seeds Books, 2003), 43.

19. Elaine Pagels, *Beyond Belief: The Secret Gospel of Thomas* (New York: Vintage, 2004), 40–41.

20. Ben Witherington III, *The Gospel Code* (Downers Grove, Ill.: InterVarsity, 2004), 101.

21. Barnstone and Meyer, *Gnostic Bible*, 48, 69, 46.

22. Pagels, *Beyond Belief*, 35.

23. Elaine Pagels, *Gnostic Gospels* (New York: Vintage, 1989), xxxv.

24. Funk et al., *Five Gospels*, 35.

25. Bart Ehrman, *Lost Christianities* (Oxford: Oxford University Press, 2003), 248.

26. Jenkins, *Hidden Gospels*, 16.

27. All interviews have been edited for conciseness, clarity, and content.

28. Helmut Koester, *Ancient Christian Gospels* (Philadelphia: Trinity Press International, 1990), xxx.

29. Davies, *Gospel of Thomas and Christian Wisdom*, 146.

30. See John Dominic Crossan, *The Historical Jesus: The Life of a Mediterranean Jewish Peasant* (San Francisco: HarperCollins, 1991), 427–34.

31. See Nicholas Perrin, *Thomas and Tatian: The Relationship between the Gospel of Thomas and the Diatessaron*, Academia Biblica 5 (Atlanta: Society of Biblical Literature, 2002); Nicholas Perrin, "NHC II,2 and the Oxyrhynchus Fragments (P.Oxy 1, 654, 655): Overlooked Evidence for a Syriac Gospel of Thomas," *Vigiliae Christianae* 58 (2004): 138–51; and Nicholas Perrin, *Thomas, the Other Gospel* (Louisville: Westminster John Knox Press, 2007).

32. From the German word *Quelle*, or "source."

33. Elaine Pagels, *Beyond Belief*, 38.

34. See http://home.epix.net/~miser17/Thomas.html (Sept. 17, 2006).

35. Witherington, *Gospel Code*, 75.

36. Jenkins, *Hidden Gospels*, 17.

37. See John Dominic Crossan, *The Cross That Spoke* (New York: Harper-Collins, 1992).

38. Evans added: "Luke was a proselyte more than likely."

39. Moody Smith, "The Problem of John and the Synoptics in Light of the Relation between Apocryphal and Canonical Gospels," in Adelbert Denaux, ed., *John and the Synoptics*, BETL 101 (Leuven: Peeters and Leuven University Press, 1992), 150.

40. See Lee Strobel and Garry Poole, *Exploring the Da Vinci Code* (Grand Rapids, Mich.: Zondervan, 2006).

41. See Stephen C. Carlson, *The Gospel Hoax: Morton Smith's Invention of Secret Mark* (Waco, Tex.: Baylor University Press, 2005).

42. Smith, *Secret Gospel*, xi. Pagels wrote the foreword to Smith's book.

43. Carlson, *Gospel Hoax*, 80.

44. Ibid., 16.

45. Ibid., 79.

46. Ibid., 77.

47. Scott Brown, who wrote his doctoral dissertation on Secret Mark, is among the scholars who continue to believe in its legitimacy: "I, for one, side with Clement, who believed that Mark himself created the Secret Gospel in Alexandria by adding more stories to the version of his gospel than are found in the New Testament" (quoted in a 2005 afterword to *Secret Gospel*).

48. Carlson, *Gospel Hoax*, 84, 85.

49. Smith, *Secret Gospel*, ix; from Pagels's foreword.

50. Ibid., 85.

51. *Against Heresies* 1.31.1.

52. See John 13:27.

53. See Mark 11 and Mark 14.

54. See "Are the Gospels Reliable?" available at www.whoisthisjesus.tv/qa.htm #scholar. (Feb. 6, 2007).

CHALLENGE #2: "The Bible's Portrait of Jesus Can't Be Trusted Because the Church Tampered with the Text"

1. Ehrman, *Misquoting Jesus*, 207, 208.

2. Richard C. Carrier, "Did Jesus Exist? Earl Doherty and the Argument to Ahistoricity," www.infidels.org/library/modern/richard_carrier/jesus puzzle.html (Nov. 23, 2006).

3. See advertising supplement on TimesSelect in the *New York Times* (Sept. 24, 2006).

4. Reportedly Ehrman wanted to name the book *Lost in Transmission*, but the publisher thought that made it sound like an automotive book.

5. Ehrman, *Misquoting Jesus*, 89 – 90.

6. Ibid., 7.

7. Ibid., 208.

8. Ibid.

9. Hoover, 6.

10. Carrier, "Did Jesus Exist?"

11. Ehrman, *Misquoting Jesus*, 9.

12. Ibid.

13. Ibid., 11.

14. Neely Tucker, "The Book of Bart," *Washington Post* (March 5, 2006).

15. Emphasis added.

16. See www.csntm.org.

17. See www.netbible.org.

18. Ben Witherington III, "Misanalyzing Text Criticism — Bart Ehrman's *Misquoting Jesus*," http://benwitherington.blogspot.com/2006/03/misanalyzing-test-criticism-bart-html (June 6, 2006).

19. Gordon D. Fee, review of *The Orthodox Corruption of Scripture* in *Critical Review of Books in Religion* 8 (1995), 204. Bart D. Ehrman's book *Misquoting Jesus* is a popularized version of *The Orthodox Corruption of Scripture*.

20. Funk et al., *Five Gospels*, 6.

21. 2 Timothy 3:16 – 17: "All Scripture is God-breathed and is useful for teaching, rebuking, correcting and training in righteousness, so that the servant of God may be thoroughly equipped for every good work."

22. See Matthew 1:22; 2:15.

23. See 2 Peter 3:15 – 16.

24. See John 10:35.

25. See Daniel B. Wallace, "Mark 2:26 and the Problem of Abiathar," www.bible.org/page.php?page_id=383. (Nov. 23, 2006).

26. Ehrman, *Misquoting Jesus*, 207 – 8.

27. See John 7:53 – 8:11.

28. Shawntaye Hopkins, "Woman Bitten by Snake at Church Dies," *Lexington Herald-Leader* (Nov. 8, 2006).

29. Frank Zindler, *The Real Bible: Who's Got It?* www.atheists.org/christianity/realbible.html (Nov. 29, 2006).

30. See Michael Baigent, Richard Lee, and Henry Lincoln, *Holy Blood, Holy Grail* (New York: Dell, 1983), 368–69.

31. Norman Geisler and William Nix, *From God to Us: How We Got Our Bible* (Chicago: Moody, 1980), 180.

32. Ehrman, *Misquoting Jesus*, acknowledgments.

33. For the entire interview with Metzger, see Lee Strobel, *The Case for Christ* (Grand Rapids, Mich.: Zondervan, 1998), 55–72.

CHALLENGE #3: PART ONE: "New Explanations Have Refuted Jesus' Resurrection"

1. Richard C. Carrier, "The Spiritual Body of Christ and the Legend of the Empty Tomb," in Robert M. Price and Jeffrey Jay Lowder, eds., *The Empty Tomb* (Amherst, N.Y.: Prometheus, 2005), 197.

2. John Shelby Spong, *Resurrection: Myth or Reality?* (San Francisco: Harper-SanFrancisco, 1995), 241.

3. See Strobel, *Case for Christ*, 191–257.

4. "Is There Historical Evidence for the Resurrection of Jesus? A Debate between William Lane Craig and Bart D. Ehrman," www.holycross.edu/departments/crec/website/resurrdebate.htm (Oct. 2, 2006).

5. See Surah 4:157–58.

6. "Who Is the True Jesus?" Videotape. Available at www.facultylinc.com/national/fslf.nsf (Oct. 1, 2006).

7. Hassan M. Fattah, "In Qaeda Video, Zawahri Condemns Bush and Pope Benedict," *New York Times* (Sept. 30, 2006).

8. Lemuel Lall, "Jesus Christ Lived in India, Was Buried in Kashmir: RSS Chief," www.hindustantimes.com/news/5922_1914198,0015002100000000.ht (Jan. 28, 2007).

9. Price and Lowder, *Empty Tomb*, 16.

10. Baigent, *Jesus Papers*, 125.

11. See Baigent, *Jesus Papers*, 124–32.

12. Tabor, *Jesus Dynasty*, back cover.

13. See Tabor, *Jesus Dynasty*, 238–40.

14. Ibid., 234.

15. N. T. Wright, *The Resurrection of the Son of God* (Minneapolis: Fortress, 2003), 718.

16. The segment "Resurrection: True or False?" appeared on PAX-TV's program *Faith under Fire*.

17. Gary Habermas and Antony Flew, *Did Jesus Rise from the Dead? The Resurrection Debate* (San Francisco: Harper & Row, 1987), xiv.

18. For the transcript of a prior interview, see Antony Flew and Gary R. Habermas, "My Pilgrimage from Atheism to Theism," www.biola.edu/antonyflew (Feb. 7, 2007).

19. For video clips of my interview with Flew, see www.LeeStrobel.com (Feb. 7, 2007).

20. Transcript available at www.holycross.edu/departments/crec/website/resurrdebate.htm (Oct. 2, 2006).

21. Paul Copan and Ronald K. Tacelli, eds., *Jesus' Resurrection: Fact or Figment?* (Downers Grove, Ill.: InterVarsity, 2000), 67.

22. 1 Corinthians 15:17.

23. Gary R. Habermas and Michael R. Licona, *The Case for the Resurrection of Jesus* (Grand Rapids, Mich.: Kregel, 2004), 1.

24. Ibid.

25. See www.holycross.edu/departments/crec/website/resurrection-debate-transcript.pd (Oct. 2, 2006).

26. John Dominic Crossan, *Jesus: A Revolutionary Biography* (San Francisco: HarperCollins, 1991), 145.

27. Tabor, *Jesus Dynasty*, 230 (emphasis in original).

28. See Deuteronomy 21:23.

29. See Acts 9:26–30; 15:1–35.

30. 1 Corinthians 15:3–7.

31. Dean John Rodgers of Trinity Episcopal School for Ministry, quoted in Richard N. Ostling, "Who Was Jesus?" *Time* (Aug. 15, 1988).

32. Acts 13:36–38.

33. Mark 8:31; 9:9, 31; 10:32–34; 14:28.

34. 1 Clement 42:3. Translation by Gary Habermas and Michael Licona.

35. Polycarp's letter to the Philippians 9:2. Translation by Gary Habermas and Michael Licona.

36. Gerd Lüdemann, *What Really Happened to Jesus?* trans. John Bowden (Louisville: Westminster John Knox, 1995), 80.

37. Fredriksen's comments came during an interview with the late ABC journalist Peter Jennings for his documentary *The Search for Jesus*, which first aired in July 2000. Emphasis added.

38. Paula Fredriksen, *Jesus of Nazareth* (New York: Vintage, 1999), 264.

39. See 1 Corinthians 9:1 and 15:8; Acts 9, 22, and 26.

40. See Matthew 12:46–50, 13:55–56; Mark 3:31–35, 6:3; Luke 8:19–21; John 2:12, 7:3, 5, 10; Acts 1:13–14; 1 Corinthians 9:5; Galatians 1:19.

41. See Mark 3:21, 31; 6:3–4; and John 7:3–5.

42. John 7:3–5: "Jesus' brothers said to him, 'Leave Galilee and go to Judea,

so that your disciples there may see the works you do. No one who wants to become a public figure acts in secret. Since you are doing these things, show yourself to the world.' For even his own brothers did not believe in him."

43. See Acts 15:12–21 and Galatians 1:19.

44. See Josephus (*Ant.* 20:200); Hegesippus (quoted by Eusebius in *EH* 2:23); Clement of Alexandria (quoted by Eusebius in *EH* 2:1, 23).

45. Reginald Fuller, *The Formation of the Resurrection Narratives* (New York: Macmillan, 1971), 37.

46. Acts 2:32.

47. William Ward, *Christianity: A Historical Religion?* (Valley Forge, Pa.: Judson, 1972), 93–94.

48. Marcus J. Borg and N. T. Wright, *The Meaning of Jesus: Two Visions* (San Francisco: HarperSanFrancisco, 1999), 124–25.

CHALLENGE #3: PART TWO: The Cross-Examination

1. "Code Red" was invented for the movie. The film won an Academy Award nomination for Best Picture, while Jack Nicholson was nominated for Best Supporting Actor.

2. Abdullah Yusuf Ali, translator, *The Qur'an* (Elmhurst, N.Y.: Tahrike Tarsile Qur'an, Inc., 1999), 61.

3. *The True Furqan* (Duncanville, Tex.: World Wide, 2006). This is not to say that pure Christian doctrine is presented in *The True Furqan*. One could write it using any doctrine, true or false, and it could still serve to answer the test presented in the Qur'an.

4. Ali, *The Qur'an*, 1.

5. Baigent, *Jesus Papers*, 125.

6. Ibid., 130 (emphasis added).

7. Richard C. Carrier, "The Spiritual Body of Christ," in Price and Lowder, *Empty Tomb*, 187.

8. Borg and Wright, *Meaning of Jesus*, 135, 131.

9. Tabor, *Jesus Dynasty*, 232.

10. Paraphrase of Luke 24:39.

11. See 1 Corinthians 9:11.

12. Emphasis added.

13. Emphasis added. See also 1 Corinthians 15:53–54.

14. Carrier, "The Spiritual Body of Christ," in Price and Lowder, *Empty Tomb*, 184.

15. Strobel, *Case for Christ*, 238.

16. See Deuteronomy 21:23.

17. Carrier, "The Spiritual Body of Christ," in Price and Lowder, *Empty Tomb*, 156.

18. Uta Ranke-Heinemann, *Putting Away Childish Things* (San Francisco: HarperSanFrancisco, 1994), 131.

19. Copan and Tacelli, *Jesus' Resurrection*, 44.

20. See Matthew 5:22–24, 35–43.

21. Jeffery Jay Lowder, "Historical Evidence and the Empty Tomb Story," in Price and Lowder, *Empty Tomb*, 267.

22. See Tabor, *Jesus Dynasty*, 228–40.

23. Craig A. Evans, *Fabricating Jesus: How Modern Scholars Distort the Gospels* (Downers Grove, Ill.: InterVarsity, 2006), 220.

24. Tabor, *Jesus Dynasty*, 25–26.

25. See www.ingermanson.com/jesus/art/stats.php (April 7, 2007).

26. Hershel Shanks and Ben Witherington III, *The Brother of Jesus* (San Francisco: HarperSanFrancisco, 2003), 11–12, 57–58.

27. See *Acts of Philip* 37, 46, 50, 51, 119.

28. See 1 Corinthians 9:5.

29. Simcha Jacobovici and Charles Pellegrino, *The Jesus Family Tomb* (San Francisco: HarperSanFrancisco, 2007), vii.

30. See www.answers.org/news/article.php?story=20070307145346542 (April 17, 2007).

31. Audrey Barrick, "Study: Most Non-Born-Again Christians Still Believe Jesus Resurrected," *Christian Post* (April 3, 2007). Interestingly, the random poll of 1,204 Americans showed that 75 percent of those who said they're not "born-again Christians" believe in Jesus' bodily resurrection.

32. Acts 2:32.

33. Robert M. Price, "By This Time He Stinketh," in Price and Lowder, *Empty Tomb*, 423.

34. Jeffery Jay Lowder, "Historical Evidence and the Empty Tomb Story," in Price and Lowder, *Empty Tomb*, 288.

35. William Lane Craig, *Assessing the New Testament Evidence for the Historicity of the Resurrection of Jesus* (Lewiston, N.Y.: Edwin Mellen, 1989), 420.

36. Carrier, "The Spiritual Body of Christ," in Price and Lowder, *Empty Tomb*, 195.

37. Copan and Tacelli, *Jesus' Resurrection*, 45.

38. See Francis S. Collins, *The Language of God* (New York: Free Press, 2006), especially 11–31 and 213–25.

CHALLENGE #4: "Christianity's Beliefs about Jesus
Were Copied from Pagan Religions"

1. Timothy Freke and Peter Gandy, *The Jesus Mysteries* (New York: Three Rivers, 1999), 9.
2. Tom Harpur, *The Pagan Christ* (New York: Walker & Company, 2004), 10.
3. See Helen Keller, *The Story of My Life*, chapter 14, www.afb.org/MyLife/book.asp?ch=P1Ch14 (Jan. 23, 2007).
4. Law.com defines plagiarism as "taking the writings or literary concepts (a plot, characters, words) of another and selling and/or publishing them as one's own product." See dictionary.law.com.
5. Brown, *Da Vinci Code*, 232.
6. Harpur, *Pagan Christ*, 51. Harpur acknowledges in his appendix A that he has been influenced by the views of Gerald Massey (1828–1907) and Alvin Boyd Kuhn (1880–1963). Said New Testament scholar Craig A. Evans: "The work of these men, especially their reconstructions of ancient history and attempts to draw lines of continuity between Egyptian religion and Christianity, is deeply flawed. No qualified historian takes the theories of these men seriously. Anyone charmed by Harpur's *Pagan Christ* should beware. We are talking old, odd stuff here. Personal philosophy and introspection it may be; history by any responsible, recognized sense it is not." See Evans, 220–21.
7. Ibid., 85.
8. Freke and Gandy, *Jesus Mysteries*, 109.
9. Tomothy Freke and Peter Gandy, *The Laughing Jesus* (New York: Three Rivers Press, 2005), 55–56.
10. Hugh J. Schonfield, *Those Incredible Christians* (New York: Bantam, 1968), xii.
11. John H. Randall, *Hellenistic Ways of Deliverance and the Making of the Christian Synthesis* (New York: Columbia University Press, 1970), 154.
12. See J. P. Holding, "Did the Mithraic Mysteries Influence Christianity?" www.tektonics.or (Jan. 23, 2007).
13. Freke and Gandy, *Laughing Jesus*, 61.
14. Freke and Gandy, *Jesus Mysteries*, 9.
15. Harpur, *Pagan Christ*, 10.
16. Ibid., 38, 39, 53.
17. Tim Callahan, *Secret Origins of the Bible* (Altadena, Cal.: Millennium, 2002), 332.
18. See Challenge #3.

19. Tryggve N. D. Mettinger, *The Riddle of Resurrection* (Stockholm: Almqvist & Wicksell, 2001), 221.

20. Ibid.

21. Ibid.

22. John D. Wineland, ed., *The Light of Discovery* (Eugene, Ore.: Pickwick, 2007), xiii.

23. Ibid., xi.

24. Komoszewski, Sawyer, and Wallace, *Reinventing Jesus*, 250.

25. Wineland, *Light of Discovery*, xi.

26. See Strobel, *Case for Christ*, 73–91.

27. See Manfred Clauss, *The Roman Cult of Mithras* (New York: Routledge, 2000), 14–15, 21–22, 28.

28. See Richard Reitzenstein, *Hellenistic Mystery Religions*, trans. John E. Steely (Pittsburgh: Pickwick, 1978).

29. A. Loisy, "The Christian Mystery," *Hibbert Journal* (1911–12), 51, quoted in Edwin M. Yamauchi, "Easter — Myth, Hallucination, or History?" *Christianity Today* (March 15, 1974).

30. Albert Schweitzer, *Geschichte der Paulinischen Forschung* (Tubingen, 1911), 151; English translation, *Paul and His Interpreters* (London, 1912), 192, quoted in Bruce Metzger, "Historical and Literary Studies: Pagan, Jewish, and Christian," www.frontline-apologetics.com/mystery_religions_early_christianity.htm (Jan. 30, 2007).

31. "The word *Hellenistic* was coined early in the nineteenth century as a name for the period of history that began with the death of Alexander the Great in 323 BC and ended with the Roman conquest of the last major vestige of Alexander's empire, the Egypt of Cleopatra, in 30 BC. Obviously if this were the exclusive use of the term, it would make little sense to talk about 'Christianity and the Hellenistic world.' But the fact is that the phrase 'the Hellenistic world' is used to refer to the whole culture of the Roman Empire. While Rome achieved military and political supremacy throughout the Mediterranean world, it adopted the culture of the Hellenistic world that preceded its rise to power. Thus, while political control of the Mediterranean world belonged to Rome, the culture continued to be Hellenistic." Ronald Nash, *The Gospel and the Greeks* (Phillipsburg, N.J.: P&R, 2003), 10–11.

32. Nash, *Gospel and the Greeks*, 1. Nash notes that in 1956, an essay by the influential H. Riesenfeld of the University of Uppsala in Sweden called the appeal to the mystery religions "outdated." See H. Riesenfeld, "Mythological Background of the New Testament Christology," in W. D. Davies

and D. Daube, eds., *The Background of the New Testament and Its Eschatology* (Cambridge: Cambridge University Press, 1956), 81–95, esp. 81.

33. Nash, *Gospel and the Greeks*, 3.

34. Ronald Nash, "Was the New Testament Influenced by Pagan Religions?" www.equip.org/free/DB109.htm (Jan. 25, 2007).

35. See Jonathan David, "The Exclusion of Women in the Mithraic Mysteries: Ancient or Modern?" *Numen* 47 (2000), 121–41.

36. See Richard Gordon, "Franz Cumont and the Doctrines of Mithraism," *Mithraic Studies* 1:236.

37. See Edwin Yamauchi, *Persia and the Bible* (Grand Rapids, Mich.: Baker, 1996), 510.

38. E. J. Yarnold, "Two Notes on Mithraic Liturgy," *Mithras: Bulletin of the Society for Mithraic Studies* (1974), 1.

39. Nash, *Gospel and the Greeks*, 137.

40. Manfred Clauss, *The Roman Cult of Mithras*, trans. Richard Gordon (New York: Routledge, 2000), 7.

41. L. Patterson, *Mithraism and Christianity* (Cambridge: Cambridge University Press, 1921), 94.

42. Gary Lease, "Mithraism and Christianity: Borrowings and Transformations," in Wolfgang Haase, ed., *Aufstieg und Niedergang der Römischen Welt*, vol. 2 (Berlin/New York: Walter de Gruyter, 1980), 1316.

43. Ibid., 1329.

44. See ibid., 1321–22.

45. See Yamauchi, *Persia and the Bible*, 520–21.

46. Richard Gordon, *Image and Value in the Greco-Roman World* (Aldershot: Variorum, 1996), 96, quoted in Holding, "Did the Mithraic Mysteries Influence Christianity?"

47. Clauss, *Roman Cult of Mithras*, 110.

48. Ibid., 113.

49. Yarnold, "Two Notes on Mithraic Liturgy."

50. Lease, "Mithraism and Christianity," 1324.

51. Ibid.

52. Ibid., 1325.

53. See Romans 6:3.

54. See John 3:3.

55. See John 1:29. Also see Challenge #5.

56. Günter Wagner, *Pauline Baptism and the Pagan Mysteries* (Edinburgh: Oliver and Boyd, 1967), 266.

57. Bruce Metzger, *Historical and Literary Studies: Pagan, Jewish and Chris-*

tian (Grand Rapids, Mich.: Eerdmans, 1968), 11: "Thus, for example, one must doubtless interpret the change in the efficacy attributed to the rite of the taurobolium. In competing with Christianity, which promised eternal life to its adherents, the cult of Cybele officially or unofficially raised the efficacy of the blood bath from twenty years to eternity."

58. Stephen Neill and Tom Wright, *The Interpretation of the New Testament 1861–1986* (Oxford: Oxford University Press, 1988), 208.

59. Yarnold, "Two Notes on Mithraic Liturgy."

60. See Edwin M. Yamauchi, "Tammuz and the Bible," *Journal of Biblical Literature* 84 (1965), 283–90.

61. See S. N. Kramer, *Bulletin of the American Schools of Oriental Research* 183 (1966), 31.

62. Samuel N. Kramer said the alleged resurrection of Tammuz was "nothing but inference and surmise, guess and conjecture." See Samuel N. Kramer, *Mythologies of the Ancient World* (Garden City, N.Y.: Doubleday, 1961), 10.

63. See P. Lambrechts, "La 'résurrection' d'Adonis," *Mélanges Isidore Lévy* (1955), 207–40, quoted in Yamauchi, "Easter—Myth, Hallucination, or History?"

64. P. Lambrechts, "Les Fêtes 'phrygiennes' de Cybèle et d'Attis," *Bulletin de l'Institut Historique Belge de Rome* 27 (1952), 141–70, quoted in Yamauchi, "Easter—Myth, Hallucination, or History?"

65. Nash, *Gospel and the Greeks*, 130.

66. Nash, "Was the New Testament Influenced by Pagan Religions?"

67. In a quote cited earlier, Freke and Gandy also mention the god Serapis. Said Nash: "During the Isis cult's later, mystery stage, its male deity is no longer the dying Osiris but Serapis; and Serapis is often thought of as a sun god. It is clear that the Serapis of the post-Ptolemaic, mystery version of the cult was not a dying god. Obviously, then, neither could he be a rising god." See Nash, *Gospel and the Greeks*, 128.

68. Bruce M. Metzger, "Methodology in the Study of the Mystery Religions and Early Christianity," in Metzger, *Historical and Literary Studies*, 21.

69. Roland de Vaux, *The Bible and the Ancient Near East* (New York: Doubleday, 1971), 236, quoted in Yamauchi, "Easter—Myth, Hallucination, or History?"

70. Wagner, *Pauline Baptism and the Pagan Mysteries*, 261.

71. See Luke 1:1–4.

72. Robert J. Miller, *Born Divine* (Santa Rosa, Calif.: Polestar, 1993), 246.

73. Ibid., 208.

74. Walter E. Bundy, *Jesus and the First Three Gospels* (Cambridge, Mass.: Harvard University Press, 1955), 11.

75. Tom Flynn, "Matthew vs. Luke: Whoever Wins, Coherence Loses," available at www.secularhumanism.org/index.php?section=library&page=flynn_25_ 1 (January 29, 2007).

76. For a discussion of the Isaiah 7:14 prophecy, see Challenge #5.

77. Robert Gromacki, *The Virgin Birth*, 2nd ed. (Grand Rapids, Mich.: Kregel, 2002), 213.

78. See Barry B. Powell, *Classical Myth*, 3rd ed. (Upper Saddle River, N.J.: Prentice Hall, 2001), 250. To examine artwork of the birth of Dionysus on an Italian vase, circa 380 BC, showing him emerging from Zeus's thigh, see 251. According to J. Ed Komoszewski, M. James Sawyer, and Daniel B. Wallace, any reference to a "virgin birth" for Dionysus comes in post-Christian sources. See Komoszewski, Sawyer, and Wallace, *Reinventing Jesus*, 242–43.

79. See Edwin M. Yamauchi, "Anthropomorphism in Ancient Religions," *Bibliotheca Sacra* 125 (1968), 99.

80. J. Gresham Machen, *The Virgin Birth of Christ* (1930; repr., Grand Rapids, Mich.: Baker, 1965), 338.

81. Ibid., 330, 336.

82. Ibid., 326.

83. Peter Green, *Alexander of Macedon* (Berkeley: University of California Press, 1991), 37.

84. Buddha lived about five hundred years before Christ. As Machen notes: "In the introduction to the Jâtaka book, which dates from the fifth century after Christ, we have the well-known story of the white elephant that entered into the body of Mâyâ, Buddha's mother, at the time when her child was conceived; and the white elephant story seems to be shown by inscriptional evidence to have been current as early as the reign of Asoka in the third century before Christ. In its earliest form, the story appears as the narration of a dream; Mâyâ *dreamed* that a marvelous white elephant entered into her side.... In later Buddhist sources, what had originally been regarded as a dream of Mâyâ came to be regarded as an actual happening.... It would be difficult to imagine anything more unlike the New Testament story of the virgin birth of Christ." See Machen, *Virgin Birth of Christ*, 339–41 (emphasis in original).

85. See Edwin M. Yamauchi, "Historical Notes on the (In)comparable Christ," *Christianity Today* (Oct. 22, 1971).

86. See "Story of Lord Krishna's Birth," Sanatan Sanstha: Sanatan Society for Scientific Spirituality, www.sanatan.org/en/campaigns/KJ/birth.htm (Jan. 28, 2007).

87. Raymond E. Brown, *The Virginal Conception and Bodily Resurrection of*

Jesus (New York: Paulist, 1973), 62; cited in Komoszewski, Sawyer, and Wallace, *Reinventing Jesus*, 247.

88. Brown, *The Virginal Conception and Bodily Resurrection of Jesus*, 65.

89. Thomas Boslooper, *The Virgin Birth* (Philadelphia: Westminster, 1962), 135, quoted in Gromacki, *Virgin Birth*, 211.

90. Quoted in Tom Snyder, *Myth Conceptions* (Grand Rapids, Mich.: Baker, 1995), 194.

91. See Joseph Klausner, *From Jesus to Paul* (New York: Macmillan, 1943), 104. Retorted Nash: "The fate of Osiris's coffin in the Nile is about as relevant to baptism as the sinking of Atlantis." See Nash, *Gospel and the Greeks*, 128.

92. Russell D. Moore, "Ronald Nash, RIP," available at merecomments.type pad.com/merecomments/2006/03/ronald_nash_rip.html (Jan. 29, 2007).

93. Nash, *Gospel and the Greeks*, 116, 117, 254.

94. Nash, "Was the New Testament Influenced by Pagan Religions?"

95. Nash, *Gospel and the Greeks*, 161–62, quoting André Boulanger, *Orphée: Rapports de l'orphisme et du christianisme* (Paris, 1925), 102. Emphasis added.

96. Nash, "Was the New Testament Influenced by Pagan Religions?" Condensed but preserving much of Nash's wording.

97. Colossians 2:8: "See to it that no one takes you captive through hollow and deceptive philosophy, which depends on human tradition and the elemental spiritual forces of this world rather than on Christ."

98. Metzger said: "It must not be uncritically assumed that the Mysteries always influenced Christianity, for it is not only possible but probable that in certain cases, the influence moved in the opposite direction." See Metzger, *Historical and Literary Studies*, 11.

99. Nash, *Gospel and the Greeks*, 162.

100. 2 Peter 1:16.

CHALLENGE #5: "Jesus Was an Imposter Who Failed to Fulfill the Messianic Prophecies"

1. Associated Press, "Comedian Jackie Mason Drops Lawsuit against Jews for Jesus Missionary Group," *International Herald Tribune* (Dec. 4, 2006).

2. Feinberg is a professor at Trinity Evangelical Divinity School. See "Did Jesus Fulfill Prophecies in Ways in Which the Jews at the Time Were Expecting?" www.whoisthisjesus.tv/qa.htm#scholars (Dec. 27, 2006).

3. Brickner quotations are from Sarah Pulliam, "'Volcanic' Response: Jews for Jesus Takes to New York City Streets," *Christianity Today* (Sept. 2006).

4. Michael Luo, "Jews for Jesus Hit Town and Find a Tough Crowd," *New York Times* (July 4, 2006).

5. "I Won't Fall Prey to Jews for Jesus," *New York Daily News* (July 12, 2006).

6. Pulliam, " 'Volcanic' Response."

7. Associated Press, "Comedian Jackie Mason Drops Lawsuit against Jews for Jesus Missionary Group." Mason discontinued litigation after receiving an apology from Jews for Jesus.

8. "I Won't Fall Prey to Jews for Jesus."

9. Gal Beckerman, "Jews for Jesus Campaign Targets NY Jews," *Jerusalem Post* (July 9, 2006).

10. Joshua Waxman, "The Limits of Identity," in "The Virtual Talmud," www.beliefnet.com/blogs/virtualtalmu (Aug. 30, 2006).

11. Aryeh Kaplan, *The Real Messiah?* (Toronto: Jews for Judaism, 2004), 14.

12. Quoted in Pinchas Stolper, "Was Jesus the Messiah?" in Kaplan, *Real Messiah?* 32.

13. Stephen Prothero, *Religious Literacy* (San Francisco: HarperSanFrancisco, 2007), 183.

14. Ibid., 150.

15. See J. Barton Payne, *Encyclopedia of Biblical Prophecy* (New York: Harper & Row, 1973).

16. Walter C. Kaiser Jr., *The Messiah in the Old Testament* (Grand Rapids, Mich.: Zondervan, 1995), 29. Kaiser cites the source as Alfred Edersheim, *The Life and Times of Jesus the Messiah*, 2 vols. (Grand Rapids, Mich.: Eerdmans, 1953), 2:710–41 (appendix 9).

17. Lee Strobel, *The Case for Faith* (Grand Rapids, Mich.: Zondervan, 2000), 131.

18. See John 4:25–26.

19. The number of messianic Jews is difficult to ascertain. Rabbi Bentzion Kravitz said in *The Jewish Response to Missionaries*: "According to a 1990 Council of Jewish Federations population study, over 600,000 Jews in North America alone identify with some type of Christianity. Over the past 25 years, more than 275,000 Jews worldwide have been converted." See www.jewsforjudaism.com/web/handbook/s_toc.htm (Dec. 28, 2006). Estimates by organizations of messianic Jews are generally lower. In my interview, Michael L. Brown put the number at about one percent of the worldwide Jewish population; this would mean there are 120,000 to 140,000 messianic Jews.

20. Quoted in Kaiser, *The Messiah in the Old Testament*, 19; citing E. Sehmsdorf, *Die Prophetenauslegung bei J. G. Eichhorn* (Göttingen: Vandenhoef,

1971), 153–54; noted in Ronald E. Clements, "Messianic Prophecy or Messianic History?" *Horizons in Biblical Theology* 1 (1979), 87.

21. Kaiser, *Messiah in the Old Testament*, 14.

22. Kaplan, *Real Messiah?* 27.

23. *Missionary Impossible*, published by Jews for Judaism, www.jewsforjudaism .com/web/byg/pdf/J4J_CMSGW16.pd (Dec. 29, 2006).

24. Ibid., 4.

25. Ibid., 16.

26. "Do All Scholars Believe Jesus Fulfilled Messianic Prophecies?" www.whois thisjesus.tv/qa.htm#scholar (Dec. 28, 2006).

27. Ibid.

28. FIRE is an acronym for Fellowship for International Revival and Evangelism.

29. See Isaiah 42:4.

30. See 2 Chronicles 7:19–22.

31. See Daniel 9:24.

32. See Haggai 2:6–9.

33. See Malachi 3:1–5.

34. For a description of the time reckoning, see Michael L. Brown, *Answering Jewish Objections to Jesus*, vol. 1, *General and Historical Objections* (Grand Rapids, Mich.: Baker, 2000), 70–71.

35. See Babylonian Talmud, Sanhedrin 98a.

36. Matthew 27:46 and Mark 15:34 report Jesus saying on the cross, "My God, my God, why have you forsaken me?" This is the first line of Psalm 22. In Jesus' day, the Psalms were not numbered; people referred to them by their opening line.

37. See Psalm 22:27–31.

38. See Deuteronomy 18:15–22.

39. Torah, which means "teaching, instruction, law," can refer to the first division of the Tanakh (the Old Testament) or the Oral Torah, which is composed of all rabbinic traditions related to the Written Torah and various legal aspects of the Jewish life. The traditions were first passed on orally before they were written down. See Browns, *Answering Jewish Objections to Jesus*, 1:255–56.

40. See Isaiah 53:10.

41. See Babylonian Talmud, Yoma 39a.

42. Ibid.

43. 1 Peter 2:24: "'He himself bore our sins' in his body on the cross, so that we might die to sins and live for righteousness; 'by his wounds you have been healed.'"

44. Midrash Ha-Chafetz to Leviticus 1:12, cited in *Torah Shelemah* 25:17 and by Joshua Berman, *The Temple: Its Symbolism and Meaning Then and Now* (Northvale, N.J.: Jason Aronson, 1995), 126.

45. Kaplan, *Real Messiah?* 4, 14.

46. See Mark 14:62.

47. See Deuteronomy 4:12, 15, 35, 6:4; Isaiah 43:10–11, 45:5–6, 46:9.

48. See Exodus 33:20.

49. See Genesis 32:30.

50. See Isaiah 6:1.

51. John 1:18 RSV.

52. John 10:30.

53. See John 10:36.

54. See Colossians 2:9.

55. See Isaiah 1:11–20; Amos 5:22–24; Psalm 51:17–19; Jeremiah 7:1–10; Micah 6:6–8.

56. *Missionary Impossible*, 4–5. Following the practice of some Jews, this document uses *G-d* rather than spell out God's name. For references to repentance, see 2 Chronicles 7:14; Ezekiel 18 and 33; Jeremiah 36:3; Isaiah 55:6–7; and Jonah 3:10.

57. Matthew 3:2.

58. Luke 5:32.

59. See Mark 6:7–13.

60. Emphasis added.

61. See 1 Samuel 15:22.

62. Kaiser, *Messiah in the Old Testament*, 155.

63. For an early example, see Acts 8:26–39.

64. See Psalm 44.

65. See John 1:46.

66. See Matthew 21:13. The term "den of robbers" was a reference to Jeremiah 7:11: "Has this house, which bears my Name, become a den of robbers to you?"

67. See Acts 8:26–39.

68. See Matthew 5:39.

69. Isaiah 1:4. Isaiah also called Israel "a seed of an adulterer" in Isaiah 14:20 and "a seed of falsehood" in Isaiah 57:4.

70. "Seed" can mean: "As marked by moral quality = persons (or community) of such a quality." See Francis Brown, S. Driver, and C. Briggs, *The Brown-Driver-Briggs Hebrew and English Lexicon* (New York: Oxford University Press, 1959), 283.

71. For the story of Louis S. Lapides, who was raised in a Jewish home but became a follower of Jesus largely based on Isaiah 53, see Strobel, *Case for Christ*, 171 – 87. Lapides is now the pastor of a California church and is the former president of a national network of messianic congregations.

72. See Matthew 1:22 – 23.

73. Rashi is an acronym for Rabbi Shlomo Yitschaki (1040 – 1105), considered the foremost Jewish commentator on the Tanakh (Old Testament) and Babylonian Talmud. Rashi did not personally believe that Isaiah prophesied a virgin birth. See Rabbi A. J. Rosenberg, *Judaica Press Complete Tanach with Rashi*, CD-ROM ed. (New York: Davka Corporation and Judaica Press, 1999).

74. See 2 Samuel 12:24 – 25.

75. See Charles A. Briggs, *Messianic Prophecy* (New York: Scribner's, 1889), 326, quoted in Kaiser, *Messiah in the Old Testament*, 112 – 13.

76. See Tovia Singer, "Judaism's Response to Christian Missionaries," www.out reachjudaism.org/like-a-lion.htm (Dec. 27, 2006).

77. See William G. Braude, *Pesikta Rabbati: Homiletical Discourses for Festal Days and Special Sabbaths*, 2 vols. (New Haven: Yale, 1968), 680 – 87.

78. James E. Smith, *What the Bible Teaches about the Promised Messiah* (Nashville: Nelson, 1993), 146, quoted in Kaiser, *Messiah in the Old Testament*, 113), cited in Michael L. Brown, *Answering Jewish Objections to Jesus*, vol. 3, *Messianic Prophecy Objections* (Grand Rapids, Mich.: Baker, 2003), 121.

79. "Did Jesus Fulfill Prophecies in Ways in Which the Jews at the Time Were Expecting?" Available at www.whoisthisjesus.tv/qa.htm#scholars (Dec. 27, 2006).

80. Kaiser, *Messiah in the Old Testament*, 232.

81. Norman L. Geisler, *Baker Encyclopedia of Christian Apologetics* (Grand Rapids, Mich.: Baker, 1999), 613.

82. See Robert Kittel, *Theologians under Hitler* (New Haven: Yale, 1985).

83. See Edward H. Flannery, *The Anguish of the Jews: Twenty-Three Centuries of Anti-Semitism* (New York: Paulist, 1985).

CHALLENGE #6: "People Should Be Free to Pick
and Choose What to Believe about Jesus"

1. *Utne Reader* (Aug. 1998).

2. Hanna Rosin, "Believers in God, If Not Church," *Washington Post* (Jan. 18, 2000).

3. David Ian Miller, "Finding My Religion," www.sfgate.com/cgi-bin/article .cgi?file=/g/a/2006/07/24/findrelig.DT (Jan. 12, 2007).

4. Rosin, "Believers in God, If Not Church."

5. James R. Edwards, *Is Jesus the Only Savior?* (Grand Rapids, Mich.: Eerdmans, 2005), 3.

6. "Mixing Religious Teachings," CBS Poll (June 29, 2005), www.cbsnews.com/stories/2005/06/29/opinion/polls/main705181.shtm (Jan. 4, 2007).

7. Cimino and Lattin, *Shopping for Faith*, 26.

8. "Mixing Religious Teachings," CBS Poll.

9. Edwards, *Is Jesus the Only Savior?* 5.

10. Rosin, "Believers in God, If Not Church."

11. Edwards, *Is Jesus the Only Savior?* 5.

12. Terry Mattingly, "Oprah and Her American Faith," www.kitsapsun.com/bsun/fe_religion/article/0,2403,BSUN_19075_5269707,00.html (Jan. 11, 2007).

13. Ibid. Also see Marcia Nelson, *The Gospel According to Oprah* (Louisville: Westminster John Knox, 2005).

14. Miller, "Finding My Religion."

15. "The Gospel According to Oprah," www.wfial.org/index.cfm?fuseaction=artNewAge.article_ (Jan. 5, 2007).

16. See John 18:38.

17. Andreas Köstenberger, gen. ed., *Whatever Happened to Truth?* (Wheaton, Ill.: Crossway, 2005), 9.

18. See Romans 2:14–15.

19. See Romans 1:18–19.

20. See Luke 10:27, as well as Matthew 22:37 and Mark 12:30.

21. Cited in C. S. Lewis, ed., *George MacDonald: An Anthology* (New York: Macmillan, 1978), 7.

22. For a discussion of the topic "A Loving God Would Never Torture People in Hell," see Strobel, *Case for Faith*, 169–94.

23. Shirley MacLaine, *Out on a Limb* (New York: Bantam, 1983), 347.

24. See Psalm 31:15.

25. See Keith Windschuttle, *The Killing of History* (San Francisco: Encounter, 2000).

26. Luke 1:3–4: "With this in mind, since I myself have carefully investigated everything from the beginning, I too decided to write an orderly account for you, most excellent Theophilus, so that you may know the certainty of the things you have been taught."

27. See Larry W. Hurtado, *Lord Jesus Christ: Devotion to Jesus in Earliest Christianity* (Grand Rapids, Mich.: Eerdmans, 2003).

28. Revised Standard Version.

29. See Matthew 7:1–5.
30. "Straightening the Record: Some Response to Critics," *Modern Theology* 6 (Jan. 1990), 187.
31. See Romans 12:19–21 and Matthew 5:43–48.
32. Bryan Appleyard, "Is Sin Good?" *Sunday Times Magazine* (April 11, 2004).
33. J. Fletcher, "Sin in Contemporary Literature," *Theology Today* 50.2 (1993), 254.
34. Alan Mann, *Atonement for a "Sinless" Society* (Waynesboro, Ga.: Paternoster, 2005), 26.
35. See Karl Menninger, *Whatever Became of Sin?* (New York: Hawthorn, 1973).
36. John Shelby Spong, *Why Christianity Must Change or Die* (San Francisco: HarperSanFrancisco, 1999), 95.
37. Edwards, *Is Jesus the Only Savior?* 151.
38. See Matthew 18:21–35.
39. Romans 6:23: "For the wages of sin is death, but the gift of God is eternal life in Christ Jesus our Lord."
40. John 3:14–15: "Just as Moses lifted up the snake in the wilderness, so the Son of Man must be lifted up, that everyone who believes may have eternal life in him."
41. See John 10:11–18.
42. See 2 Corinthians 5:18–19.
43. John Stott, *The Cross of Christ* (Downers Grove, Ill.: InterVarsity, 1986), 160.
44. See Romans 8:3–4.
45. Dan Kimball, *They Like Jesus, but Not the Church* (Grand Rapids, Mich.: Zondervan, 2007), 30.
46. Cathleen Falsani, *The God Factor* (New York: Sarah Crichton, 2006), 9.
47. See Hebrews 10:24–25.
48. See Galatians 5:22–23.
49. Köstenberger, *Whatever Happened to Truth?* 76.
50. 1 John 5:13 (emphasis added).

CONCLUSION: "Discovering the Real Jesus"

1. Michka Assayas, *Bono: In Conversation with Michka Assayas* (New York: Riverhead, 2005), 206.
2. Anne Rice, "Author's Note" in *Christ the Lord: Out of Egypt* (New York: Knopf, 2005), 305–22.

3. Ibid., 312.
4. This idea of skepticism not equaling scholarship comes from Evans, *Fabricating Jesus*, 17.
5. Ibid., 15.
6. Ibid., 15–16.
7. Ibid., 16.
8. Ibid.
9. Quotes by Charlesworth, Dunn, Meier, O'Collins, and Theissen are found in the opening, unnumbered pages of Evans, *Fabricating Jesus*.
10. Ben Witherington III, *What Have They Done with Jesus?* (San Francisco: HarperSanFrancisco, 2006), 1.
11. Ibid., 2.
12. Larry Hurtado, *Lord Jesus Christ: Devotion to Jesus in Earliest Christianity* (Grand Rapids, Mich.: Eerdmans, 2003), 2.
13. Ibid., 3.
14. Ibid., 2.
15. See Richard Bauckham, *Jesus and the Eyewitnesses: The Gospels as Eyewitness Testimony* (Grand Rapids, Mich.: Eerdmans, 2006). The quote from Wright appears on the back cover.
16. Evans, *Fabricating Jesus*, 17.
17. Ibid., from opening, unnumbered pages.
18. C. S. Lewis, *Mere Christianity*, rev. and amp. ed. (New York: HarperCollins, 2001), 196–97.
19. Three verses from the New Testament book of Romans are often used to sum up the Gospel. Romans 3:23: "For all have sinned and fall short of the glory of God." Romans 6:23: "For the wages of sin is death, but the gift of God is eternal life in Christ Jesus our Lord." Romans 10:13: "Everyone who calls on the name of the Lord will be saved."
20. Don Everts, *Jesus with Dirty Feet* (Downers Grove, Ill.: InterVarsity, 1999), 26–27.

Acknowledgments

Thanks for pausing at this page so I can let you know how indebted I am to the many people who helped me create this book. I am thankful that the scholars I interviewed—Craig A. Evans, Daniel B. Wallace, Michael Licona, Edwin Yamauchi, Michael L. Brown, and Paul Copan—were willing to share their time and expertise with me. Also, Mark Mittelberg, my ministry partner for twenty years, was invaluable as always, contributing advice, feedback, and encouragement along the way. Garry Poole and my daughter, Alison Morrow, helped hone the final manuscript. My precocious granddaughter, Abigail Morrow, provided much-needed diversions from time to time. Everyone at Zondervan—especially Doug Lockhart, Scott Bolinder, John Sloan, Bob Hudson, Leslie Speyers, Mark Rice, Scott Heagle, and the editorial, design, marketing, publicity, and sales teams—offered incredible support. I'm blessed to be associated with such a great publisher. Finally, my wife, Leslie; our son, Kyle, and his wife, Kelli; and our daughter, Alison, and her husband, Dan Morrow, were constant sources of love and encouraging words. God's best to all of you!

Index

Meet Lee Strobel

Atheist-turned-Christian Lee Strobel, the former award-winning legal editor of the *Chicago Tribune*, is a *New York Times* bestselling author of nearly twenty books and has been interviewed on numerous national television networks, including ABC, PBS, CNN, and Fox.

Described by the *Washington Post* as "one of the evangelical community's most popular apologists," Lee shared the prestigious Charles "Kip" Jordon Christian Book of the Year award in 2005 for a curriculum he coauthored about the movie *The Passion of the Christ*. He also has won Gold Medallions for his books *The Case for Christ*, *The Case for Faith*, *The Case for a Creator*, and *Inside the Mind of Unchurched Harry and Mary*.

Lee was educated at the University of Missouri (Bachelor of Journalism degree, 1974) and Yale Law School (Master of Studies in Law degree, 1979). He was a professional journalist for fourteen years at the *Chicago Tribune* and other newspapers, winning Illinois' top honors for investigative reporting (which he shared with a team he led) and public service journalism from United Press International.

A former teaching pastor at two of America's largest churches, Lee also was executive producer and host of the weekly national television program *Faith under Fire*. In addition, he taught First Amendment law at Roosevelt University. In 2007 he was honored by the conferring of a Doctor of Divinity degree from Southern Evangelical Seminary.

Lee and Leslie have been married for thirty-five years and live in Southern California. Their daughter, Alison, is a novelist whose second book, *Violette Between*, was published in 2006. Their son, Kyle, holds two master's degrees (philosophy of religion and New Testament) and is pursuing a doctorate in theology at the University of Aberdeen in Scotland. His first book, *Metamorpha: Jesus as a Way of Life*, was published in 2007.

Lee's free e-newsletter, "Investigating Faith," is available at LeeStrobel .com.

Share Your Thoughts

With the Author: Your comments will be forwarded to the author when you send them to *zauthor@zondervan.com*.

With Zondervan: Submit your review of this book by writing to *zreview@zondervan.com*.

Free Online Resources at
www.zondervan.com

Daily Bible Verses and Devotions: Enrich your life with daily Bible verses or devotions that help you start every morning focused on God. Visit www.zondervan.com/newsletters.

Free Email Publications: Sign up for newsletters on Christian living, academic resources, church ministry, fiction, children's resources, and more. Visit www.zondervan.com/newsletters.

Zondervan Bible Search: Find and compare Bible passages in a variety of translations at www.zondervanbiblesearch.com.

Other Benefits: Register to receive online benefits like coupons and special offers, or to participate in research.